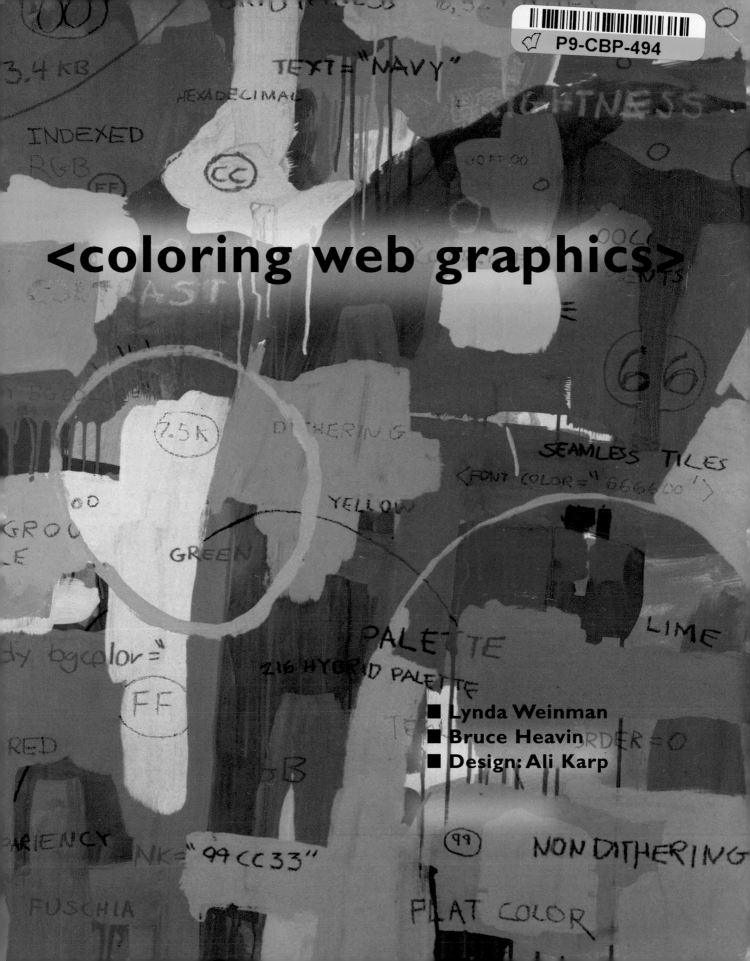

<coloring web graphics>

- Lynda Weinman
- Bruce Heavin
- Design: Ali Karp

Coloring Web Graphics
By Lynda Weinman & Bruce Heavin

Published by: New Riders Publishing
201 West 103rd Street
Indianapolis, IN 46290 USA

Warning and Disclaimer

Trademark Acknowledgments

Publisher: Don Fowley
Publishing Manager: David Dwyer
Marketing Manager: Mary Foote
Managing Editor: Carla Hall

Coloring Web Graphics Credits

Product Development Specialist
John Kane

Software Specialist
Steve Flatt

Project Editor
Jennifer Eberhardt

Acquisitions Coordinator
Stacey Beheler

Administrative Coordinator
Karen Opal

Cover Artwork, Spread Illustrations, and Photography
Bruce Heavin

Cover Production
Aren Howell

Book Designer
Ali Karp

Production Manager
Kelly Dobbs

Production Team Supervisor
Laurie Casey

Production Analysts
Jason Hand
Erich Richter

Production Team
Barbara Borri
Joe Millay
Gwen Stramler
Megan Wade
Steven Weinman

Indexer
Sharon Hilgenberg

■ Lynda Weinman and Bruce Heavin. (photos: Tom Delmundo)

■ Lynda Weinman

Lynda Weinman writes full-time for a living now, but in the past has been a designer, animator, magazine contributor, computer consultant, instructor, moderator, and lecturer. She lives in California with her seven-year-old daughter, 2 cats, 1 snake, and 5 computers. She has taught Web Design, Interactive Media Design, Motion Graphics, and Digital Imaging classes at Art Center College of Design in Pasadena, California (though she is currently taking a break from teaching). Lynda contributes regularly to *The Net*, *MacUser*, *Step-by-Step Graphics*, *New Media*, and *Full Motion* magazines. She likes the Web so much, she even has a domain for her name:

■ http://www.lynda.com

■ Bruce Heavin

Bruce Heavin is an acclaimed painter and illustrator whose mastery of color is evident in all of his work. His clients include Adobe, E! Entertainment Television, *Outside*, *Computer Life*, *MacUser*, and *Keyboard* magazines. He is responsible for the distinctive covers of all of Lynda's Web design books, which were created using acryllic paints and crayons. Bruce's work combines computer techniques and traditional painting techniques. He has designed graphics for numerous Web sites and CD-ROMs, including pieces for DreamWorks SKG Interactive Web site. He's almost always available for illustration assignments (hint hint), and works out of his home on a Mac PPC 8500. A portfolio of Bruce's images are on-line at his Web site.

■ http://www.stink.com

■ Lynda with her daughter Jamie in a serious moment
(photo: Bruce Heavin)

■ This book is dedicated to Jamie Cat

■ Book Designer Ali—a rare
moment away from her Mac

Lynda's Acknowledgements

To **Bruce** who is the coolest, funniest, most talented, most supportive person I've ever met. I love you!

To **Jamie** who is the coolest, funniest, most talented, most cherished daughter I've ever met. I love you!

To **Ali Karp** who never slept, rested, or dated during this entire project. Her dedication, skill, and perfectionism never ceased to amaze me. You rule.
■ alink@earthlink.net

To **Ali's Mom** who went way beyond the call of motherly duty.

To **John Kane** who is a peach of a fellow. Thanks for listening to everything, always being there, and being so darned good at your new job!

To **David Dwyer** for all the opportunities he has given me. Thank you for believing in this project, David!

To **Crystal Waters** for her friendship, humor, love, and support.

To **Joy Silverman** for inspiring me and being my role model.

To Homegurrrl's Web Design Mailing listmember **Amy Rosenthal** for her generosity with the FreeHand and Painter CLUTs she painstakingly made and shared in this book's CD. Not to mention talking to me late at night about palettes and CLUTs and other geeky stuff.

To **Mary Thorpe** for being her incredible, helpful self.

To my **friends** and **family** for their patience, understanding, love, and support.

To **Ivan Hoffman** for being so thorough and caring.

To **Helene Atkin** for NPR!

Very special thanks to **PhotoDisc** ■ http://www.photodisc.com for the use of their incredible stock footage collection to demonstrate image compression in this book!

< coloring

Bruce's Acknowledgements

To **Lynda**. You bring out the best in me. You are the most beautiful person. I love you.

Joe Maller for the late night support and his never-ending ability to push me way too far on any given project. I think those efforts resulted in this book going way beyond what I had originally intended.
■ http://www.joemaller.com

Don Barnett for his incredible insight into ideas for media and animation. Perhaps one of the greatest multimedia designers ever! You're the person who can do what nobody else can. Keep proving them wrong!
■ http://www.cris.com/~nekton/barnett.html

Kathy Tafel for putting up with my antics while working at *The Net* magazine; figuring out how to work with color images on the Web and compressing them down beyond belief. And yes, I can still make the smallest GIFs, hands down!

Crystal Waters for the occasional words of help. I'll never call on Fridays at 9-10 pm again.
■ http://www.typo.com

To **family and friends** for their support.

In memory of **Dwight Harmon** who unknown to the world, changed the face of art forever. Your encouragement and wisdom continues on.

■ Bruce Heavin, back when he was a Pilgrim

■ Illustration for
Los Angeles Times Magazine

■ Illustration for
Outside magazine

■ Illustration for
The Net magazine

■ contents at a glance

Introduction: **xv**
How This Book Works

1. **Computer Color Overview:**   **1**
How screen-based color differs
from print-based color.

2. **Browser-Safe Color:**   **17**
Defines browser-safe colors, hybrid
colors, and when to use them.

3. **Web File Formats:**   **37**
Explains how GIF and JPEG compress
images and how to make small, fast,
high-quality Web graphics.

4. **Color Principles:**   **53**
Color theory for Web design; the
importance of hue, value, saturation,
contrast, brightness, and texture.

5. **Imaging Techniques:**
How to load swatches, make images   **71**
small, create your own swatches and
CLUTs, plus much more.

6. **Color Groupings/Swatches/Directory:**   **93**
A printed directory of the contents
of the CD-ROM.

7. **Color-Related HTML Tags:**   **117**
Learn how to color your pages, text,
links, tables, and more.

Glossary: **136**
A place to find definitions for color-
related terms and processes.

Index   **284**

Introduction

1 Computer Color Overview   2

Computer Color	4
Web Color	5
RGB Versus CMYK	6
Calibration and Gamma	7
More Facts About Gamma	7
High Resolution Versus Low Resolution	8
Bit-Depth	10
Dithering and Banding	12
Monitor's Bit-Depth	14
How to Change Your Monitor's Bit-Depth	15
Hexadecimal Color?	16

2 Browser-Safe Color   18

Introduction to Browser-Safe Specs	20
Why Work Within a Limited Palette?	21
Hexadecimal-Based Artwork	21
Illustration-Based Artwork	22
Photograph-Based Artwork	23
Browser-Safe Color Summary	24
What Does the Browser-Safe Palette Look Like?	25
What Are Hybrid-Safe Colors?	28
How Do You Work with Browser-Safe and Hybrid Colors?	29
The Book's CD-ROM	29
Photoshop Swatch Palettes	30
Imaging Programs other than Photoshop	30
Paint Shop Pro .pal file	31
Browser-Safe Color Charts Organized by Hue	32
Brower-Safe Color Charts Organized by Luminance	34

3 Web File Formats — 36

Color and Web File Formats	38
GIF Compression	39
"GIF" Pronunciation	39
Making Small GIFs	40
GIFs for Illustration-Sytle Imagery	41
GIFs for Photographic Imagery	43
Interlaced GIFs	48
Transparent GIFs	50
PNG	51
Animated GIFs	52
Popular GIF animation authoring tools	52
Some good animated GIF references	52
JPEG	54
Progressive JPEGs Versus Standard JPEGs	58
Progressive JPEGs	58
HTML for Embedding Images	59

4 Color Principles — 60

Color Principles	62
Color Terminology	64
The Importance of Value	66
How to Control the "Read" of an Image	66
The Importance of Brightness and Contrast	67
The Importance of Saturation	68
The Importance of Texture and Noise	69
How to Unify Colors	70
Everything Is Relative	71

5 Imaging Techniques   74

Imaging Techniques	76
How to Load a Browser-Safe Swatch Palette into Photoshop	77
How to Append a Swatch Set	77
How to Use the Browser-Safe Swatch Sets	77
How to Add/Replace a Color to a Swatch Set	78
How to Subtract Colors from a Browser-Safe Swatch Set	78
How to Save a New Swatch Set	78
Swatch Sets for Imaging Programs Other Than Photoshop?	79
How to Load the Browser-Safe Palette into Paint Shop Prop	80
How to Load a Browser-Safe Palette into Photo-Paint	81
How to Load a Browser-Safe Palette into Painter	82
What Is a CLUT and What Do You Do with One?	83
Applying Browser-Safe Colors to Existing Artwork	83
Reducing Colors in GIF Files Using Photoshop	84
Photoshop's Indexed Color Dialog Box	85
Photoshop Resolution Settings	85
Photoshop Palette Settings	86
Photoshop Dither Settings	86
Reducing Colors in Photo-Paint	87
Reducing Colors in Paint Shop Pro	88
The Windows 16 Palette	88
How to Ensure Your Artwork Stays Browser Safe	89
Removing Unwanted Browser-Safer Colors in Photoshop	91
Common Problems with GIF Transparency	92
URLs for Transparency Tricks and Tips	93
How to Create a Common Palette for Animated GIFs	94
How to Use a Custom Palette in GifBuilder	96

Loading a Common Palette into GIF Construction Set   96

Making a Super Palette in DeBabelizer   97

   Photoshop 4.0   97

Vector-Based Artwork   98

Working with CorelDraw   98

Working with Adobe Illustrator   99

Working with FreeHand   100

Working with Color Picker-Based Applications   101

Custom Palettes for Shockwave Documents   102

Hybrid Color Background Tile Creation in Photoshop   103

Coloring Hybrid Tiles in Photoshop   104

Coloring Pattern Tiles in Photoshop   104

   Photoshop Shortcuts   104

Previsualizing Tiles in Photoshop   105

How to Create Your Own Seamless Tile in Photoshop   106

Using a Logo for a Tile Background   108

Previsualizing Web Pages in Photoshop   109

6 Color Groupings/Swatches/Directory 110

How This Chapter Works   112

The Coloring Web Graphics CD-ROM   113

File Organization   114

Red   116

Green   136

Blue   156

Cyan   176

Magenta   196

Yellow   216

Monochromatic   236

Oddball   252

Analagous   256

Clipart   260

< coloring

7 Color-Related HTML Tags   266

Color-Related HTML Tags   268
The Basic Structure of HTML   268
Adding Color to a Web Page   269
Using Color Names Instead of Hex   270
Warning: Color Names Are Rarely Browser Safe   272
Coloring Individual Lines of Text   274
Coloring Links   275
Inserting a Background Image   276
Adding Color to Tables   277

Glossary   278
Index   284

Introduction

Why Buy an Entire Book about Web Color?

If you're going to create Web pages, you're going to need to work with color. The truth is, anyone who creates a Web page is forced into the role of visual designer, whether they consider themselves qualified or not. What many Web designers do not realize is that color is handled differently by different browsers, by different computer platforms, and by different operating systems. Because of this, one has to contend with an assortment of new and foreign concepts such as hexadecimal code, color cubes, dithering, and palette shifting.

Most of us don't think of color as abstract mathematical numbers or strange new terms; we choose color using our emotions and intuition. Color is a science, but color is also an art form. Keeping this in mind, *Coloring Web Graphics* puts the art back into the decision-making process, while respecting the sciences involved.

As Web designers, it should be our goal to make creative design decisions with the full understanding of the possibilities and limitations of the Web as its own medium. Because the Web has numerous limitations and constraints, creative thinking is required to solve its problems. Blaming technology or software tools doesn't solve visual problems; rather, we must put our creativity to the test in order to find workarounds within the Web's strange new rules.

Control Freaks

Most designers want one thing when it comes to images, alignment, and overall composition: C-O-N-T-R-O-L! It drives us nuts to accept that there isn't a method to achieve this. We have no possible way to dictate the computer platform with which our Web pages are viewed. We have no control over the bit-depth and the amount of colors on the screen of the user. We have no way to adjust viewers' monitors (brightness/contrast). We have no way to force others to use desired plug-ins.

You can ask your users to make their screen soooo wide. You can ask your users to turn off underlining for links. You can ask users to choose certain fonts for their browsers. You can request others to use certain browsers. You can ask users to do practically anything so that your site looks as you intended, but the reality is that many won't bother. This book takes a different approach, one that advocates learning how to make our visuals—be it the color of our text, images, movies, or animated buttons—flexible enough to hold up under a multitude of situations.

This book teaches you all about color on the Web. It describes all kinds of color-related Web concepts such as bit-depth and color cubes, dithering and palettes, and hexadecimal colors. Though these subjects might not seem appealing at first, understanding them will put you in control of how your pages are viewed by others. The only way to harness that precious control everyone wants is through knowledge and understanding of how the Web handles color.

This Book's Goals

Our goal with this book is to present this material in as non-intimidating and useful manner possible. Bruce and I are artists, and we've made a conscious effort to make our information oriented to other artists (and non-artists who find themselves suddenly in the role of the artist).

For example, we know that the browser-safe colors are in a 6x6x6 color cube. Knowing that doesn't help anyone understand how to work with those colors artistically or make images with them. We consider our role to be translators of technical information, to make Web color accessible to people who want to use these colors. It's not so important to know where a certain color of blue is on an abstract cube; it's much more important to see it with the other blues, or understand what other blue colors might work, or how to make an image read with the specific blue, or how to make sure the same blue is viewed across multiple computer platforms.

■ **note**

A CMYK Warning!

Alas, this book has created a cruel twist of information delivery! It's all about computer color, computer screen delivery, and RGB colors, and yet it's printed on paper using inks and CMYK color! Well, we don't think paper is dead, or that books are a lost cause in this age of digital domination. Books do certain things better than computers, and computers do certain things better than books. Besides, nothing beats having an easily transportable, batteryless information source with no RAM requirements or technical expertise required to use it!

In all seriousness, this book was written with the intent to be a useful guide to Web designers. We can't help that two very different technologies abound—one for printed color and one for computer screen-based color. The problem is inherent in the two opposing mediums—the colors in the book will not perfectly match the digital files' colors on your computer screen. Our advice? Use the book as a reference, and use the digital files from the *Coloring Web Graphics* CD-ROM as your true guides.

Foreword from Bruce Heavin

I first started to design for the Web when I was asked to create imagery for *The Net* magazine's site in 1995. I had no prior experience with the medium as I searched the Web for examples using my America Online browser on my Macintosh 640AV. I was just an illustrator with ideas, and a new medium to call my toy.

Things began to disturb me as it became more and more apparent that the images I made were not the same as what I saw over AOL's browser. Later I got another service and used Netscape and things looked a lot better, but problems still existed and some colors tended to dither miserably while a select few didn't. Color perplexed and plagued me. GIF image file sizes fluctuated wildly all over the board as I loved to play with different bit-depths, image-editing programs, and types of images to see how to get the files as small as possible. My greatest success in GIF file compression was a single GIF experiment that was 64k in size but would expand to be 128 megs when opened in Photoshop!

Lynda Weinman had just started on a book, *Designing Web Graphics*. I worked with her to find colors that wouldn't dither across multiple platforms. We eventually found these colors and named them the "browser-safe" color palette. We covered lots of ground in her first book, but have since discovered that designers need a lot more information relating specifically to color. Thus *Coloring Web Graphics* was born. Until now, most people saw the possibilities of color on the Web as limited to a 6X6X6 cube that isn't friendly to designers or artists. Within the book we will present the colors in ways that make sense to the point that you won't have to think about a 6X6X6 palette.

One of the main objectives I set out with in making this book was that I wanted to get the choices of color away from looking like an unusable, mysterious color cube and into a usable spectrum of color, values, and saturation.

Computer graphics should not only belong to the computer programmer and the engineer, but should be usable for the artist as well. The tools we use for making Web sites shouldn't puzzle us, but empower us to do exactly what we set out to do. Web design can become intimidating and useless when the available tools are more difficult to deal with than that of our content, concepts, and designs. It is important to understand how to set up your computer with all the right tools and have the knowledge to use them. The biggest challenge for creating graphics on the Web should be our ideas, concepts, and compositions. It is my hope to leave you all with just that after you finish this book.

Foreword from Lynda Weinman

I have always found the subject of color more than a little baffling. I've never studied formal color theory, and have learned how to work with color intuitively using my gut instincts. As a result, I've never had the confidence that I used color "properly," or was in full control over communicating ideas with color.

I am certain that I am not alone in my color insecurities. I have watched many newcomers begin Web pages and make color choices that were not optimum, or worse—make colors that were subject to change depending from which platform and browser they were viewed. My guess is that anyone who has to use color and make color decisions would welcome a little guidance from a master.

As an instructor at Art Center, many extraordinary students crossed my path, and often influenced me as much as I influenced them. One of these students was Bruce Heavin who, in addition to having a wonderful and original painting style, had some of the best mastery of color I had ever seen.

Bruce graduated several years ago, and we stayed in touch. When it came time to decide on a cover for my first book, *Designing Web Graphics*, New Riders Publishing acted on my suggestion to commission Bruce to paint it. While working on the book, Bruce took a heightened interest in the book's content after he was asked to design his first Web site.

Certain that the browsers were using a fixed palette that no one had published or distributed, Bruce came over to my house and went to work between Mac and PC trying to identify which colors were being used by Netscape in 256-color environments. We identified the browser-safe color palette by trial and error—and later discovered that it was a mathematical cube that was used in many browsers and across many platforms.

Long story short—Bruce has an amazing wealth of knowledge about color; specifically, color on the computer. I figured if we combined his knowledge with my background in teaching digital design techniques we could come up with a pretty useful resource for Web designers. Fortunately our publisher, New Riders, agreed, and you're holding the results in your hand.

How This Book Works

This book was written so that it doesn't have to be read in a linear order. Feel free to flip around, pick up ideas here and there, and leave the rest for some other time.

The CD-ROM

Note that the software on the CD-ROM is not freeware. By purchasing this book, you have purchased the software on the CD-ROM. This software is not intended for distribution to anyone other than the owner of this book. You may use the clip art, with the hope that you will respect the third-party folders that request shareware fees. If you use shareware art on your site, be a champ and pay up! The files located in the SWATCH folder may not be posted to your Web or FTP site, published electronically or in print, or distributed in any manner without the express permission of Lynda Weinman and and Bruce Heavin.

What You'll Find on the CD-ROM

The *Coloring Web Graphics* CD-ROM has three main directories: CLUTS, SWATCHES, and CLIPART. The organizational structure is printed at the beginning of Chapter 6, "Color Groupings/Swatches/ Directory." Some of the things you'll find are

- Browser-Safe Color Lookup Tables (CLUTs) to load into Photoshop, Painter, FreeHand, Photo-Paint, and Paint Shop Pro.
- Swatches that include suggested color themes for your Web pages.
- Browser-safe clip art for use on your Web pages.

■ What the Chapters Cover

Chapter 1: Computer Color Overview

Understand how computers display color, and the differences between color in print and on the Web. This chapter examines dithering, screen bit-depth, gamma, and monitor settings.

Chapter 2: Browser-Safe Color

This chapter describes what browser-safe color is, why it's useful, and when (and when not) to use it.

Chapter 3: Web File Formats

This chapter covers how to make small, fast, and high-quality Web graphics. A thorough review of GIF and JPEG compression, with lots of visual charts to help you understand how to optimize your own images.

Chapter 4: Color Principles

This chapter covers the essential parts of color theory that relate specifically to Web design. Learn how hue, saturation, value, contrast, brightness, and texture affect your Web-bound artwork.

Chapter 5: Imaging Techniques

This chapter has step-by-step tutorials to teach you how to use browser-safe colors in Photoshop, Paint Shop Pro, Photo-Paint, FreeHand, GifBuilder, GIF Construction Set, Director, and Illustrator.

Chapter 6: Color Groupings/Swatches/Directory

Here's where you'll find the guide to the *Coloring Web Graphics* CD-ROM. Use this print-based directory to find the file on the CD that you or your clients want to use.

Chapter 7: Color-Related HTML Tags

This chapter addresses how to add color-related tags to HTML pages, within WYSIWYG or text-based editors.

Glossary

Can't remember what a certain Web color-related term means? You've come to the right place.

The Coloring Web Graphics Web Site

Every good book deserves a good Web site. Especially books about the Web. There is no better medium with which to update information, correct mistakes, or notify readers about new, cool (or not-so-cool) stuff.

Check out our site at ■ http://www.lynda.com/coloringbook/, or go to the front page of www.lynda.com where you'll find links to this book and other Web design-related books.

Feel free to visit Bruce's personal site too. His work can be found at ■ http://www.stink.com.

And, we both love e-mail (though we can't promise to answer everyone!), so feel free to write us about *Coloring Web Graphics*.
Bruce Heavin: bruce@stink.com
Lynda Weinman: lynda@lynda.com

■ New Riders Publishing

The staff of New Riders Publishing is committed to bringing you the very best in computer reference material. Each New Riders book is the result of months of work by authors and staff who research and refine the information contained within its covers.

As part of this commitment to you, the NRP reader, New Riders invites your input. Please let us know if you enjoy this book, if you have trouble with the information and examples presented, or if you have a suggestion for the next edition.

Please note though: New Riders staff cannot serve as a technical resource for Web graphics or for questions about software or hardware-related problems. Please refer to the documentation that accompanies your software or to the applications' Help systems.

If you have a question or comment about any New Riders book, there are several ways to contact New Riders Publishing. We will respond to as many readers as we can. Your name, address, or phone number will never become part of a mailing list or be used for any purpose other than to help us continue to bring you the best books possible.

You can write us at the following address:

New Riders Publishing
Attn: Publisher
201 W. 103rd Street
Indianapolis, IN 46290

If you prefer, you can fax New Riders Publishing at:

(317) 817-7448.

You can also send electronic mail to New Riders
at the following Internet address:

jkane@newriders.mcp.com

NRP is an imprint of Macmillan Computer Publishing.
To obtain a catalog or information, or to purchase any
Macmillan Computer Publishing book, call (800) 428-5331
or visit our Web site at ■ http://www.mcp.com.

Thank you for selecting *Coloring Web Graphics*!

Computer Color Overview

Computer Color

Creating color artwork for the Web is very different than other color delivery mediums because you're publishing your work to people's screens instead of printed pages. Computer screen-based color is composed of projected light and pixels instead of ink pigments, dot patterns, and screen percentages.

In many ways, working with screen-based color can be more fun than working with printed inks. No waiting for color proofs, or working with CMYK values that are much less vibrant than RGB. No high-resolution files. No dot screens to deal with.

Yes, working on the computer for computer delivery is a lot easier in some ways, but don't be fooled into thinking that what you see on your screen is what other people will see on theirs. Just like its print-based counterpart, computer screen-based color has its own set of nasties and gremlins.

Working with computer screen-based color introduces a whole new vocabulary of terms, such as additive light, bit-depth, gamma, calibration, dithering, and banding. Working with computer screen-based color for the Web introduces even more involved concepts, such as cross-platform compatibility, video cards, and different operating systems.

Let's start at the beginning and define some terms before we get too far into this stuff. In this chapter, we'll take you through a short tour of some of the core issues related to computer and Web-based color. It's our goal throughout this book to stay away from ultra-technical information and communicate the essence of what you need to know in order to produce colors on Web pages that appear true to how you intended them.

Web Color

Everything that is wonderful about the Web—global accessibility, cross-platform compatibility, networked distribution, and ever-improving technology—has a trade-off somewhere down the color graphics creation road. On a printed page, everyone sees the same colors (with the exception of those who are visually impaired). A printed page has fixed dimensions. A printed page is designed once and forever stays the same. A printed page cannot be changed once it is finished.

The Web differs from the printed page in more ways than you might imagine. It is not enough to approach Web authoring with good ideas and great artwork. Understanding the medium is necessary in order to ensure that others view your designs and colors as you intended.

Here's a short list of the things that are different about the Web as a publishing medium, as it pertains to color:

- People view your artwork with monitors that have a wide variety of bit-depth settings.
- Various computer monitors have differing color calibration and gamma default settings.
- Different operating systems affect the way colors are displayed.
- Different Web browsers affect the way color is displayed.
- People judge your site not only by its artistic content, but by its speed. Color can affect speed, believe it or not!

Creating color images and screens for the Web can be done without understanding the medium's limitations, but the results may not be what you were hoping for. The focus of this chapter is to describe the Web and computer color environment, and to clue you in on known pitfalls and solutions that will offer you maximum control over how your artwork is ultimately seen.

RGB Versus CMYK

So how does color make it to your computer screen? Your monitor displays light in the form of pixels. Pixel colors are created from red, green, and blue lights that mix together optically to form other colors. Once combined, these three colors create a color space called RGB. Another common color space is called CMYK, which is formed from cyan, magenta, yellow, and black. CMYK color space on a computer was invented to simulate printing inks, and is used commonly by print designers. Web designers are screen-based, hence we use RGB color space only.

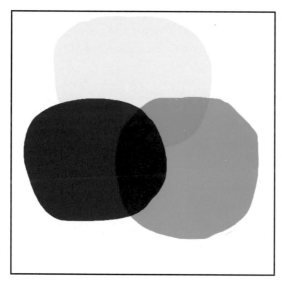

CMYK colors are subtractive, meaning that mixing multiple colors creates black. This color space was created for computer graphics that will be printed on paper.

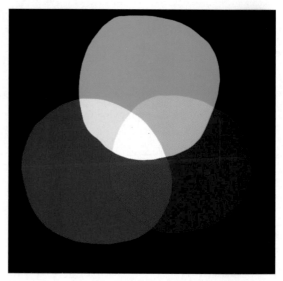

RGB color is additive, meaning that mixing multiple colors creates white. This color space was created for computer graphics that will be viewed on the computer screen.

An understanding of RGB versus CMYK can be summarized:

- CMYK color is used to simulate printing inks.
- CMYK is used by print designers.
- Web designers are screen-based.
- RGB color space is used by all computer screens.

Therefore, Web designers always use RGB and never CMYK! Note: Photoshop and Paint Shop Pro use RGB color space as their default. Instructions on how to change an image from CMYK to RGB in Photoshop follow in Chapter 5, "Imaging Techniques."

Calibration and Gamma

If you've ever owned two television sets, you know the color from set to set can vary wildly. Anyone who works for a company with more than one computer knows that the colors shift between systems—even between identical operating systems and identical hardware.

Some attempt to regulate color screens through *calibration*, or adjusting a monitor's color, brightness, and contrast settings. One of the problems with color on computer screens is that very few monitors are calibrated accurately to one another. Shades of a color often vary wildly from computer to computer, and from platform to platform.

Across different computer platforms, the calibration problem is amplified by gamma differences. Gamma dictates the brightness and contrast of the computer's display. Macs, for example, are typically much brighter than PCs because of the differences in Macintosh's native gamma settings. Both calibration and gamma pose variables that are impossible to control in Web design.

■ **note**

More Facts About Gamma

If you're interested in learning more about gamma, check out the following URLs:

■ http://www.inforamp.net/~poynton/

■ http://www.w3.org/pub/WWW/TR/PR-png
960701.html#GammaAppendix

■ ftp://ftp.inforamp.net/pub/users/poynton/doc/
Mac/Mac_gamma.pdf

■ http://www.boutell.com/boutell/png/PNG-
GammaAppendix.html

Here is the same Web page, photographed on 4 different platforms and monitors:

mac

pc

sgi

sun

Though these numbers vary widely from different sources, it is generally reported that Mac and SGI monitors are close to the same but PCs are much darker.

Here are some average factory settings:

■ SGI monitors=1.7 gamma

■ Mac monitors=1.8 gamma

■ PC monitors=2.5 gamma

High Resolution Versus Low Resolution

Since your delivery medium is a computer screen, and not a printed page, high-resolution files are not part of Web design life. High resolution is defined as anything that can't be displayed at its intended size at a 1:1 magnification on a computer screen. Average computer screens display 72 pixels per inch, so anything prepared at 72 ppi (pixels per inch) or dpi (dots per inch) is defined as a low-resolution file, and anything above is considered high resolution.

For those of you who have worked with high-resolution graphics files before, you might remember that in order to view them 1:1, you generally have to use the magnifying glass tool many times, resulting in a huge cropped image on your computer screen. The reason for this is that a computer screen can't physically display a high-resolution file. High-resolution graphics are intended to be printed on high-resolution printers, not displayed on standard computer monitors. If you put a high-resolution file on the Web it can only display at 1:1 magnification, meaning it will appear much bigger than you intended.

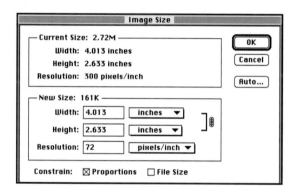

Here's a graphic measuring approximately 4 x 2 inches at 72 dots per inch.

The 72 dpi image is true to its correct size in inches when posted to a Web page.

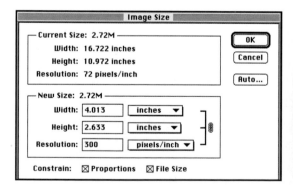

Here's an example of setting up a high-resolution image. It measures approximately 4 x 2 inches at 300 dots per inch.

It's quite a bit larger than 4 x 2 inches on the Web. What happened? The browser converted the graphic to 72 dpi, so it is more than three times bigger than intended.

Most likely, your goal for working at high resolution would be to ensure the highest possible quality for your image, though in actuality you would defeat that purpose.

You should always work at "screen resolution" when authoring images for the Web (or any other screen-based medium, such as television or interactive multimedia). The accepted measurement of screen resolution is 72 dpi—or 72 dots per inch.

Whenever working on images for the Web, set your graphics to be measured in pixels, not inches. Inches are needed when creating artwork that will be printed on paper, and pixels are the standard unit of measurement for screen-bound images.

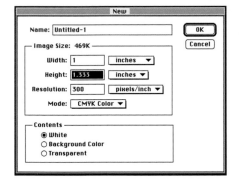

In Photoshop, most print designers are used to working in CMYK, at high resolutions.

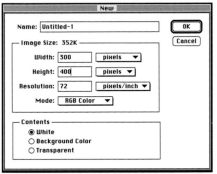

Web designers using Photoshop should always set the color space to RGB, and the dpi to 72.

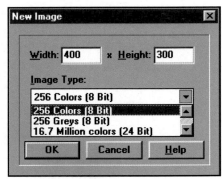

Paint Shop Pro defaults to RGB at 72 dpi, so you don't have to worry about changing settings for Web graphics.

Bit-Depth

Uh oh, the dreaded bit-depth topic! For those math-phobic people, this will most likely be an intimidating-sounding subject. Bear with us. Bit-depth is very important in understanding Web graphics. Bit-depth refers to how many colors reside in an image. The number of colors in an image can have a HUGE impact on file size. Here's how bit-depth is calculated:

32-bit	16.7+ million colors plus an 8-bit (256-level) grayscale mask
24-bit	16.7+ million colors
16-bit	65.5 thousand colors
15-bit	32.8 thousand colors
8-bit	256 colors
7-bit	128 colors
6-bit	64 colors
5-bit	32 colors
4-bit	16 colors
3-bit	8 colors
2-bit	4 colors
1-bit	2 colors

Here's a visual guide to bit-depth settings:

8-bit 256 colors

7-bit 128 colors

6-bit 64 colors

5-bit 32 colors

4-bit 16 colors

3-bit 8 colors

2-bit 4 colors (includes b&w and 2 colors)

1-bit 2 colors (b&w only)

Dithering and Banding

When an image with millions of colors is converted to an image with 256 colors or less, image quality is lost. Basically, when colors are removed from the image, some sacrifices have to be made. This can take place in two forms: dithering or banding. Here are some definitions to remember:

- Dithering is the positioning of different colored pixels within an image that uses a 256-color palette to simulate a color that does not exist in the palette. A dithered image often looks noisy, or composed of scattered pixels.

- An Adaptive Palette is used to convert an image to 256 colors based on existing colors within the image. Generally, adaptive-based dithering looks the best of all dithering methods.

- Screen Dithering is what happens when a 24-bit or 16-bit image is viewed on a computer with a 256-color card. The image's color is reduced to 256 colors, and the "dither" looks uniform, as if a pattern was used.

- Banding is a process of reducing colors to 256 or less without dithering. It produces areas of solid color, and generates a posterized effect.

Understanding the terminology of dithering and banding is important in Web design, as these are often effects that are undesirable. Bringing down the quality of images is necessary at times for speed considerations, but riding the line between low file size and good enough quality means that you will often encounter unwanted results. These new terms help define the problems you'll encounter when creating Web graphics, and will be used throughout the rest of the book.

Screen dithering takes the form of a repeated pattern and creates a moiré appearance.

The dots within a "screen dithered" image look uniform, based on a generalized screen pattern.

This is an example of "image dithering" using an adaptive palette. It will typically look a lot better than "screen dithering" because the dither pattern is based on the content of the image, not a preset screen.

Even though the image is composed of pixellated dots, they are less obvious and objectionable because there's no obvious pattern or screen.

The banding in this image is obvious. It looks like a posterization effect.

Here's a close-up of the banding. Instead of the dots you'll find in dithering methods, the computer takes the image and breaks it into regions of solid color.

Monitor's Bit-Depth

So far, we defined bit-depth as it relates to images. There are actually two instances where understanding bit-depth is important. The first is to understand the bit-depth of an image, and the second is to understand the bit-depth of your end viewer's monitor. This time we're discussing the monitor's bit-depth, not the bit-depth of images.

Most professional digital artists have 24-bit monitors (that can display up to 16.7 million colors). The average computer user (hence the average member of your Web-viewing audience) has an 8-bit (256 color) monitor. This makes sense if you think about it, because the majority of computer monitors are owned by average people, who bought the least expensive version of their computer system, not professional graphics artists who might have greatly enhanced systems.

Herein lies a huge problem. The majority of people who create artwork for Web sites are viewing the artwork under better conditions than the average end user. This makes for a communication gap; one that this book hopes to bridge rather than to skim over, or worse—ignore.

If a computer system only has an 8-bit color card, it cannot physically view more than 256 colors at once. When people with 256-color systems view your Web screens, they cannot see images in 24-bit, even if they want to.

Here's an example of a 24-bit image that has not been converted to 256 colors, when viewed on a 256-color system. This demonstrates an example of screen dithering.

■ step-by-step

How to Change Your Monitor's Bit-Depth

We recommend that you always run a bit-depth preview test on your Web pages before you send them out for the world to see. Change your monitor settings to 256 colors, and you'll see how your artwork translates under those conditions.

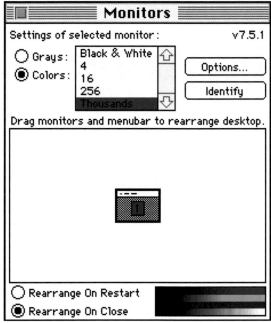

Macintosh: Open the control panel called "Monitors" or "Sights and Sound." (Control panel items are located in your System Folder.)

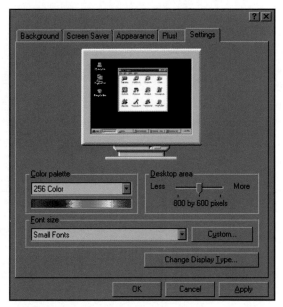

Windows 95: Access your display properties by using your right mouse button and selecting Display properties.

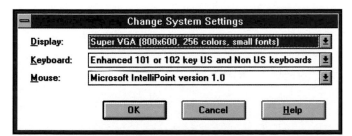

Windows 3.1: From Program Manager, display the Change System Settings dialog box by double-clicking on the Windows Setup icon (generally found in the Main program group) and Choosing Change System Settings from the Options menu.

Hexadecimal Color?

Before the Web came along, few people other than programmers, math students, and mathematicians had any need to work with hexadecimal numbers. Just think, before the Web came along there were all kinds of things you'd never done before! You can now add converting RGB values to hexadecimal values to your list.

Hexadecimal numbers in Web design are used to convert RGB values so HTML can understand which colors you've chosen. To describe the color R:255 G:00 B:51, the hexadecimal code would look like: FF0033. Here's the most minimal sample code for an HTML page that has the following color scheme:

```
<html>
<body bgcolor="003333" text="33CCCC" link="336699"
vlink="006666" alink="00CC99"
</body>
</html>
```

These swatches demonstrate the RGB-to-hex conversion process.

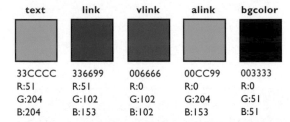

text	link	vlink	alink	bgcolor
33CCCC	336699	006666	00CC99	003333
R:51	R:51	R:0	R:0	R:0
G:204	G:102	G:102	G:204	G:51
B:204	B:153	B:102	B:153	B:51

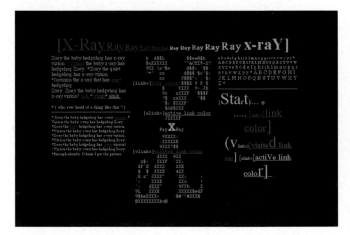

Here are the results of the hexadecimal HTML code to create background, text, link, visited link, and active link colors.

00=00	01=01	02=02	03=03	04=04	05=05	06=06	07=07	08=08
09=09	10=0A	11=0B	12=0C	13=0D	14=0E	15=0F	16=10	17=11
18=12	19=13	20=14	21=15	22=16	23=17	24=18	25=19	26=1A
27=1B	28=1C	29=1D	30=1E	31=1F	32=20	33=21	34=22	35=23
36=24	37=25	38=26	39=27	40=28	41=29	42=2A	43=2B	44=2C
45=2D	46=2E	47=2F	48=30	49=31	50=32	**51=33**	52=34	53=35
54=36	55=37	56=38	57=39	58=3A	59=3B	60=3C	61=3D	62=3E
63=3F	64=40	65=41	66=42	67=43	68=44	69=45	70=46	71=47
72=48	73=49	74=4A	75=4B	76=4C	77=4D	78=4E	79=4F	80=50
81=51	82=52	83=53	84=54	85=55	86=56	87=57	88=58	89=59
90=5A	91=5B	92=5C	93=5D	94=5E	95=5F	96=60	97=61	98=62
99=63	100=64	101=65	**102=66**	103=67	104=68	105=69	106=6A	107=6B
108=6C	109=6D	110=6E	111=6F	112=70	113=71	114=72	115=73	116=74
117=75	118=76	119=77	120=78	121=79	122=7A	123=7B	124=7C	125=7D
126=7E	127=7F	128=80	129=81	130=82	131=83	132=84	133=85	134=86
135=87	136=88	137=89	138=8A	139=8B	140=8C	141=8D	142=8E	143=8F
144=90	145=91	146=92	147=93	148=94	149=95	150=96	151=97	152=98
53=99	154=9A	155=9B	156=9C	157=9D	158=9E	159=9F	160=A0	161=A1
162=A2	163=A3	164=A4	165=A5	166=A6	167=A7	168=A8	168=A9	170=AA
171=AB	172=AC	173=AD	17=AE	175=AF	176=B0	177=B1	178=B2	179=B3
180=B4	181=B5	182=B6	183=B7	184=B8	185=B9	186=BA	187=BB	188=BC
189=BD	190=BE	191=BF	192=C0	193=C1	194=C2	195=C3	196=C4	197=C5
198=C6	199=C7	200=C8	201=C9	202=CA	203=CB	**204=CC**	205=CD	206=CE
207=CF	208=D0	209=D1	210=D2	211=D3	212=D4	213=D5	214=D6	215=D7
216=D8	217=D9	218=DA	219=DB	220=DC	221=DD	222=DE	223=DF	224=E0
225=E1	226=E2	227=E3	228=E4	229=E5	230=E6	231=E7	232=E8	233=E9
234=EA	235=EB	236=EC	237=ED	238=EE	239=EF	240=F0	241=F1	242=F2
243=F3	244=F4	245=F5	246=F6	247=F7	248=F8	249=F9	250=FA	251=FB
252=FC	253=FD	254=FE	**255=FF**					

Here is a handy chart to use when dealing with RGB number conversions (0-255) to hex. The browser-safe colors are highlighted.

%	RGB	HEX
100%	255	FF
80%	204	CC
60%	153	99
40%	102	66
20%	51	33
0%	0	0

Some programs request RGB percentages, instead of specific RGB values. Refer to this chart for conversions.

Browser - Safe Color

Introduction to Browser-Safe Specs

What is all this fuss over browser-safe colors, anyway? Let's look at what the function of a browser is, first. Browser software is your window into the Web. You can't see Web pages without the browser, so the browser plays a huge role in how your images are displayed; especially when viewed on 256-color systems.

Fortunately, the most popular browsers—Netscape, Mosaic, and Internet Explorer—all share the same palette-management process. They work with the system palettes of each respective platform: Mac, Windows, and Win95. This means that any artwork you create will be forced into a variety of different palettes, depending on which operating system it is viewed from.

Thankfully, there are common colors found within the 256-system palettes— 216 common colors, in fact. Each operating system reserves 40 colors out of the possible 256 for its own use. This means that if you stick to the 216 common colors, they will be universally honored between browsers, operating systems, and computer platforms.

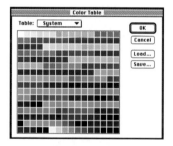
Mac System Palette

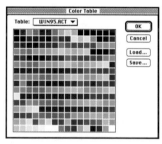
Win95 Palette

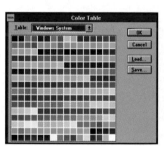
Windows Palette

Even though these three palettes look entirely different, they share 216 common colors. If you use the shared colors, referred to in this book as "browser-safe" colors, you will eliminate a lot of cross-platform inconsistencies of color artwork published over the Web.

Why Work Within a Limited Palette?

Although it is wonderful and nice to design using a large monitor and a 16 million+ color range, most people who view your work will only have computers capable of seeing images in 256 colors on a monitor that can't go beyond 640X480 in size. When we work with colors other than that of the 216 browser-safe colors, the browsers will convert the colors anyway. This will have an adverse effect on your artwork, as the following examples demonstrate.

Hexadecimal-Based Artwork

Web-page color schemes generally are chosen using hexadecimal values, which can lead to the following problem. If you choose a hexadecimal value for a one-color background based on the color that appears on your millions-of-colors monitor, you may well have chosen a value that is not browser safe. If that's the case, and the end user views the image on a 256-color monitor, the browser will convert it to one of the 216 safe colors—it will shift the color you've chosen to its own palette.

The site pictured here uses the hexadecimal code:

```
<BODY BGCOLOR="090301" TEXT="436E58"
LINK="CF7B42" VLINK="323172" ALINK="ffffff".
```

You should be able to tell, just by looking, that these colors are not browser safe! That's because browser-safe hex combinations are always formed from variations of 00, 33, 66, 99, CC, and FF.

PC 8-bit display

Mac 8-bit display

This comparison demonstrates the kind of color shifting that occurs with hexadecimal-based artwork on 8-bit systems if the colors used are not browser safe.

Illustration-Based Artwork

With illustration-based artwork, if you created logos, cartoons, or drawings in colors outside of the 216, you guessed it—the browser converts them anyway! Instead of shifting the color, which is what will happen with hexadecimal-based color, the browser will dither the artwork. Ugh!

On a millions-of-colors display, you might not notice any differences between these two different colored versions of Lynda's Homegurrl Page logo.

On an 8-bit display, look at what happens to the top version: it is filled with unwanted dots, caused by dithering. Why? The colors in the bottom logo are browser safe, and the colors in the top are not.

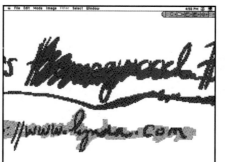

Here's a close-up of the non-browser-safe dithered version on the left, compared to the browser-safe nondithered version on the right.

Photograph-Based Artwork

Photographs are the one type of artwork that really does not benefit from using browser-safe colors. You see, browsers convert photographs to their own fixed palette, but they do a great job of it, unlike the terrible job they do with hexadecimal-based and illustration-based artwork.

Here are some comparisons that support this case:

Viewed in 24-bit   **Viewed in 8-bit**   **Viewed in 24-bit**   **Viewed in 8-bit**

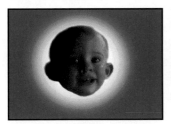  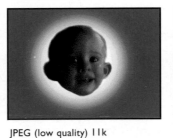 

adaptive 8-bit file 35k   JPEG (low quality) 11k

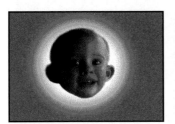   

browser-safe palette 50k   system palette 52k

The images on the left of this study were all viewed from a browser in 24-bit. Which ones on the left have the highest quality? The JPEG, which is a 24-bit file; and the adaptive file, which is an 8-bit file based on the colors within the image, not an outside palette as in the case of the images saved with the system or browser-safe palette. The right-side images show how these photographs looked within a browser viewed from a millions+ color system (24-bit). The right-side images all look worse than when viewed in the 24-bit browser, but are there any significant quality benefits from having saved them with different methods? We think not. The results of this study? It is not necessary to convert photograph-based images to the browser-safe palette, or even an 8-bit palette. The browser does its dithering dirty work regardless of how you prepare the image. It's best to leave the image in an adaptive palette or 24-bit file format so that the photographs will have the added advantage of looking better in 24-bit browser environments. JPEGs will always produce the smallest file size for photographs and have the added advantage of being a 24-bit file format, unlike GIF, which cannot save images at higher bit-depths than 8-bit (256 colors).

Browser-Safe Color Summary

So, you may think that all this hubbub over browser-safe colors need not apply to you. If you think your site will only be viewed from millions-of-colors monitors (24-bit), you might be right. It's always important to decide who your audience is before you design a site, and create artwork that is appropriate for your viewers.

Our recommendation is this: If you are going to pick colors for backgrounds, type, text, links, and illustrations, why not choose cross-platform compatible colors? We agree that the notion of working with 216 colors is pretty limited, especially in light of how sophisticated computer graphics systems are today. We've tried to make working browser safe a bit more attractive by creating suggested color families and palettes for you to choose from. It is our hope that the tools this book offers, in terms of organizing these 216 colors in the pages that follow and showing you how to make hybrid variations of them, will make working browser safe more attractive than not.

What Does the Browser-Safe Palette Look Like?

The 216-color palette for the Web has only 6 red values, 6 green values, and 6 blue values that range in contrast. Sometimes this palette is referred to as the 6X6X6 palette, or the 6X6X6 cube. This palette is a predetermined palette that, as of yet, can't be changed. It's the way browsers are pre-programmed, and designers have no HTML controls over the way that browsers handle palette managment.

The RGB values found within the 216-color palette have some predictable similarities: the numbers are all formed from variations of 00, 51, 102, 153, 204, and 255.

The hexadecimal values found within the 216-color palette have some pre-dictable similarities too: they are all formed from variations of 00, 33, 66, 99, CC, and FF.

The Front Side of the Mathematical Cube

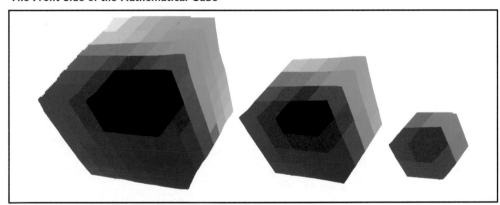

Outer cube: full saturation; Middle cube: middle saturation; Inner cube: low saturation

The Back Side of the Mathematical Cube

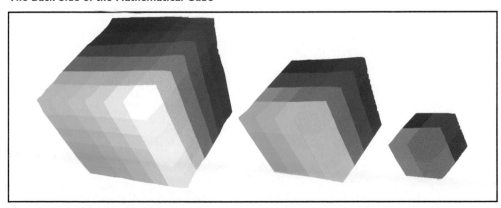

Outer cube: full saturation; Middle cube: middle saturation; Inner cube: low saturation

It should be no surprise that these colors were picked by math, not beauty. Knowing the pattern of the numeric values is useful, because you can easily check your code or image documents to see if they contain these values.

Here's a version of the browser-safe palette, straight out of the computer.

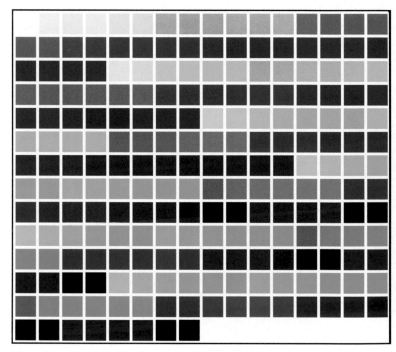

Notice how these colors have no sense of organization? It's that math versus beauty thing again!

The browser-safe palette can be organized many different ways. It's our feeling that by organizing the colors differently—by hue, by value, by saturation, by lights, by darks—that these colors form usable palettes to design with.

These three swatch set examples take the 216 colors and provide color ramps from red to every other color in the browser-safe palette. The swatch set on the left shows a fully saturated palette, while the swatch set on the right shows a desaturated palette. By organizing these colors in a visual manner rather than a mathematical manner, Web designers can work with these colors and make better choices than by picking them out of a disorganized mathematical array.

In the example below, the colors are arranged in a usable palette for Web artists. You can load these palettes (which are inside the SWATCHES/ODDBALL folder on the *Coloring Web Graphics* CD-ROM) into any paint program and use the Eyedropper tool to pick browser-safe colors.

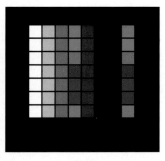

Low saturation (mfd)

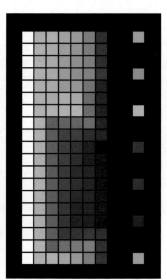

Middle saturation (rmd)

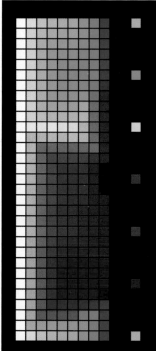

Full saturation (rmfs)

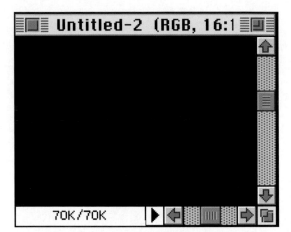

At a magnified view, you can see that Don made a pixel-by-pixel pattern of 3 different browser-safe colors.

At a 1:1 view, the pattern looks solid, and creates an optical illusion of a color found outside the palette, even though it is still technically browser safe. We call these colors *hybrid colors* within this book.

What Are Hybrid-Safe Colors?

Hybrid-safe colors were originated by Don Barnett and Bruce Heavin when working on a prototype Web site for DreamWorks Interactive SKG ■ http://www.cris.com/~Nekton/sources/net_barn.htm.

Don Barnett wanted to use colors that didn't shift or dither in 256-color environments, but he didn't like any of the 216 colors he had to choose from. He came up with the idea of forming a pre-dithered pattern, on a pixel-by-pixel basis, of multiple browser-safe colors. This created an optical mixture of colors, tricking the eye into thinking it was a new color outside of the 216 limited palette.

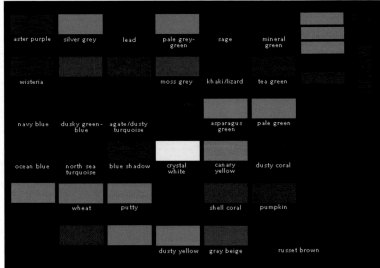

This page of hybrid colors was created by Don Barnett for the DreamWorks Interactive SKG site. This file is on the *Coloring Web Graphics* CD-ROM, inside the CLIPART\TILES\DONB folder. Instructions on how to make hybrid colors and insert them into HTML are found in Chapter 5, "Imaging Techniques."

How Do You Work with Browser-Safe and Hybrid Colors?

Ok, you might be thinking; you've convinced me that I might as well use these colors. But, how?

Hybrid color files must be loaded into the <body background> tag of an HTML document.

Here is the basic, most rudimentary HTML you would need in order to load hybrid color files into the background of your Web pages:

```
<html>
<body background="hybrid.gif">
</body><html>
```

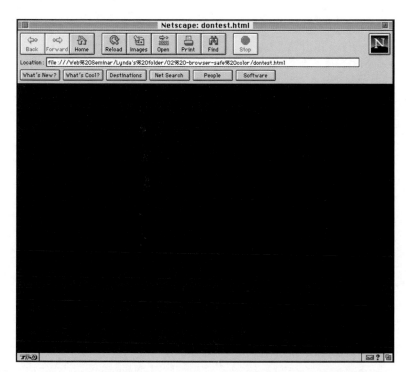

On the left is the source file for the HTML. It is repeated unlimited times, depending on how big the browser window is. To the right of the source file is the final screen in Netscape, filled repeatedly with a browser-safe seamless tile.

■ **note**

The Book's CD-ROM

Bruce Heavin, with some help from Don Barnett, Joe Maller, and Lynda Weinman, has created zillions of files found on the CD-ROM that pertain to the browser-safe and hybrid 216 palettes. These files are cataloged, and thumbnail views of them are presented in Chapter 6, "Color Groupings/ Swatches/Directory." They come in a few different flavors and categories, and this section of the book explains how to use them. Detailed instructions for palette creation, seamless tile creation, and working with palettes are found in Chapter 5, "Imaging Techniques."

■ step-by-step

Photoshop Swatch Palettes

Photoshop Swatch palettes have the extension .aco at the end of them. To use these files, follow these steps:

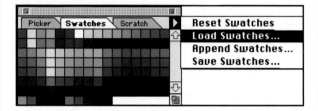

Step 1. Open Photoshop.

Step 2. Choose Palette, Show Swatches to display the Swatch Palette.

Step 3. Click on the right arrow and select Load Swatches.

Now you can open any .aco document found in the SWATCHES/ACO folder on the *Coloring Web Graphics* CD-ROM.

Note: You can load multiple swatch sets into the Photoshop Swatch Palette by choosing Append Swatches instead of Load Swatches.

■ note

Imaging Programs other than Photoshop

All of the Photoshop Swatch palettes have also been saved as .gif files, which can be found in the SWATCHES/GIF folder of the *Coloring Web Graphics* CD-ROM. Most imaging programs, including Paint Shop Pro and Corel Photo-Paint, can open GIF files. Use the eyedropper tool in these programs to select colors from the palettes.

■ step-by-step

Paint Shop Pro .pal file

With Paint Shop Pro, you can make and load custom palettes. Paint Shop Pro does not recognize the Photoshop .aco extension, however. JASC, the company that makes Paint Shop Pro, distributes a browser-safe 216 palette called netscape.pal. It's on our *Coloring Web Graphics* CD-ROM, inside the CLUTS/PSP folder.

To load the netscape.pal palette, follow these steps:

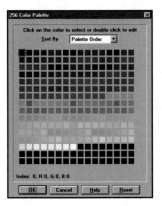 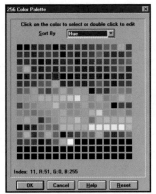 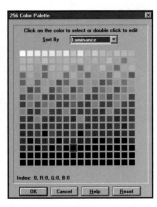

Select Load Palette from the Colors menu, then select the netscape.pal file. When you double-click on the foreground color in the Tools Palette, it brings forward the palette window.

One of the extra-special-nifty things that Paint Shop Pro does is organize any .pal file by palette, hue, or luminance value. We wish Photoshop could do this too!

Browser-Safe Color Charts Organized by Hue

330000 R=051 G=000 B=000	**660000** R=102 G=000 B=000	**990000** R=153 G=000 B=000	**CC0000** R=204 G=000 B=000	**FF0000** R=255 G=000 B=000	**663333** R=102 G=051 B=051	**993333** R=153 G=051 B=051	**CC3333** R=204 G=051 B=051
CC0033 R=204 G=000 B=051	**FF3366** R=255 G=051 B=102	**990033** R=153 G=000 B=051	**CC3366** R=204 G=051 B=102	**FF6699** R=255 G=102 B=153	**FF0066** R=255 G=000 B=102	**660033** R=102 G=000 B=051	**CC0066** R=204 G=000 B=102
CC0099 R=204 G=000 B=153	**FF33CC** R=255 G=51 B=204	**FF00CC** R=255 G=000 B=204	**330033** R=051 G=000 B=051	**660066** R=102 G=000 B=102	**990099** R=153 G=000 B=102	**CC00CC** R=204 G=000 B=204	**FF00FF** R=255 G=000 B=255
FF99FF R=255 G=153 B=255	**FFCCFF** R=255 G=204 B=255	**CC00FF** R=204 G=000 B=255	**9900CC** R=153 G=000 B=204	**CC33FF** R=204 G=051 B=255	**660099** R=102 G=000 B=153	**9933CC** R=153 G=051 B=204	**CC66FF** R=204 G=102 B=255
330099 R=051 G=000 B=153	**6633CC** R=102 G=051 B=204	**9966FF** R=153 G=102 B=255	**3300CC** R=051 G=000 B=204	**6633FF** R=102 G=051 B=255	**3300FF** R=051 G=000 B=255	**000000** R=000 G=000 B=000	**000033** R=000 G=000 B=051
666699 R=102 G=102 B=153	**6666CC** R=102 G=102 B=204	**6666FF** R=102 G=102 B=255	**9999CC** R=153 G=153 B=204	**9999FF** R=153 G=153 B=255	**CCCCFF** R=204 G=204 B=255	**0033FF** R=000 G=051 B=255	**0033CC** R=000 G=051 B=204
3399FF R=051 G=153 B=255	**6699CC** R=102 G=153 B=204	**99CCFF** R=153 G=204 B=255	**0099FF** R=000 G=153 B=255	**006699** R=000 G=102 B=153	**3399CC** R=051 G=153 B=204	**66CCFF** R=102 G=204 B=255	**0099CC** R=000 G=153 B=204
00CCCC R=000 G=204 B=204	**33CCCC** R=051 G=204 B=204	**66CCCC** R=102 G=204 B=204	**99CCCC** R=153 G=204 B=204	**00FFFF** R=000 G=255 B=255	**33FFFF** R=051 G=255 B=255	**66FFFF** R=102 G=255 B=255	**99FFFF** R=153 G=255 B=255
006633 R=000 G=102 B=051	**339966** R=051 G=153 B=102	**00CC66** R=000 G=204 B=102	**66CC99** R=102 G=204 B=153	**33FF99** R=051 G=255 B=153	**99FFCC** R=153 G=255 B=204	**00FF66** R=000 G=255 B=102	**009933** R=000 G=153 B=051
009900 R=000 G=153 B=000	**339933** R=051 G=153 B=051	**669966** R=102 G=153 B=102	**00CC00** R=000 G=204 B=000	**33CC33** R=051 G=204 B=051	**66CC66** R=102 G=204 B=102	**99CC99** R=153 G=204 B=153	**00FF00** R=000 G=255 B=000
66CC33 R=102 G=204 B=051	**99FF66** R=153 G=255 B=102	**66FF00** R=102 G=255 B=000	**336600** R=051 G=102 B=000	**669933** R=102 G=153 B=051	**66CC00** R=102 G=204 B=000	**99CC66** R=153 G=204 B=102	**99FF33** R=153 G=255 B=051
333300 R=051 G=051 B=000	**666600** R=102 G=102 B=000	**666633** R=102 G=102 B=051	**999900** R=153 G=153 B=000	**999933** R=153 G=153 B=051	**999966** R=153 G=153 B=102	**CCCC00** R=204 G=204 B=000	**CCCC33** R=204 G=204 B=051
CC9900 R=204 G=153 B=000	**FFCC33** R=255 G=204 B=051	**996600** R=153 G=102 B=000	**CC9933** R=204 G=153 B=051	**FFCC66** R=255 G=204 B=102	**FF9900** R=255 G=153 B=000	**663300** R=102 G=051 B=000	**996633** R=153 G=102 B=051
CC3300 R=204 G=051 B=000	**FF6633** R=255 G=102 B=051	**FF3300** R=255 G=051 B=000	**333333** R=051 G=051 B=051	**666666** R=102 G=102 B=102	**999999** R=153 G=153 B=153	**CCCCCC** R=204 G=204 B=204	**FFFFFF** R=255 G=255 B=255

| FF3333 R=255 G=051 B=051 | 996666 R=153 G=102 B=102 | CC6666 R=204 G=102 B=102 | FF6666 R=255 G=102 B=102 | CC9999 R=204 G=153 B=153 | FF9999 R=255 G=153 B=153 | FFCCCC R=255 G=204 B=204 | FF0033 R=255 G=000 B=051 |

| 993366 R=153 G=051 B=102 | FF3399 R=255 G=051 B=153 | CC6699 R=204 G=102 B=153 | FF99CC R=255 G=153 B=204 | FF0099 R=255 G=000 B=153 | 990066 R=153 G=000 B=102 | CC3399 R=204 G=051 B=153 | FF66CC R=255 G=102 B=204 |

| 663366 R=102 G=051 B=102 | 993399 R=153 G=051 B=153 | CC33CC R=204 G=051 B=204 | FF33FF R=255 G=051 B=255 | 996699 R=153 G=102 B=153 | CC66CC R=204 G=102 B=204 | FF66FF R=255 G=102 B=255 | CC99CC R=204 G=153 B=204 |

| 9900FF R=153 G=000 B=255 | 330066 R=051 G=000 B=102 | 6600CC R=102 G=000 B=204 | 663399 R=102 G=051 B=153 | 9933FF R=153 G=051 B=255 | 9966CC R=153 G=102 B=204 | CC99FF R=204 G=153 B=255 | 6600FF R=102 G=000 B=255 |

| 000066 R=000 G=000 B=102 | 000099 R=000 G=000 B=153 | 0000CC R=000 G=000 B=204 | 0000FF R=000 G=000 B=255 | 333366 R=051 G=051 B=102 | 333399 R=051 G=051 B=153 | 3333CC R=051 G=051 B=204 | 3333FF R=051 G=051 B=255 |

| 3366FF R=051 G=102 B=255 | 003399 R=000 G=051 B=153 | 3366CC R=051 G=102 B=204 | 6699FF R=102 G=153 B=255 | 0066FF R=000 G=102 B=255 | 003366 R=000 G=051 B=102 | 0066CC R=000 G=102 B=204 | 336699 R=051 G=102 B=153 |

| 33CCFF R=051 G=204 B=255 | 00CCFF R=000 G=204 B=255 | 003333 R=000 G=051 B=051 | 006666 R=000 G=102 B=102 | 336666 R=051 G=102 B=102 | 009999 R=000 G=153 B=153 | 339999 R=051 G=153 B=153 | 669999 R=102 G=153 B=153 |

| CCFFFF R=204 G=255 B=255 | 00FFCC R=000 G=255 B=204 | 00CC99 R=000 G=204 B=153 | 33FFCC R=051 G=255 B=204 | 009966 R=000 G=153 B=102 | 33CC99 R=051 G=204 B=153 | 66FFCC R=102 G=255 B=204 | 00FF99 R=000 G=255 B=153 |

| 33CC66 R=051 G=204 B=102 | 66FF99 R=102 G=255 B=153 | 00CC33 R=000 G=204 B=051 | 33FF66 R=051 G=255 B=102 | 00FF33 R=000 G=255 B=051 | 003300 R=000 G=051 B=000 | 006600 R=000 G=102 B=000 | 336633 R=051 G=102 B=051 |

| 33FF33 R=051 G=255 B=051 | 66FF66 R=102 G=255 B=102 | 99FF99 R=153 G=255 B=153 | CCFFCC R=204 G=255 B=204 | 33FF00 R=051 G=255 B=000 | 33CC00 R=051 G=204 B=000 | 66FF33 R=102 G=255 B=051 | 339900 R=051 G=153 B=000 |

| CCFF99 R=204 G=255 B=153 | 99FF00 R=153 G=255 B=000 | 669900 R=102 G=153 B=000 | 99CC33 R=153 G=204 B=051 | CCFF66 R=204 G=255 B=102 | 99CC00 R=153 G=204 B=000 | CCFF33 R=204 G=255 B=051 | CCFF00 R=204 G=255 B=000 |

| CCCC66 R=204 G=204 B=102 | CCCC99 R=204 G=204 B=153 | FFFF00 R=255 G=255 B=000 | FFFF33 R=255 G=255 B=051 | FFFF66 R=255 G=255 B=102 | FFFF99 R=255 G=255 B=153 | FFFFCC R=255 G=255 B=204 | FFCC00 R=255 G=204 B=000 |

| CC6600 R=204 G=102 B=000 | CC9966 R=204 G=153 B=102 | FF9933 R=255 G=153 B=051 | FFCC99 R=255 G=204 B=153 | FF6600 R=255 G=102 B=000 | 993300 R=153 G=051 B=000 | CC6633 R=204 G=102 B=051 | FF9966 R=255 G=153 B=102 |

Browser-Safe Color Charts Organized by Luminance

FFFFFF R=255 G=255 B=255	**FFFFCC** R=255 G=255 B=204	**FFFF99** R=255 G=255 B=153	**CCFFFF** R=204 G=255 B=255	**FFFF66** R=255 G=255 B=102	**CCFFCC** R=204 G=255 B=204	**FFFF33** R=255 G=255 B=051	**CCFF99** R=204 G=255 B=153
99FF99 R=153 G=255 B=153	**CCFF00** R=204 G=255 B=000	**CCCCFF** R=204 G=204 B=255	**66FFFF** R=102 G=255 B=255	**FFCC66** R=255 G=204 B=102	**99FF66** R=153 G=255 B=102	**CCCCCC** R=204 G=204 B=204	**66FFCC** R=102 G=255 B=204
33FFFF R=051 G=255 B=255	**CCCC66** R=204 G=204 B=102	**66FF66** R=102 G=255 B=102	**FF99CC** R=255 G=153 B=204	**99CCCC** R=153 G=204 B=204	**33FFCC** R=051 G=255 B=204	**CCCC33** R=204 G=204 B=051	**66FF33** R=102 G=255 B=051
FF9966 R=255 G=153 B=102	**99CC66** R=153 G=204 B=102	**33FF66** R=051 G=255 B=102	**CC99CC** R=204 G=153 B=204	**66CCCC** R=102 G=204 B=204	**00FFCC** R=000 G=255 B=204	**FF9933** R=255 G=153 B=051	**99CC33** R=153 G=204 B=051
9999FF R=153 G=153 B=255	**33CCFF** R=051 G=204 B=255	**CC9966** R=204 G=153 B=102	**66CC66** R=102 G=204 B=102	**00FF66** R=000 G=255 B=102	**FF66CC** R=255 G=102 B=204	**9999CC** R=153 G=153 B=204	**33CCCC** R=051 G=204 B=204
00FF00 R=000 G=255 B=000	**CC66FF** R=204 G=102 B=255	**6699FF** R=102 G=153 B=255	**00CCFF** R=000 G=204 B=255	**FF6666** R=255 G=102 B=102	**999966** R=153 G=153 B=102	**33CC66** R=051 G=204 B=102	**CC66CC** R=204 G=102 B=204
FF6600 R=255 G=102 B=000	**999900** R=153 G=153 B=000	**33CC00** R=051 G=204 B=000	**FF33FF** R=255 G=051 B=255	**9966FF** R=153 G=102 B=255	**3399FF** R=051 G=153 B=255	**CC6666** R=204 G=102 B=102	**669966** R=102 G=153 B=102
996699 R=153 G=102 B=153	**339999** R=051 G=153 B=153	**CC6600** R=204 G=102 B=000	**669900** R=102 G=153 B=000	**00CC00** R=000 G=204 B=000	**CC33FF** R=204 G=051 B=255	**6666FF** R=102 G=102 B=255	**0099FF** R=000 G=153 B=255
339933 R=051 G=153 B=051	**CC3399** R=204 G=051 B=153	**666699** R=102 G=102 B=153	**009999** R=000 G=153 B=153	**FF3300** R=255 G=051 B=000	**996600** R=153 G=102 B=000	**339900** R=051 G=153 B=000	**FF00FF** R=255 G=000 B=255
CC3333 R=204 G=051 B=051	**666633** R=102 G=102 B=051	**009933** R=000 G=153 B=051	**FF0099** R=255 G=000 B=153	**993399** R=153 G=051 B=153	**336699** R=051 G=102 B=153	**CC3300** R=204 G=051 B=000	**666600** R=102 G=102 B=000
6633CC R=102 G=051 B=204	**0066CC** R=000 G=102 B=204	**FF0033** R=255 G=000 B=051	**993333** R=153 G=051 B=051	**336633** R=051 G=102 B=051	**CC0099** R=204 G=000 B=153	**663399** R=102 G=051 B=153	**006699** R=000 G=102 B=153
9900CC R=153 G=000 B=204	**3333CC** R=051 G=051 B=204	**CC0033** R=204 G=000 B=051	**663333** R=102 G=051 B=051	**006633** R=000 G=102 B=051	**990099** R=153 G=000 B=153	**333399** R=051 G=051 B=153	**CC0000** R=204 G=000 B=000
990033 R=153 G=000 B=051	**333333** R=051 G=051 B=051	**660099** R=102 G=000 B=153	**003399** R=000 G=051 B=153	**990000** R=153 G=000 B=000	**333300** R=051 G=051 B=000	**3300FF** R=051 G=000 B=255	**660066** R=102 G=000 B=102
330066 R=051 G=000 B=102	**0000CC** R=000 G=000 B=204	**330033** R=051 G=000 B=051	**000099** R=000 G=000 B=153	**330000** R=051 G=000 B=000	**000066** R=000 G=000 B=102	**000033** R=000 G=000 B=051	**000000** R=000 G=000 B=000

FFFF00 R=255 G=255 B=000	**FFCCFF** R=255 G=204 B=255	**99FFFF** R=153 G=255 B=255	**CCFF00** R=204 G=255 B=102	**FFCCCC** R=255 G=204 B=204	**99FFCC** R=153 G=204 B=204	**CCFF33** R=204 G=255 B=051	**FFCC99** R=255 G=204 B=153
FFCC33 R=255 G=204 B=051	**99FF33** R=153 G=255 B=051	**CCCC99** R=204 G=204 B=153	**66FF99** R=102 G=255 B=153	**FFCC00** R=255 G=204 B=000	**99FF00** R=153 G=255 B=000	**FF99FF** R=255 G=153 B=255	**99CCFF** R=153 G=204 B=255
FF9999 R=255 G=153 B=153	**99CC99** R=153 G=204 B=153	**33FF99** R=051 G=255 B=153	**CCCC00** R=204 G=204 B=000	**66FF00** R=102 G=255 B=000	**CC99FF** R=204 G=153 B=255	**66CCFF** R=102 G=204 B=255	**00FFFF** R=000 G=255 B=255
33FF33 R=051 G=255 B=051	**CC9999** R=204 G=153 B=153	**66CC99** R=102 G=204 B=153	**00FF99** R=000 G=255 B=153	**FF9900** R=255 G=153 B=000	**99CC00** R=153 G=204 B=000	**33FF00** R=051 G=255 B=000	**FF66FF** R=255 G=102 B=255
CC9933 R=204 G=153 B=051	**66CC33** R=102 G=204 B=051	**00FF33** R=000 G=255 B=051	**FF6699** R=255 G=102 B=153	**999999** R=153 G=153 B=153	**33CC99** R=051 G=204 B=153	**CC9900** R=204 G=153 B=000	**66CC00** R=102 G=204 B=000
6699CC R=102 G=153 B=204	**00CCCC** R=000 G=204 B=204	**FF6633** R=255 G=102 B=051	**999933** R=153 G=153 B=051	**33CC33** R=051 G=204 B=051	**CC6699** R=204 G=102 B=153	**669999** R=102 G=153 B=153	**00CC99** R=000 G=204 B=153
00CC66 R=000 G=204 B=102	**FF33CC** R=255 G=051 B=204	**9966CC** R=153 G=102 B=204	**3399CC** R=051 G=153 B=204	**CC6633** R=204 G=102 B=051	**669933** R=102 G=153 B=051	**00CC33** R=000 G=204 B=051	**FF3399** R=255 G=051 B=153
FF3366 R=255 G=051 B=102	**996666** R=153 G=102 B=102	**339966** R=051 G=153 B=102	**CC33CC** R=204 G=051 B=204	**6666CC** R=102 G=102 B=204	**0099CC** R=000 G=153 B=204	**FF3333** R=255 G=051 B=051	**996633** R=153 G=102 B=051
9933FF R=153 G=051 B=255	**3366FF** R=051 G=102 B=255	**CC3366** R=204 G=051 B=102	**666666** R=102 G=102 B=102	**009966** R=000 G=153 B=102	**FF00CC** R=255 G=000 B=204	**9933CC** R=153 G=051 B=204	**3366CC** R=051 G=102 B=204
009900 R=000 G=153 B=000	**CC00FF** R=204 G=000 B=255	**6633FF** R=102 G=051 B=255	**0066FF** R=000 G=102 B=255	**FF0066** R=255 G=000 B=102	**993366** R=153 G=051 B=102	**336666** R=051 G=102 B=102	**CC00CC** R=204 G=000 B=204
FF0000 R=255 G=000 B=000	**993300** R=153 G=051 B=000	**336600** R=051 G=102 B=000	**9900FF** R=153 G=000 B=255	**3333FF** R=051 G=051 B=255	**CC0066** R=204 G=000 B=102	**663366** R=102 G=051 B=102	**006666** R=000 G=102 B=102
663300 R=102 G=051 B=000	**006600** R=000 G=102 B=000	**6600FF** R=102 G=000 B=255	**0033FF** R=000 G=051 B=255	**990066** R=153 G=000 B=102	**333366** R=051 G=051 B=102	**6600CC** R=102 G=000 B=204	**0033CC** R=000 G=051 B=204
003366 R=000 G=051 B=102	**3300CC** R=051 G=000 B=204	**660033** R=102 G=000 B=051	**003333** R=000 G=051 B=051	**330099** R=051 G=000 B=153	**660000** R=102 G=000 B=000	**003300** R=000 G=051 B=000	**0000FF** R=000 G=000 B=255

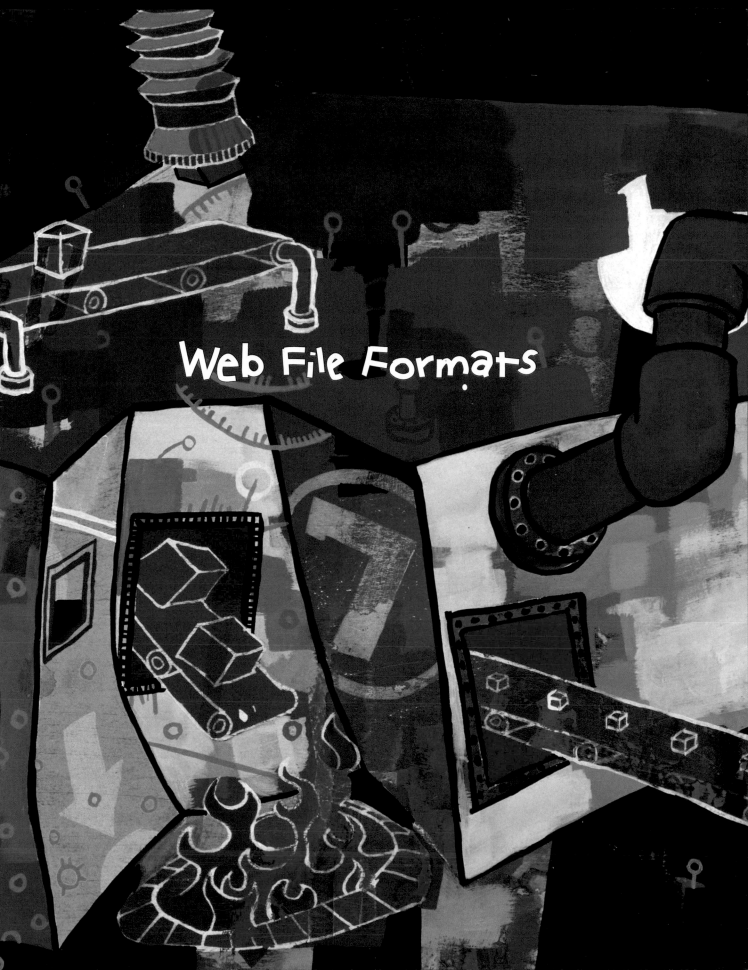

Web File Formats

Color and Web File Formats

What does color have to do with file formats, you may ask? Lots! We will examine file formats for the Web from a few different color-related angles in this book, such as how to make color images small in file size so that they download quickly, and how file formats and color palettes affect the visual integrity of Web-bound artwork.

There are two main file formats for the Web so far: JPEGs and GIFs. Both of these file formats have been widely adopted because they compress images dramatically. On the Web, small files (not just in dimensions, but in file size) result in speedy graphics. It's no longer necessary to only create compelling visuals and information—the speed with which your site is viewed is also subject to critique. As anyone who has ever surfed the Web knows, if a site is too slow, most of us will click onward and elsewhere.

Working with compression methods isn't anything anyone has ever had to think much about before the Web. So, if you're new to Web graphics authoring, and these file formats are unfamiliar to you, don't sweat it. They're new to just about everyone.

JPEG stands for Joint Photographic Experts Group, and GIF stands for Graphic Interchange Format. These names tell you, in each respective acronym, which format is best for which kind of image. JPEGs were designed to compress photographs, and GIFs were designed to compress graphics.

There will be times when you will want to make a photograph into a GIF, such as with transparent GIFs and animated GIFs, and times when you want to make a graphic into a JPEG, such as when a logo or graphic is combined with a photograph. This chapter serves as a valuable reference whenever you question which file format to use and why.

GIF Compression

Unlike most other computer graphic file formats, GIF (Graphic Interchange Format) was designed specifically for online delivery, as it was originally developed for CompuServe in the late 1980s. The file format compresses graphics beautifully, but can also be used for photographic images. Whenever you create graphics, such as logos, illustrations, or cartoons, we recommend the GIF file format.

GIF uses a compression scheme called LZW, which is based on work done by Lempel-Ziv & Welch. The patent for LZW compression is owned by a company called Unisys, which charges developers like Netscape and Photoshop licensing and royalty fees for selling products that use the GIF file format. End users, such as ourselves (Web designers) and our audience (Web visitors), do not have to pay licensing fees or worry about any of this. There is some speculation that the GIF file format may be less prevalent at some point because of the fees, but we hope not. GIFs are accepted by all browsers, GIFs are small, and GIFs do things that many other file formats do not, such as animation, transparency, and interlacing.

The GIF file format, by definition, can only contain 256 colors or less. This is not the case with JPEGs, which by definition contain millions of colors (24-bit). Because GIFs are an indexed-color file format (256 colors or less), it's extremely beneficial to have a thorough understanding of bit-depth settings and palette management when preparing GIF images. We provide such an understanding in this chapter, and we offer specific instructions on how to create images using these file formats in Chapter 5, "Imaging Techniques."

There are two different flavors of GIF: GIF87a and GIF89a. GIF87a supports transparency and interlacing, while GIF89a supports transparency, interlacing, and animation (more information on these features follows). As of this book's printing, the major browsers (Netscape, Microsoft Internet Explorer, and Mosaic) all support both GIF format specifications. You don't really have to refer to the names GIF89a or GIF87a unless you want to sound techie. Most of us simply call these files by the features used, be it a transparent GIF, animated GIF, or plain vanilla GIF.

GIF compression is lossless, meaning that the GIF compression algorithm will not cause any unwanted image degradation. The process of converting a 24-bit image to 256 or fewer colors will cause image degradation on its own, however, so don't get too excited yet!

■ note

"GIF" Pronunciation

First of all, how is GIF pronounced? Some people say it with a soft g as in jiffy, and some with a hard g as in gift. You have our blessing to say it either way. Because no one seems to agree, perhaps it could be said that there is no correct pronunciation?

Making Small GIFs

The GIF file-compression algorithm offers impressive file size reduction, but the degree of file size savings has a lot to do with how you create your GIF images. Understanding how GIFs compress is the first step in this process.

LZW compression looks to patterns of data. Whenever it encounters areas in an image that do not have changes, it can implement much higher compression. This is similar to another type of compression called run-length compression (used in BMP, TIFF, and PCX formats), but LZW writes, stores, and retrieves its code a little differently. Similar to many types of run-length compression, though, GIF compression searches for changes along a horizontal axis, and whenever it finds a new color, it adds to the file size.

 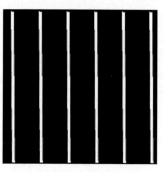 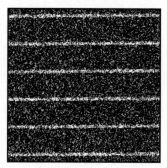

Here's an original image saved as a GIF image that contains horizontal lines. It is 6.7k.

Here's the identical image, only flipped on its side so the lines are vertical. It's a whopping 42% bigger at 11.5k!

Try adding noise to the original? You'll be adding 88% to the file size. This one is 56k!

So what does the line test really teach? That artwork that has horizontal changes compresses better than artwork that doesn't. That anything with noise will more than quadruple your image's file size. That large areas of flat color compress well, and complicated line work or dithering does not.

GIFs for Illustration-Style Imagery

GIFs work much better for graphics than photographs. By graphics, we mean illustrations, cartoons, or logos. Such graphics typically use areas of solid color, and GIFs handle compression of solid color better than the varied colors found in photographs.

With all GIFs, the fewer colors (lower bit-depth), the smaller the resulting file. You should remember this fact when considering whether to improve image quality through anti-aliasing.

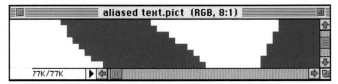

Here's an example of aliased text. It resulted in a file that totaled 3.8k when saved as a GIF.

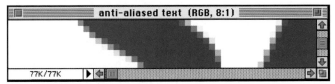

Here's an example of anti-aliased text. It resulted in a file that's 5k when saved as a GIF. The anti-aliasing caused the file to be 24% larger!

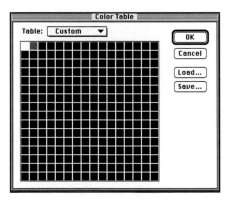

Close-up View: Aliasing does not disguise the jaggy nature of pixel-based artwork.

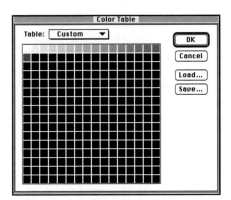

Close-up View: This close-up shows how anti-aliasing creates a blended edge. This blending disguises the square-pixel-based nature of computer-based artwork.

The aliased artwork used only 4 colors.

The anti-aliased artwork used 18 colors.

Most computer artists have never considered working with aliased artwork. It's assumed that artwork will always look better if it has anti-aliased edges. This is simply not true! Artists have never had to factor size of files into their design considerations before. Having something load 24% faster is nothing to balk at. In many cases, aliased artwork looks just as good as anti-aliased artwork, and choosing between the two approaches is something that Web designers should consider whenever possible.

As well as considering whether to use aliased or anti-aliased graphics, you should also always work with browser-safe colors when creating illustration-based artwork for the Web. Examples of how browser-safe colors improve the quality of illustrations were shown in Chapter 2, "Browser-Safe Color." You'll find precise instructions for choosing browser-safe colors for creating custom illustrations in Chapter 5, "Imaging Techniques."

Artwork by Yuryeong Park for the Hot Hot Hot site ■ http://www.hothothot.com. The entire site is done in aliased graphics, and no page exceeds 30k, even though all pages have many images per page.

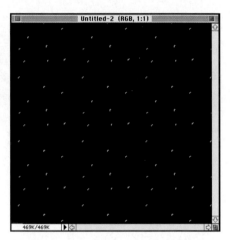

A background tile, previewed in Photoshop, created by Don Barnett. The source tile is only 1.7k. The savings from aliased graphics can really add up!

Here's an example of a 700 x 1134 pixel GIF file created by Bruce Heavin that totals only 7.1k! Why? Lots of solid color and no anti-aliasing. This image has only 4 colors.

GIFs for Photographic Imagery

GIFs are definitely designed to handle graphics better than photographs. That doesn't mean that there won't be times when you
have to turn photographs into GIFs anyway. You may want to use
transparency or animation, which are two features that JPEGs do
not offer.

GIFs can be saved at any bit-depth from 8-bit down to 1-bit. The
bit-depth refers to how many colors the image contains. Generally,
the lower the bit-depth, the smaller the GIF.

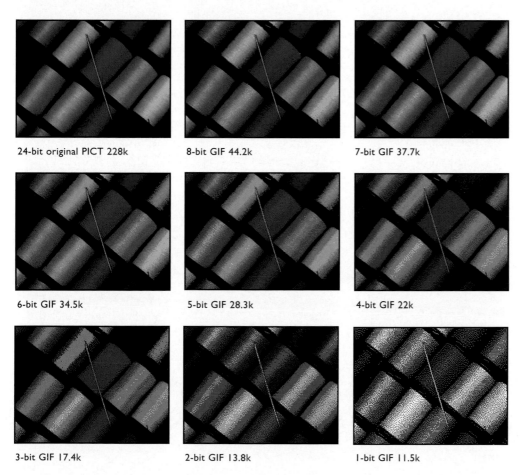

24-bit original PICT 228k   8-bit GIF 44.2k   7-bit GIF 37.7k

6-bit GIF 34.5k   5-bit GIF 28.3k   4-bit GIF 22k

3-bit GIF 17.4k   2-bit GIF 13.8k   1-bit GIF 11.5k

Your job when preparing a GIF is to take it down to its lowest bit-depth level and still maintain acceptable
image quality. Depending on how important this image is, acceptable quality falls somewhere between 6-bit and
4-bit, which offers a 22-50% file size reduction over the 8-bit version.

The questions you will have to answer, based on the content of the images you are creating, are how many colors to assign to an image, and which dithering and color mapping method to choose from.

Color mapping refers to the colors that are assigned to a GIF image and can either be taken from the image or a pre-determined palette of colors:

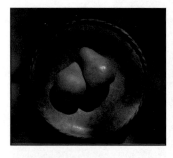
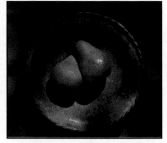
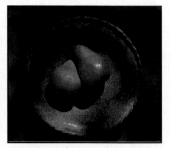

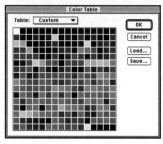
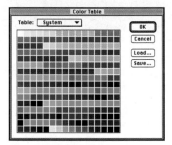
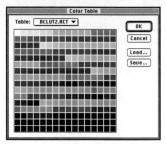

adaptive palette

mac system palette

216 browser-safe palette

The adaptive palette looks the best because the colors are based on the content of the image. Paint Shop Pro calls this type of palette a nearest color palette. Photoshop calls it an adaptive palette.

The system palette image looks much worse. Even though it has the same number of colors as the adaptive palette, the colors are unrelated to the image and detract from the quality.

The browser-safe palette looks worst of all. Not only does it use fewer colors, but just like the system palette, the colors are unrelated to the image.

It's clear that an adaptive or nearest color palette gives the best results to the image, but what about when it's seen in a browser? The following color table shows the results:

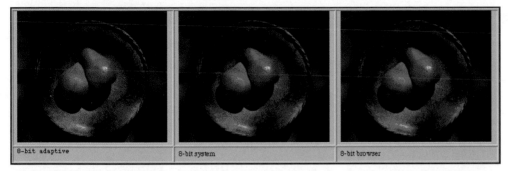

This example demonstrates how the images display in an 8-bit Web browser. See any differences? The differences are minor, if any, aren't they? This is what visitors to your site would see if they had only an 8-bit display.

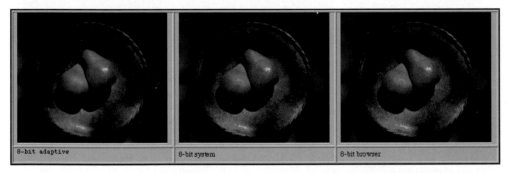

This example demonstrates how the images display in a 24-bit Web browser. The adaptive GIF looks the best, does it not? The moral of the story? Use adaptive palettes for photographs saved as GIFs, and let the 8-bit browsers out there remap your colors on-the-fly for you. This allows your 24-bit viewing audience to see these images at their best, and your 8-bit viewing audience is none the worse off.

Making a choice between dithering methods also plays a huge role in creating smaller GIFs. Any type of "noise" introduces added file size. Unfortunately, whenever you're working with photograph-based GIFs, dithering of one type or another must be employed to reduce the 24-bit color.

GIF saved with dithering 30.1k

GIF without dithering 23.7k

GIF saved with dithering 40.2k

GIF saved in Photoshop's dither none method 38.2k

In this example, the GIF that did not use dithering is an impressive 21% smaller. The only problem is, it looks awful! Sometimes file savings does not warrant loss of quality. Whenever a photograph contains glows, feathered edges, or subtle gradations, you will have to use dithering when converting from 24-bit to 8-bit in order to maintain quality.

There's almost no perceivable difference between these two images, regardless of whether a dithering method is used to convert to 8-bit color or Photoshop's dither none method was chosen. Why? This image has a lot of solid areas of color to begin with. The file savings between 40.2k and 38.2k is not huge either, but the non-dither method will still yield a smaller file size.

Instructions for how to set up dither and no-dither methods for Photoshop and Paint Shop Pro are in Chapter 5, "Imaging Techniques." Both programs offer the capability to set the "dithering" or "no-dithering" method.

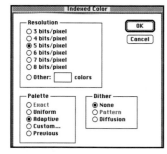

In Photoshop, you could choose from the dither methods of None, Pattern, or Diffusion. None would create the smallest possible GIF files, but that doesn't ensure they'll look good.

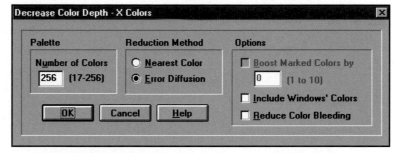

In Paint Shop Pro, you would dither a photograph by choosing Error Diffusion. You would not dither by choosing Nearest Color.

To summarize, in order to make smaller GIFs, you should:

■ Try to save the file at the lowest possible bit-depth, while monitoring quality.

■ Try to avoid dithering, if the image can withstand it. In Photoshop, within the Index Color window, choose Dithering:None. In Paint Shop Pro, inside the Decrease Colors window, choose Nearest Color.

There is never one pat answer for making the smallest possible GIFs. Choices between bit-depth and dithering methods should always be based on the image's content. In general, images with subtle gradations will need to be dithered. Images with areas of solid color will look fine without dithering.

Interlaced GIFs

If you've surfed the Web much, you've encountered interlaced GIFs. They're those images that start out blocky and appear less and less blocky until they come into full focus.

These examples simulate the effect of interlacing on a browser. The image starts chunky and comes into focus over time. This allows the end viewer to decide whether to wait for your graphic to finish or click onward.

In theory, interlacing is supposed to make it possible for your end viewer to get a rough idea of your visuals, and to make a decision whether to wait or click onward before the image finishes rendering. Again—in theory, this is supposed to save time. Unfortunately, if the end viewer is forced to wait for the entire image to finish coming into focus to read essential information, it is often a frustrating experience. In other words, interlaced images save time if you don't have to wait for them to finish.

Our recommendation is that you do not use interlaced GIFs for important visual information that is critical to viewing your site. An imagemap or navigation icon for example, must be seen in order to fulfill its function. While interlaced GIFs serve their purpose on nonessential graphics, they only frustrate end users when used on essential graphics.

Another problem with interlacing is when it's used with transparency. Interlaced, transparent GIFs will often not finish the final render pass and will look chunky and unprofessional.

Graphics & Multimedia	CAD	Internet	Networking
Macromedia	AutoCad	Webmaster	Windows NT
Web-Design	MicroStation	Java	NetWare
3D Studio MAX	AutoCAD LT	WebDesign	MCSE
		VRML	CNE
		Shareware	Operating Systems
			Security

Here's a compelling reason to avoid transparent, interlaced GIFs for main navigation artwork. Sometimes the interlacing doesn't finish rendering and then you're left with unreadable artwork.

Transparent GIFs

Transparent GIFs are used to create the illusion of irregularly shaped artwork. All computer-made images end up in rectangular-shaped files; it's the nature of the medium. Certain file formats, such as GIF, can store masked regions, which create the illusion of shapes other than rectangles. This "masked region" appears to be transparent.

For example, you could create a red circle inside a blue square computer document. By instructing the blue background color of the circle to disappear, or be transparent, the red circle appears to be free floating over another image. Transparency works by creating masked regions that are instructed to disappear when combined with other files.

Here's an example of artwork from Lynda's Homegurrrl site that has been defined to be transparent. The gray color was instructed to drop out within transparency software. Precise instructions for creating transparent artwork in popular image-editing programs are found in Chapter 5, "Imaging Techniques."

Transparency comes in two forms: 8-bit transparency and 1-bit transparency. 8-bit transparency is the best, but it isn't supported by GIFs or by Web browsers. 8-bit transparency is what is used by the file formats Photoshop, TGA, and PICT. 8-bit transparency is also called alpha channel-based transparency and can support up to 256 different levels of opacity (which is why it looks so great!). GIFs support 1-bit transparency, which makes it a much more limited type of masking.

This screen shows the transparent artwork in context. Once the GIF transparency is recognized within the browser software, the browser allows the rectangular artwork to appear irregularly shaped.

This image represents the type of compositing you can do in Photoshop with 8-bit transparency, where it can easily display differing levels of transparency, glows, and blurs. GIF transparency is unfortunately much more crude than this.

■ note

PNG

The only type of Web file format that supports 8-bit transparency is PNG, which was not widely implemented at the time this chapter was written. If you are interested in more information about PNG, try ■ http://quest.jpl.nasa.gov/PNG/png.html. GIF is much more common than PNG, and supported by far more browsers, so it is still much more practical to get your GIF-making chops up to speed and make the best of what it offers.

Animated GIFs

Animated GIFs are part of the GIF89a specification. They are formally called multiblock GIFs because multiple images can be stored as separate blocks within a single GIF document. When the GIF document is viewed, the multiple images display, one at a time, and produce streaming animation.

Streaming is a wonderful and appropriate method for displaying animation over the Web. Streaming means that each frame of the animation displays one after the other, so that your end user doesn't have to wait for the whole file to download before seeing anything. Other animation formats in the past required that the entire movie download before a single frame could be viewed.

Animated GIFs function much like automated slide shows. They can include custom palette information and be set to play at different speeds. They can include interlacing and transparency, too! The beauty of animated GIFs is that they require no plug-ins, and the authoring tools to create them are often free and easy to learn. As well, major browsers (Netscape, Internet Explorer, and Mosaic) support them, so you can include them in Web pages without worrying about compatibility or accessibility. Specific instruction on how to create animated GIFs and apply custom palettes is available in Chapter 5, "Imaging Techniques."

Just like other GIF files, the number of colors and amount of noise in the frames affect the overall file size. If you have a 100-frame animation with each frame totaling 5k, your animated GIF will be 500k. It simply multiplies in size according to how many frames you create and the file size of the individual frame of artwork. On the other hand, your end viewer is really only waiting for 5k servings at a time, so it's nothing like the painful waiting that a standard 500k GIF would incur!

■ note

Popular GIF animation authoring tools

GIF Construction Set/bookware (Windows/Win95)
■ http://www.mindworkshipcom/alchemy/alchemy.html

GIFBuilder/freeware (Mac)
■ http://iawww.epfl.ch/Staff/Yves.Piguet/clip2gif-home/GifBuilder.html

Some good animated GIF references

Royal Frazier's awesome site
■ http://member.aol.com/roalef/gifanim.htm

GIFBuilder's FAQ
■ http://iawww.epfl.ch/Staff/Yves.Piguet/clip2gif-home/GifBuilder Doc/GifBuilder-FAQs.html

Here's a 30-frame animation, found on Lynda's Homegurrl site at ■ http://www.lynda.com/anim.html. It's hard to tell the subtle changes from frame to frame when viewed in sequence, but once the frames are played in motion over time, the '50s man appears to be bobbing his head, waving his finger, and has little lines flowing from the side of his head. It totals **64k** in size. Why? It's only two colors, with no anti-aliasing.

JPEG

The JPEG (pronounced jay-peg) file format offers a 24-bit alternative to the 8-bit GIF file format. This is especially great for photographic content because 24-bit photographs do not dither!

 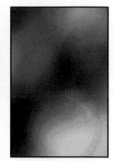

JPEG 7.9k   GIF 22.3k

JPEG 13.7k   GIF 46.9k

JPEG 18.6K   GIF 34.4k

JPEG handles images with subtle gradations beautifully. This is in part because the file format allows the image to remain in 24-bit. Compare the 8-bit GIF to the 24-bit JPEG. They will not only be bigger in file size (in these examples anywhere from 47%-70%!), but they look worse, too!

JPEG was developed specifically for photographic-style images. It looks to areas with subtle tonal and color changes and offers the best compression when it encounters that type of imagery. It actually does not compress solid color well at all!

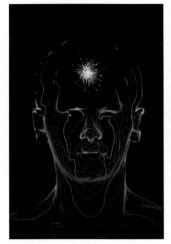 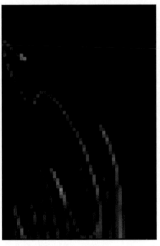 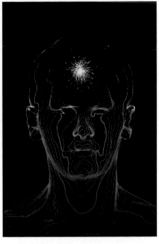

Here's an image with a lot of solid color, saved as a JPEG. It is 49.5k.

Here's a close-up of JPEG artifacts.

Not only does the GIF look better (no artifacts!), but it is also 39% smaller at 24.2k.

JPEG is a lossy compression algorithm, meaning that it removes information from your image, and therefore causes a loss in quality. JPEG does a great job of doing this, so the difference in information data is often not visible or objectionable. It does introduce artifacts in some instances, especially where it encounters solid colors. This is a byproduct of its lossy compression methods.

Unlike the GIF file format, JPEGs require both compression and decompression. This means that JPEG files need to decompress when they're viewed. Even though a GIF and a JPEG might be identical sizes, or sometimes even when the JPEG is smaller, the JPEG might take longer to download or view from a Web browser because of the added time required to decompress.

Another difference between GIF and JPEG is the fact that you can save JPEGs in a variety of compression levels. This means that more or less compression can be applied to an image, depending on which looks best.

The following examples were taken from Photoshop. Photoshop employs the JPEG compression settings of max, high, medium, and low. In Photoshop, these terms relate to quality, not the amount of compression.

max   high   med   low

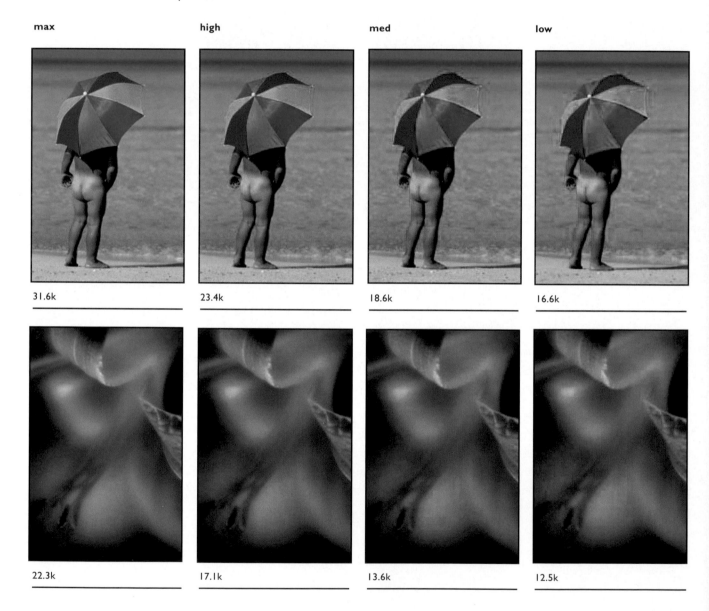

31.6k   23.4k   18.6k   16.6k

22.3k   17.1k   13.6k   12.5k

coloring

You can see by this test that there's not a whole lot of difference between low quality and high quality, except with graphics. As we've said, leave graphics for GIF and photographs for JPEGs. Although there are good reasons for saving photographs as GIF (animation, transparency, and interlacing), there are no good reasons for saving graphics as JPEGs, unless the graphics are combined with photographs. With photographic content in general, don't be afraid to try low-quality settings; the file size saving is usually substantial, and the quality penalties are not too steep.

max high med low

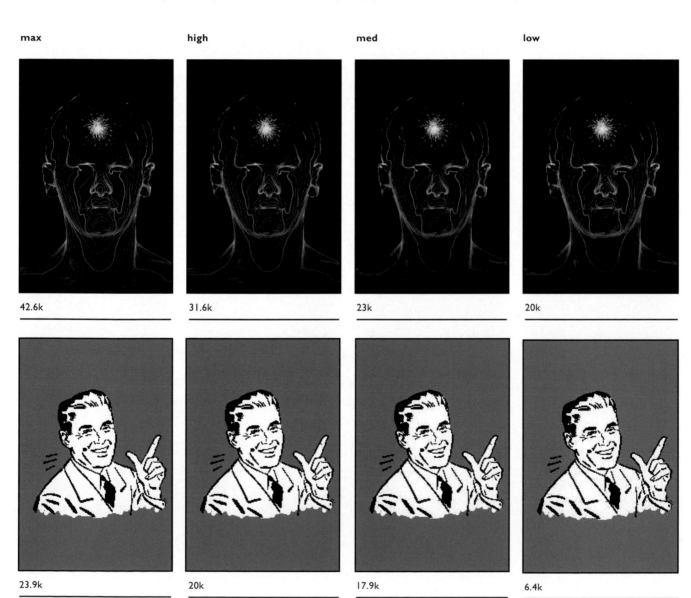

42.6k 31.6k 23k 20k

23.9k 20k 17.9k 6.4k

Progressive JPEGs Versus Standard JPEGs

Progressive JPEGs are a new entrée into our Web graphics file format vocabulary. This type of JPEG boasts much higher compression rates than regular JPEG and supports interlacing (where the graphic starts chunky and comes into focus). They were initially introduced by Netscape, and are now additionally supported by MSIE and Mosaic. Progressive-JPEG-making tools for Mac and PCs are listed at: ■ http://www. in-touch.com/pjpeg2.html#software.

Pro-JPEGs boast superior compression to regular JPEGs. They also give you a wider range of quality settings. Instead of Photoshop's standard Max, High, Medium, and Low settings, pro-JPEGs can be set in quality from 0-100. We simulated a comparison here, using the settings of 100, 75, 25, and 0.

max 28.9k

high 12.4k

med 10.5k

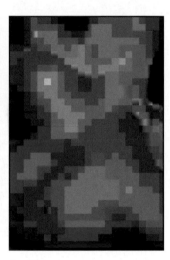

low 8.7k

■ note

Progressive JPEGs

There are many tools for creating progressive JPEGs. We used a plug-in to Photoshop called ProJPEG, made by Boxtop Software and available from ■ http://www.aris.com/boxtop/ProJPEG/welcome.html. The great thing about this plug-in is it allows you to preview the results before you commit. Yee haw!

HTML for Embedding Images

Regardless of whether you're using a regular GIF, animated GIF, transparent GIF, interlaced GIF, JPEG, or Progressive JPEG format, the HTML is usually the same.

You must first learn to save the file with the proper extension. Here's a handy list:

GIF	.gif
Interlaced GIF	.gif
Transparent GIF	.gif
Animated GIF	.gif
JPEG	.jpg
Progressive JPEG	.jpg

To insert a graphic into an HTML page, use this tag:
`<img src="myimage.gif">`

To link an image to another image or HTML page, use this tag
`<a href="www.destination_url.com"><img src="myimag.jpg"></a>`

To get rid of the border of an image that's been linked, do this:
`<a href="www.destination_url.com"><img src="myimag.jpg" border=0></a>`

The HTML is the easy part—it's understanding how to optimize graphics, choosing which file format for which type of image, and making the images and content that will be much harder to master!

Girl

dirt

pool

corn

Sky

firetruck

Oranges

Color Principles

Grass

night

Color Principles

Anyone who has ever seriously studied color theory will most likely report that it is an overwhelmingly technical and deeply complex subject. General color theory is way too involved to cover given the size and purpose of *Coloring Web Graphics*. For this reason, we have chosen to break down color theory concepts into understandable and practical bytes, geared toward helping artists and non-artists understand how to work with color, with a Web-specific focus. The overriding principle of this chapter is that it is not necessary to understand all the technical aspects of color. It is far more important to understand how color works in context and in relationship to other colors, and how to use this information to make well-designed Web pages.

Some people suggest that color has "meaning," such as red means mad or blue means cold. Depending on who you talk to, in different cultures and different countries, and even different age groups, the meanings of specific colors can vary. Some cultures use black for mourning for instance, whereas others use black for weddings. We believe that response to color is personal and subjective, and we see no purpose here in documenting or reporting the underlying meanings behind color.

It's not to say that color doesn't mean very specific things to people. Color is often associated with symbolism. Color definitely evokes emotions. What one person likes another might dislike. Color is subjective, and it is not for us to say what is "good" color and what is "bad" color.

Instead, we want to share principles and observations about color that are helpful when making color decisions with artwork and Web pages. This chapter sheds light on color terminology and contains useful tips and practices related to computer screen-based color.

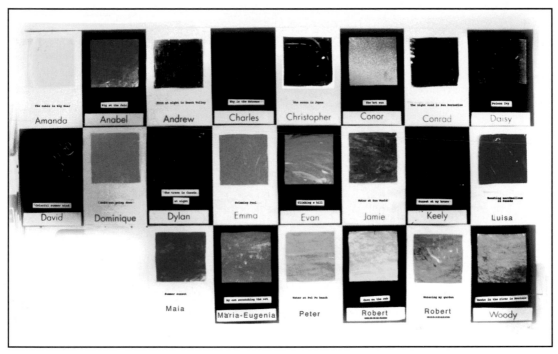

By strange coincidence Jamie, Lynda's daughter, was studying color this term in grade school. Here's an example of 6- and 7- year-olds' renditions of color meanings. From top left to bottom right—some of the children's color definitions: The cabin in big bear, Pig at the fair, Moon at night in Deer Valley, Sky in the Bahamas, The ocean in Japan, The hot sun, The night sand in San Bernadino, Poison Ivy, Colorful summer wind, Gold sun going down, The trees in Canada at night, Swimming pool, Climbing a hill, Water at Sea World, Sunset at my house, Roasting marshmallows in Canada, Summer sunset, My cat scratching the vet, Water at Poi Pu Beach, Corn on the cob, Watering my garden, and Rocks in the river in Montana. Who is to say what a color means to someone? These children's free associations are not only charming; they reveal that defining color is both personal and subjective.

Color Terminology

Like any science, color has specific terminology. Use this visual glossary as a reference for explanations of key terms used when describing color.

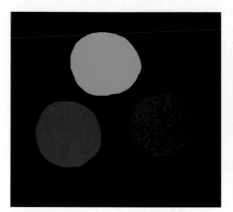

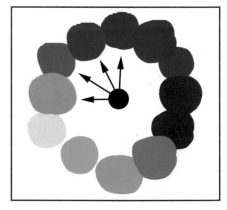

Primary Colors are calculated differently on the computer than with traditional paint and pigment. As a child, you may have learned that primary colors are red, blue, and yellow. From those primary colors, any other color can be mixed. On the computer, however, primary colors are made of projected light. When mixing color with light, the hues red, green, and blue are required as the basis to create all the other colors in the visible RGB color spectrum.

Secondary Colors are the colors in between primary colors. Secondary colors on the computer are created by mixing the primary colors with light. If you mix red and green, you will get yellow; blue and green will create cyan; and red and blue will form magenta.

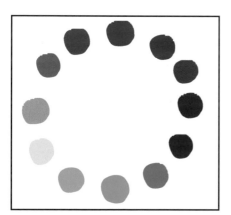

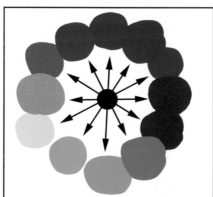

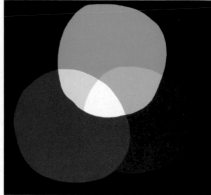

The **Color Wheel** Defines all the Hues in the Visible Spectrum.

Complementary Colors are created from opposing color hues on the color wheel.

Analogous Color brackets a color hue on either side of the color wheel. If you were to pick red, for example, its analogous neighbors would be orange to one side and purple to the other.

Here's an example of red being pushed in two directions: cool to the left, and warm to the right.

tValue is the term used to describe the range from light to dark in your image.

low contrast

normal contrast

high contrast

Contrast is the degree of separation between values.

brightness adjustment

normal adjustment

darkness adjustment

Brightness adds white, or tints your image, whereas the lack of brightness adds black, or tones your image.

Saturation defines the intensity of color.

Hue defines a linear spectrum of the color wheel.

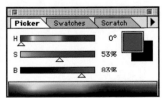

Combining Hue, Value, and **Saturation** can create any color in the RGB color space.

■ note

How to Control the "Read" of an Image

The notion of "reading" might evoke associations of textbooks and phonics lessons, but images also have to tell stories, convey information, and provide hierarchy. There are many methods for making images "read," and this section of this chapter concentrates on the role of **value**, **contrast** and **brightness**, **saturation**, and **texture** and **noise** and their affect on the readability of images or Web pages.

The Importance of Value

Value plays the most important role in the overall read of any image, page, or composition. This principle applies to everything from illustrations to photographs to 3D renderings to text.

Notice how it's impossible to read the text in this example because the text's value is similar to the value of the background.

This example shows balanced text color values, which enables the text to be readable.

Value is especially important in context of Web graphics. Differences in computer platforms, gamma settings, or a monitor's calibration can wreak havoc on the readability of images. A dark image created on one machine will come out black, or appear tinted on another. Macintosh computers are generally lighter than Windows-based machines. Web pages can now also be viewed over television screens, which will introduce a whole new set of headaches to deal with, which we will understand better once Web-based television is more prevalent.

So how do we know if we are making an image with values that will display properly on other machines? Well, we don't know, but we can make sure that our image has a good range from black to white. Don't place all the important information in the dark areas, because they might go to black and fade out on someone's PC. And the same goes for light areas. We can't have absolute control over how someone will see our images, so making them as readable as possible in terms of value should be your highest priority. Always view your images on other platforms to see if your images achieve their intended values. A great exercise is to temporarily throw your monitor in grayscale mode and then view your image to see if its values are reading as you expected.

The Importance of Brightness and Contrast

An image with low contrast can be a tough thing to read. Contrast is also important in relation to text legibility. Your background needs to contrast the value of your text so that it will separate from the background in order to be an easy read.

24-bit or 8-bit display   grayscale display   b&w display

Does your Web page stand the brightness and contrast test? Don't count on people viewing your images on color monitors only; there are tons of portable computers that have grayscale and limited 1-bit displays.

Black-and-white monitors on some computers and laptops have the tendency to use an automatic setting of 50% contrast threshold when it comes to displaying type. This will make viewing text that doesn't have the wide degree of separation very difficult. Any portion of the image that is above middle gray will go to black, and any part of the image that is below 50% gray will go to white. Because of this, you may want to consider making your most important information very high in contrast so that it can be read under all monitor conditions.

When you place text upon a background tile with a lot of high contrast noise, the text may become next to invisible, if not unreadable. Here are a few solutions:

- Choose similar values for the colors within the tile, thereby reducing your tile's contrast. The text that goes on a background will read better if it contains a distinct value. If the background is light, make the text dark. If the text is dark, make the background light. If the foreground is about 50% gray in value, you can choose to make your background dark or light.

- Make your text larger so that it reads solid against noise.

- Instead of using HTML-based text, make your text an image. If you have dark text against a dark background, give it a light outline, or glow. If you have light text against a light background, give it a dark outline, or dropshadow.

The Importance of Saturation

Color saturation is the measurement of color intensity. Full saturation represents the purest color attainable without adding any tint or any tone (black or white). Desaturation is the lack of color intensity—the more desaturated a color on the computer in RGB color space, the closer to gray it becomes. On the computer screen, red, green, and blue in their purest forms are fully saturated colors.

Images with too much color and saturation can lead to a visual headache and cause all the colors to scream for equal attention. Toned, tinted, or varied grayed-out colors can provide a visual contrast from fully saturated colors.

Some suggested methods to vary saturation for effective design include:

- Using saturation as a visual compositional device that suggests areas of interest or lack of.
- Bringing attention to some text, button, or element.
- Separating on-screen items by contrasting saturation levels.

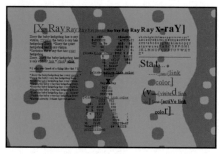

This image has an excessive amount of saturation. The background tile totally overwhelms the text.

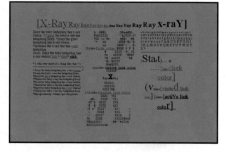

Notice how the saturated links show up, and everything that is desaturated merges into the background.

The Importance of Texture and Noise

Texture, patterns, and noise can help you organize your page in the same way you can organize and design composition with color, value, and saturation. When viewing images with texture, we tend to interpret and group textures and patterns into more general shapes. If our minds can't organize the patterns, we interpret it as visual noise and tend to pass over it for something more identifiable.

Here's an example of the noisy textured background competing with the readability.

It's improved by increasing the contrast between the text and noisy background.

Our eyes distinguish this pattern by its texture, rather than its color differences. Texture, if handled properly, is another device with which to create visual interest and readability.

If you have areas of texture next to a lack of texture, they will contrast and become more visible and obvious with greater degrees of change. The more the value ranges in a texture, the more obvious it will become to the eye. Problems can occur when background textures are too wild in contrast of value, color, and saturation because it fights the text and imagery for attention, thus losing your viewer. If textures have too much and obvious noise and contrast, text at normal sizes tends to get lost.

How to Unify Colors

One solution toward unifying colors is that the colors all need to have something that ties them together: a color, saturation level, or value. Another way to unify colors is by pushing the entire image toward a hue, tint, tone, saturation, or value.

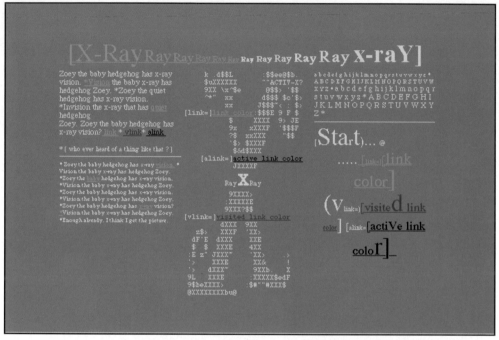

Here's an example of creating "unified color." Bruce created this color example by using one of the analogous color swatch sets, found in Chapter 6, "Color Groupings/Swatches/Directory."

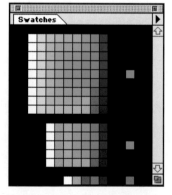

Here's an example of one of the analogous color swatches (file name: ga.aco or ga.gif, located in the SWATCH folder on the *Coloring Web Graphics* CD-ROM) that Bruce used for the unified color example.

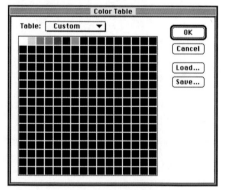

These are the eight colors that Bruce chose from the green analogous color swatch set.

Everything Is Relative

Color is never actual; it is relative to whatever color it's placed next to. A color that seems yellow-green to the eye at first might switch and appear to be yellow when a similar color with more green is placed right next to it. Why is this? We perceive color by its relative relationships to the surrounding colors. The same goes for relationships of value and saturation.

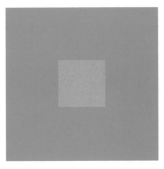

blue-green alone

yellow-green alone

When placed together, the yellow-green looks more yellow and the blue-green looks more blue.

If we show a middle gray by itself we see it for what it is. However, if we place a noticeably lighter gray next to the existing one, the existing one will appear darker. Our minds need reference in relationship to color and value in order to get its bearings.

In actuality, they are two very different shades of colored gray. This demonstrates our minds' tendency to judge color in relationship to other colors.

In this example the grays look identical.

We also tend to view value in relative terms. If an entire image is dark without much contrast, our minds will explore the image and define the lightest areas in the image to be the lights and the darkest areas in the image to be dark, thus completing an entire range. Now this image would look good and register on a dark page. But if you make elements on your page that go lighter than the lightest area on the image, then the image is perceived to be dark.

With a darker element on the screen, such as this black background, the image appears more washed out.

Since this image has pure blacks and pure whites, the black background and white type balance out, without appearing lighter or darker in relationship to anything else.

In this example, black reads as black in this image, but white reads as middle gray.

With white text, the image looks darker than before. Since there is no white in this photograph, the image reads as darker than when the type was gray.

This text color represents the black point of this image on this page.

Black and white points of an image are relative, as the examples above demonstrate.

Here's an example of a grayscale ramp with a solid middle-gray bar in the middle. Notice how the bar looks like it gradates as well. This is an optical illusion caused by our perceptual inclination to judge value in relationship to other values.

When the middle-gray bar is viewed by itself, it doesn't look gradated anymore.

For the most part, our minds always view imagery in relative terms. Texture seems to be stronger when placed next to areas of no or different texture. Green-blue wants to be greener when placed next to a blue. Understanding the balance between these relationships is key to making images that communicate through color and value. Everything is relative to everything else. Understanding this key enables you to create images and Web pages that have balance, readability, and control.

Imaging Techniques

A lot of what has been discussed in this book is useless unless you know how into put it into practice. There are lots of popular imaging programs for Web graphics, so we've included tips and techniques related to color for many software packages in this chapter. Bruce and I both use Photoshop, which is the imaging tool of choice in most professional Web design circles (as well as most other professional design-related circles!). We do understand, however, that not everyone is a professional, nor can everyone afford imaging programs with professional price tags, so we've mixed a healthy dose of Photoshop tutorials alongside tutorials for other imaging programs, such as Paint Shop Pro, Photo-Paint, Painter, FreeHand, Director, GifBuilder, and GIF Construction Set.

The core of this book's purpose is to help you choose colors from a limited color family that look good and work consistently over Web browsers. Chapter 6, "Color Groupings/Swatches/Directory," is a visual directory to guide you through the contents of the *Coloring Web Graphics* CD-ROM. You may choose to work with any of the files on our CD-ROM or to create your own artwork when following along with the tutorials found in this chapter.

How to Load a Browser-Safe Swatch Palette into Photoshop

Custom swatch palettes are one of the key components of our CD-ROM. They enable you to choose from browser-safe colors that are organized by color relationships rather than by mathematics. These swatch palettes load into Photoshop Mac/Win/Win95 versions 2.0-4.0. To load palettes into Photoshop's Swatch Palette, follow these steps:

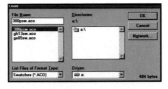

Step 1: Choose Windows, Palettes, Show Swatches. Using the upper right arrow, choose Load Swatches from the pull-down menu.

Step 2: Select from any of the files within the SWATCHES\ACO folder on the *Coloring Web Graphics* CD-ROM. The custom swatch set appears as a new set inside Photoshop's Swatch Palette.

How to Append a Swatch Set

Let's say you would like to have more than one swatch set open at a time. You can append as many swatch sets as memory allows.

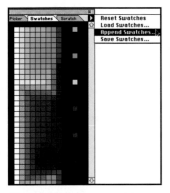

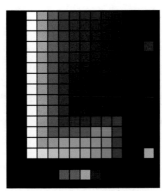

Step 1: Using the upper right arrow, choose Append Swatches.

Step 2: The new swatch set will appear below the existing swatch set. If you want to save the appended swatch set, use the upper right arrow and choose Save Swatch. On PCs these files must use an .aco file-name extension.

How to Use the Browser-Safe Swatch Sets

Use browser-safe colors when you are creating custom artwork, illustrations, cartoons, and logos for Web delivery.

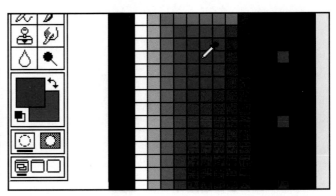

Use the Eyedropper Tool to click on a color within the swatch set. This causes the color to appear in the Foreground Color area of the Photoshop Toolbox. Choose any paint tool, and it will use the color you selected from the swatch set.

How to Add/Replace a Color to a Swatch Set

There may be times when you wish to edit a browser-safe swatch set, such as when you want to make your own limited browser-safe palette for certain favorite colors, or for any other purpose that might arise. This example shows how to add a color to an existing set. The same process would apply if you wished to make a set from scratch using all your own color choices.

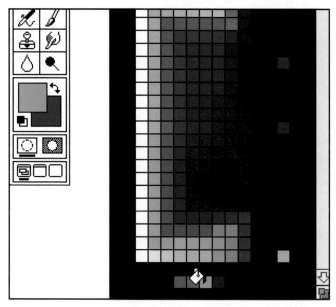

Make sure the new color you wish to add is in the Foreground Color area of the Photoshop Toolbox. Hold down the Shift Key, and your cursor will change to the Paint Bucket Tool. Click to fill one or more color cells. If you want to insert new colors and leave the existing colors in place, use the Shift-Option keys on the Mac, or Shift-Alt keys on the PC. This will cause the existing colors to shift to the right.

How to Subtract Colors from a Browser-Safe Swatch Set

You may also wish to cut certain colors out of the browser-safe color swatch sets if you are making your own favorite browser-safe color set, or for whatever other reason might arise.

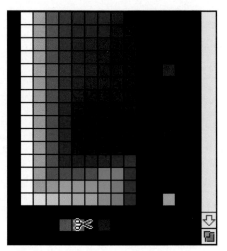

Begin by positioning your cursor over the color you wish to remove. On a Mac, hold down the Command key, and your cursor will change to the Scissor Tool. On a PC, hold down the Ctrl key to display the Scissors Tool. Click to remove the color. The remaining cells of color will move to the left.

How to Save a New Swatch Set

Once you get the hang of making swatch sets, you may want to save your own library.

Click on the Swatch Palette arrow to select Save Swatches. It's important to put the .aco extension at the end of your file names. Macs don't require this extension, but if you ever want a PC-based Photoshop user to be able to use the custom set you created, its file name must include this extension.

Swatch Sets for Imaging Programs Other Than Photoshop?

All the Photoshop swatch files on the *Coloring Web Graphics* CD-ROM are also available as GIF files. This means that any imaging program that can read GIF files can view and select from these suggested color families.

The GIF versions of the swatch sets are located inside the SWATCH\GIF folders on the *Coloring Web Graphics* CD-ROM. These files follow the same naming conventions of the Photoshop swatch files shown in Chapter 6, with the exception of the file-name extension: instead of .aco, these files have a .gif extension.

Simply open these files and use the eyedropper tool to select from a browser-safe swatch set in any imaging program that supports this type of color picking.

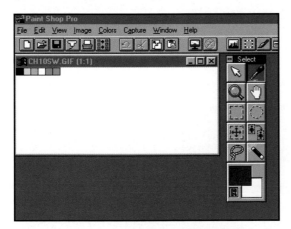

To use the color swatches on the *Coloring Web Graphics* CD-ROM in programs other than Photoshop, open any file within the SWATCHES\GIF folder. You can use the eyedropper tool to select colors from these swatches, just like in Photoshop.

How to Load the Browser-Safe Palette into Paint Shop Pro

We include a browser-safe palette for Paint Shop Pro, called netscape.pal, located in the CLUT folder of the *Coloring Web Graphics* CD-ROM. The following instructions show how to load the palette.

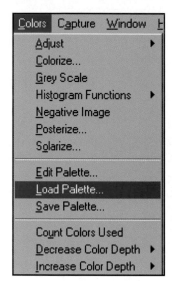

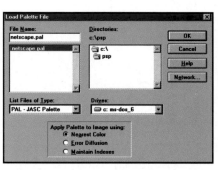

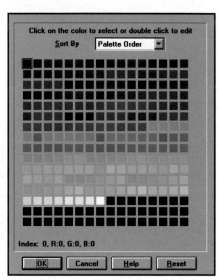

Step 1: Under the Color menu, select Load Palette.

Step 2: Select the file netscape.pal, located in the CLUT folder on the *Coloring Web Graphics* CD-ROM.

Step 3: The palette will appear. It can be sorted by Palette Order, Hue, and Luminance by changing the Sort By setting.

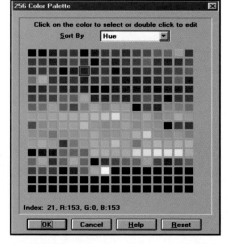

Step 4: Double-click on the foreground color in the Toolbar. In this example, it's a turquoise color.

Step 5: The color palette that you just loaded becomes active. Double-click on a browser-safe color you would like to paint with. Click OK, or press the Return key.

Step 6: The browser-safe color appears in the foreground color picker. Select any painting tool, and it will use this color.

How to Load a Browser-Safe Palette into Photo-Paint

Photo-Paint 6.0 supports the capability to load a custom palette into its color table. We have supplied a file called 216clut.cpl, available inside the CLUT folder on the *Coloring Web Graphics* CD-ROM.

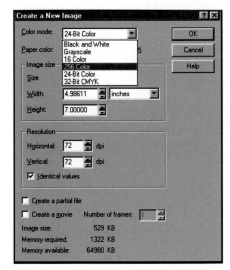

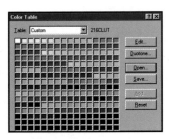

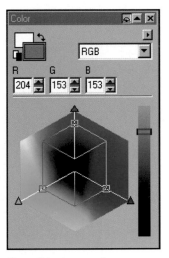

Step 1: Open a 256-color document, or create a new file using 256 colors.

Step 2: Under the Image menu, select Color Table.

Step 3: The Color Table window will open, where you can load and save custom palettes. To load the browser-safe palette, choose it from the CLUT folder on the *Coloring Web Graphics* CD-ROM. The file name is 216clut.cpl. This places the colors in the palette bar at the bottom of the screen and inside the Color window.

Photo-Paint has a really neat interface when you pick a color, showing you the color cube and where your selection is being pulled from.

How to Load a Browser-Safe Palette into Painter

Painter enables you to work with its own version of swatch sets, called Color Sets. You'll find a browser-safe CLUT for Painter located inside the CLUT\PAINTER folder on the *Coloring Web Graphics* CD-ROM. Drag this file into Painter's Color, Weaves, Grads folder on your hard drive before you begin. (Special thanks to Amy Rosenthal for creating and sharing this palette.)

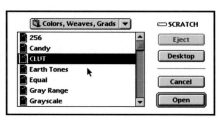

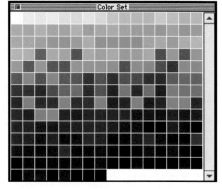

Step 1: Open the Art Materials Palette, highlight Sets, and then click on the Library button.

Step 2: Load the CLUT file.

Step 3: A new browser-safe Color Set appears.

What Is a CLUT and What Do You Do with One?

A CLUT is an acronym for Color LookUp Table. A color lookup table is the file that assigns the specific colors to any 8-bit or lower bit-depth computer image. CLUTs can be applied to images two different ways in Photoshop.

Note that any of the Photoshop .aco swatch files on the *Coloring Web Graphics* CD-ROM can be used as CLUT files within the Color Table window.

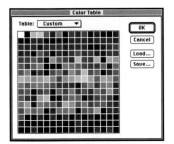

If your image is already in Index mode, go to the Mode menu and choose Color Table, which opens the Color Table dialog box. By clicking the Load or Save button, you can create and apply custom CLUTs to images.

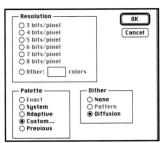

If your image is not in 256 colors yet, choose Index Color under the Mode menu to display the Indexed Color dialog box. Selecting the Custom radio button in the Palette section and clicking on OK opens the Color Table window.

■ warning

Applying Browser-Safe Colors to Existing Artwork

There are times when you might have an image that you wish to convert to browser-safe colors. This can be done by using the technique described above. However, it's very rare for an image to look good when a new CLUT is applied to an existing image. Photoshop determines how to subsitute the new colors, and it might not yield the results you expected. It's always best to create artwork with browser-safe colors first, and not rely on post-processing techniques to fix existing artwork.

Reducing Colors in GIF Files Using Photoshop

Chapter 3, "Web File Formats," described the file-saving advantages of working with limited color palettes whenever using the GIF file format. Here's how to implement procedures that create the smallest possible GIF files.

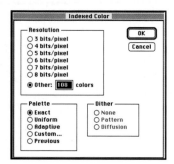

Step 1: An RGB image has to be converted to Indexed Color mode before it can be saved as a GIF. Under the Mode menu, choose Indexed Color.

Step 2: You can type any number into this dialog box. Try to go so low that the image looks bad, and then back off a step. This ensures that you've pushed the limits to how few colors are needed in order to make a small file that still maintains acceptable quality.

Photoshop's Indexed Color Dialog Box

The Indexed Color dialog box has three important functions: setting the resolution, the palette, and the dither. The **resolution** affects the bit-depth of the image. The **palette** sets which colors are used, and the **dither** tells the program which color reduction method to use—dithering, screen, or no dithering.

As Chapter 3, "Web File Formats," describes, the factors of resolution, palette, and dither all play an important role in creating optimized (small in file size) Web images. In order to implement your knowledge about file size savings, it's necessary to understand how to adjust resolution, palette, and dither settings in Photoshop.

Photoshop Resolution Settings

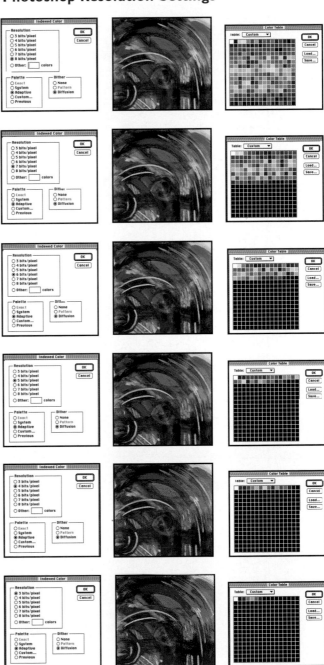

When you convert from RGB to Indexed Color mode, you are presented with the dialog box on the left. The middle row of images shows the results of the respective color depth changes. The Color Table images on the right show the resulting colors contained within each image.

Photoshop Palette Settings

Adaptive

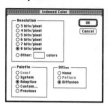  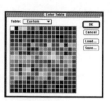

System

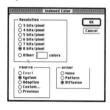  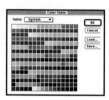

Custom

Exact

  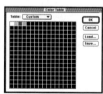

Previous

  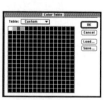

An **Adaptive** palette picks from 256 colors that are most commonly found in the original image. A **System** palette assigns a fixed palette to the original image. A **Custom** palette enables you to assign a custom palette to the image, such as the browser-safe palette. An **Exact** palette allows you to select from the exact colors found within the image. This works only with images that contain less than 256 colors; otherwise Photoshop has to substitute colors based on whatever settings you request. A **Previous** palette applies whatever palette was last used.

Photoshop Dither Settings

None

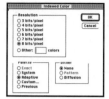 

Diffusion

 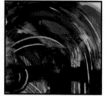

A **None** dither method uses flat colors to represent colors. In some images, this creates a posterization effect, or banding. When saving GIF files, images without dithering will always be smaller than images with dithering. Sometimes, you need to choose dithering, even though it creates a larger GIF file, because it will improve the quality of the image. A **Diffusion** dither method uses dithering (alternating pixels of different colors to create the illusion of colors not found within the palette). Adding diffusion dither to a GIF image will always increase file size, but sometimes the quality advantages are worth it. **Screen** dither (not shown) produces a uniform pattern dither, increases GIF files sizes, and rarely improves the image's appearance.

Reducing Colors in Photo-Paint

Photo-Paint has an interface similar to Photoshop's Indexed Color dialog box.

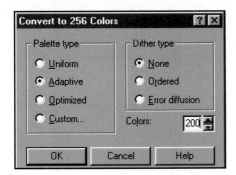

- A **Uniform** palette type produces the same palette over and over again. This is the appropriate type when you are using Photo-Paint's batch processing feature and want to convert a series of images to the same palette.

- An **Adaptive** Palette type produces a color palette based on the colors found within the image. It is similar to the Exact setting in Photoshop.

- An **Optimized** Palette type produces the best 256 colors for re-creating the image. This feature is the same as Photoshop's adpative palette setting.

- A **Custom** Palette type enables you to assign a specific palette (like the browser-safe 216) to an image.

- A **None Dither** type produces a banding effect.

- An **Ordered Dither** type produces a screen dither effect.

- An **Error diffusion** dither type produces a random dither based on the image itself.

- **Colors** determines at what bit-depth the image is saved.

Reducing Colors in Paint Shop Pro

Here is Paint Shop Pro's version of decreasing color-depth options.

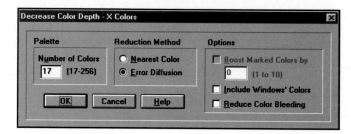

- **Number of Colors** dictates the color depth of the image.

- The **Nearest Color** reduction method is the same as Dither None in Photoshop and Photo-Paint. It will create a banded appearance.

- **Error Diffusion** will create dithering based on the image itself.

- **Boost Masked Colors** allows you to select colors within the document and have the palette weigh toward favoring those colors.

- **Include Windows' Colors** ensures that the 16 colors within Windows are reserved in the image's color table.

- **Reduce Color Bleeding** reduces the left-to-right color bleeding that sometimes occurs with the Error Diffusion Settings.

■ note

The Windows 16 Palette

Sixteen colors are reserved for a native palette assigned to Windows machines. Unfortunately, only the last six colors are browser safe. There are some cases where you might want to use these colors in a Windows-based Intranet, where cross-platform compatibility is not an issue. The win16.clut is located in the CLUT\WIN16 folder on the *Coloring Web Graphics* CD-ROM.

The 16 reserved native colors for Windows systems. Only the last 6 colors are browser safe.

How to Ensure Your Artwork Stays Browser Safe

If you work with browser-safe colors when you create artwork, you still have the important task of ensuring that those colors remain browser safe during the file format conversion process.

Unfortunately, files that are converted to JPEGs do not retain precise color information. The lossy compression method used throws away information, and unfortunately some of that information has to do with color control. Because of this, there is no way to accurately control color using the JPEG file format.

Here's an example of a solid browser-safe color, with the hex readout of 204, 204, 51.

When saved as a GIF file, this color stayed browser safe.

When saved as a JPEG, the color shifted from 204, 204, 51 to 202, 205, 52. It is no longer browser safe, as evidenced by the dither when displayed in Netscape under 8-bit monitor conditions.

We emphasized in Chapter 3, "Web File Formats," that JPEGs are not good for graphics. Not only do they compress graphics poorly, but they introduce artifacts into images, which alters color information.

What this means is that you cannot accurately match foreground GIFs to background JPEGs, foreground JPEGs to background GIFs. Even if you prepare images in browser-safe colors, they will not remain browser safe when converted to JPEG, no matter what you do. We've already established that JPEGs are not good for solid colors in Chapter 3. This is one more reason not to use JPEGs when dealing with flat-style illustration, logos, cartoons, or any other graphical image that would not lend itself to having unwanted dithering.

Next follows an example where an image was created that used a photographic background and browser-safe colors for the type.

Here's a 24-bit image that uses a photographic-style background with flat-style lettering. The letters were created using browser-safe colors.

This is an example of the image saved with an adaptive palette as a GIF.

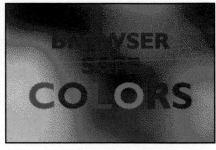

This is an example of the image saved with the browser-safe palette as a GIF.

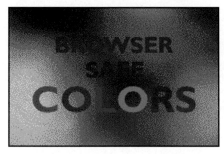

When viewed from Netscape in 256 colors, the adaptive palette version caused the lettering to dither.

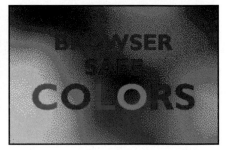

When viewed from Netscape in 256 colors, the browser-safe palette version caused the lettering to look fine.

GIFs, on the other hand, do offer precise color control. If you create an image using browser-safe colors that is less than 256 colors, Photoshop will let you save it with an Exact Palette. The only problem is when you create images that exceed 256 colors. In order to save these types of images as GIFs, some of the colors must be discarded.

This is when it's useful to use a Custom Palette setting in Photoshop and load the bclut2.aco file from the CLUT file on the *Coloring Web Graphics* CD-ROM. You can't trust an adaptive palette to preserve browser-safe colors.

Removing Unwanted Browser-Safe Colors in Photoshop

At times you will apply the browser-safe palette to a file in order to ensure that the colors within honor the 216 color range. The problem is, you might want to reduce the number of colors to less than 216 in order to create smaller GIF files.

The following example shows you how to apply a browser-safe palette and then reduce the color depth.

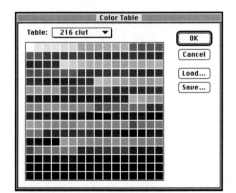

Bruce created an illustration in colors other than browser safe.

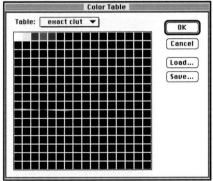

He converted them to browser-safe colors, using the 216 browser-safe CLUT file (called bclut2.aco) located in the CLUT folder on the *Coloring Web Graphics* CD-ROM.

The image is now browser safe, but it is also 216 colors! That's a few too many colors than are necessary for this image. By leaving the image this way it would generate a 16.8k GIF.

There was no reason for the image to include all 216 colors. By changing the image back to RGB mode and then back to Indexed Color mode, Bruce chose Exact Palette the second time. This image only needs to be assigned 7 colors! When saved as a GIF with only 7 colors, the image is 13k, a 22.6% savings that didn't affect visual image quality in the least.

Common Problems with GIF Transparency

If you've navigated the Web much, you've seen GIF images with fringing, halos, and matte lines around the edges. This is a common problem with transparency because images with soft edges (anti-aliasing, feathers, glows, and drop shadows) pick up parts of the color they were created against.

The principle of the problem is easy to understand. Since the mask is only 1-bit or one color, any artwork that requires blended edges, such as anti-aliased, gradated, feathered, and glowing artwork, will pick up parts of the color they were created against. You will need to take some extra measures to make the masks work.

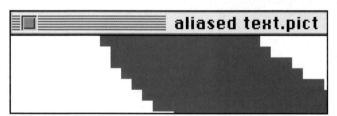

The top image shows a close-up of an anti-aliased edge. Notice how its jaggy edges blend into the white background. The bottom image shows an aliased edge. It doesn't blend to the background color. Because transparency is limited to 1-bit, or one color, it picks up the residual color around the edges of an anti-aliased graphic. This causes unwanted fringing around the edges, and creates a halo or matte line when used on a Web page.

![SAMPLE TEXT examples showing four types of edges]

This figure shows four types of edges for artwork: aliased, anti-aliased, with a shadow, and with a glow.

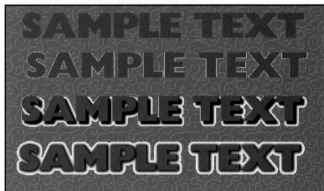

When the different examples of edges are made into transparent GIFs using 1-color transparency, notice how every example except the aliased top version picked up the background color they were made against. That's because the images with soft edges picked up parts of the white color they were created against. This created an unsightly problem, which is commonly called a halo, fringe, or matte line in the industry.

One popular solution is to build artwork against the same color background that it will be seen against in the Web browser. The artwork will look terrible when you make it, but it will look fine once overlayed against the final background in a Web browser.

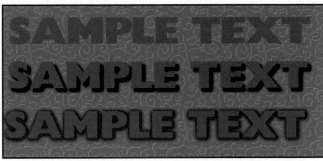

The end result looks quite acceptable now. Look ma, no matte lines!

There are tons of transparency programs for the Mac and PC. Too many programs to cover in this book, in fact! If you use the technique of creating your anti-aliased images against your target background color and then use any transparency program, you'll fix the problem of bad edges.

Here's an example of the identical artwork with anti-aliased, shadowed, and blurry edges against the same color background of the target page.

When the transparency is set, the files look pretty terrible. They won't look good again until they are laid over a green background. If prepared this way, you will correct their predisposition to favor any other color, which will eliminate unwanted fringes, halos, and matte lines.

■ **note**

URLs for Transparency Tricks and Tips:

Online Transparent GIF creation:
■ http://www.vrl.com/Imaging/invis.html

Thomas Boutell's WWW FAQ on Transparency:
■ http://sunsite.unc.edu/boutell/faq/tinter.htm

Chipp Walter's Excellent GIF transparency tutorial:
■ http://204.96.160.175/IGOR/photosho.htm

How to Create a Common Palette for Animated GIFs

The GIF89a format spec allows not only for animation, but for custom palette handling as well. It's possible to assign a common palette to all the images within an animation. This is advisable because some of the browsers have been known to cause palette flashing on animated GIFs that don't use a uniform color lookup table. Palette flashing causes your artwork to suddenly switch from having a normal appearance to flashing rainbow/psychedelic colors at whim. It's not a pretty sight, trust us!

Making a common palette for a series of images is sometimes referred to as a super palette. In Photoshop, the idea is that you import a series of images into one single file, convert it to indexed color, and then save the palette from the Color Table dialog box. Once you've saved the palette, you can reapply the palette you saved to each individual image through the Custom or Previous settings in Photoshop. Here's a step-by-step example from Bruce.

Step 1: Here are six individual frames of artwork Bruce designed for his animation sequence.

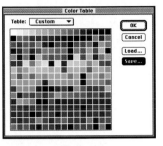

Step 2: Once all the images were in one file, Bruce changed the mode from RGB to Indexed Color.

Step 3: Under the Image menu, Bruce chose Color Table.

Step 4: He saved the custom CLUT by clicking on Save.

Step 5: This is what the CLUT file looks like on the Mac desktop. Windows users must save these files with an .aco extension.

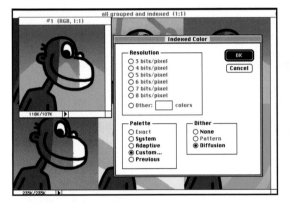

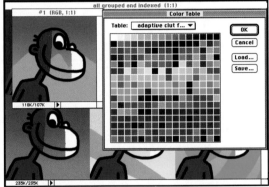

Step 6: Bruce then opened each individual image and applied the Custom Palette.

Step 7: Inside the Color Table dialog box, Bruce chose to load the CLUT he saved.

The end result of this process created six independent images that all share a common palette. The palette is optimized specifically for these images. This technique will ensure the best possible looking color fidelity for animated GIFs.

How to Use a Custom Palette in GifBuilder

GifBuilder ■ http://iawww.epfl.ch/Staff/Yves.Piguet/clip2gif-home/GifBuilder.html is a popular GIF animation tool for the Macintosh. It has lots of great features, including the ability to work with custom palettes.

In this example, Bruce chose the Best Palette option in GifBuilder. Notice the dithering inside the red body of the monkey.

Using GifBuilder's Load Palette feature, Bruce applied the Photoshop CLUT he saved from the earlier exercise. It yields superior results.

Loading a Common Palette into GIF Construction Set

GIF Construction Set for Windows ■ http://www.mindworkshop.com/alchemy/alchemy.html doesn't accept Photoshop palettes. It does, however, adopt whatever palette the artwork was set to. If you create artwork that is mapped to a common palette and then import this artwork into GIF Construction Set, you'll get excellent results.

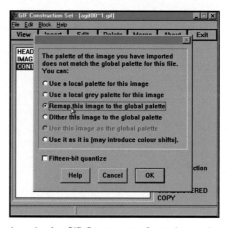

In order for GIF Construction Set to honor the image's common palette, the setting "Remap this image to the global palette" must be chosen.

Making a Super Palette in DeBabelizer

DeBabelizer is renowned as an excellent Mac-based batch image processor. (Windows version coming soon.) The term *batch proccessing* describes the capability to repeat a computer operation, such as "changing a palette," in an automated manner. DeBabelizer does many of the things Photoshop does, but the batching capability lets you apply the results over an entire folder of images at a time.

DeBabelizer has a routine called Super Palette that examines the contents of images contained within a folder of color images, and creates a common CLUT automatically. It then applies the CLUT to each of the individual images that were contained in the folder. This can be a great timesaver, overdoing it on a file-by-file basis in Photoshop. DeBabelizer has a confusing interface, but its functionality is essential to anyone author-ing vast quantities of images for multimedia or Web design.

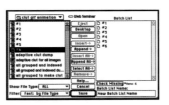

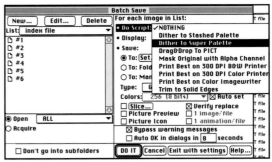

The first step to using DeBabel-izer for a Super Palette is to do a Batch, Save. This saves a path to the contents of a folder, and instructs the program to run whatever script is chosen over a series of images or folders.

You create your Batch List by click-ing on individual files or folders.

Once you've set up a Batch List, the choice to Dither to a Super Palette is one of the many scripting options avail-able to you. The Super Palette does the same process automatically that Bruce did to each image in the "How to Create a Common Palette for Animated GIFs" section of this chapter.

■ note

Photoshop 4.0

The latest version of Photoshop introduced a new scripting feature that should make the task of creating common palettes a lot easier. It may provide some competition for DeBabelizer's Super Palette feature, but will have to be custom programmed. This feature ships as a default script in DeBabelizer.

Vector-Based Artwork

The two most popular image file formats for the Web—GIF and JPEG—are bitmap-based formats. Bitmap artwork is composed of pixel-based artwork, meaning that every pixel takes up memory and is accounted for in the file format. Vector file formats are based on code that instructs the computer to draw the artwork, and furnishes information like the radius of a circle or the length of a line.

Most vector-based drawing programs enable you to move objects around on the screen and align artwork with grids using precise control and offer much more elaborate type lay-out treatments than their bitmap counterparts. For this reason, many artists work with vector-based software programs to begin with, and later export their artwork into bitmap programs where the images can be saved as GIFs and JPEGs. This section of this chapter evaluates processes for creating browser-safe vector-based artwork in three popular vector-based imaging programs: Adobe Illustrator, Macromedia's FreeHand, and CorelDraw.

For more in-depth information about these three programs, check out the following URLs:

- http://www.adobe.com/prodindex/illustrator/main.html
- http://www.macromedia.com/software/freehand/index.html
- http://www.corel.com/products/graphics&publishing/draw7/index.htm

Working with CorelDraw

At the time of this chapter, the current shipping version of CorelDraw supported the capability to output files in RGB. The only problem was that it didn't allow you to specify the palette. The next version, 7.0, promises to allow custom palette assignments. It's best to create artwork in CorelDraw that is close to the colors you want to use, and then to bring the artwork into Photo-Paint to convert the colors to the browser-safe CLUT. The Photo-Paint 216 palette is called 216clut.cpl. and is available in the CLUT\PP folder on the *Coloring Web Graphics* CD-ROM.

Working with Adobe Illustrator

Adobe Illustrator is an extremely useful program in that it does many things better than Photoshop. Some of the reasons to use Illustrator are its better handling of text, and its capability to position artwork accurately and create object-oriented artwork that is resolution independent.

The only problem using Illustrator for Web graphics is that it works only in CMYK. It's impossible to load the browser-safe color chart or swatch sets into a CMYK environment. Most artists who use Illustrator for browser-safe color artwork create the artwork in black and white in Illustrator and then import the artwork into Photoshop where they use the browser-safe swatches for re-coloring the images.

Note that version 6.0 of Illustrator will let you save GIF files and convert them to a specified palette, including one that contains the 216 browser-safe colors.

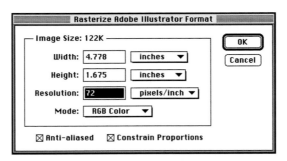

Illustrator is a popular software program because of its superior type handling, accurate positioning features, and resolution-independent drawing tools. Unfortunately it works only in CMYK color, so it's impossible to author Web color images directly. Create artwork in black and white first, and save it as a native Illustrator file.

When you open the file in Illustrator, you'll be prompted to rasterize the artwork. This converts the artwork from the Illustrator vector format to the Photoshop bitmap format.

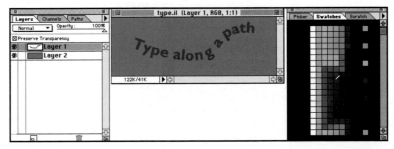

Once the artwork is rasterized in Photoshop, it can be painted with the browser-safe color swatches, just like artwork that originated in Photoshop.

Working with FreeHand

Artists who use FreeHand for its excellent type-handling tools and vector-drawing tools are in luck! FreeHand allows users to work directly in RGB, and will support the 216 palette.

FreeHand works with RGB percentages rather than specific RGB values. It's possible to mix browser-safe colors right in RGB within FreeHand. Just remember these conversions:

%	RGB	HEX
100%	255	FF
80%	204	CC
60%	153	99
40%	102	66
20%	51	33
0%	0	0

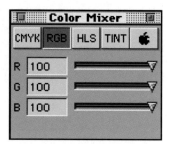

Thanks to the generousity of Amy Rosenthal, we have also included the browswer-safe palette that she painstakingly made for FreeHand on the *Coloring Web Graphics* CD-ROM. This file is inside the CLUT\FHAND folder, and it's named clut.bcs. The following steps will enable you to access this palette in FreeHand: values. It's possible to mix browser-safe colors right in RGB within FreeHand.

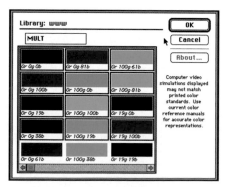

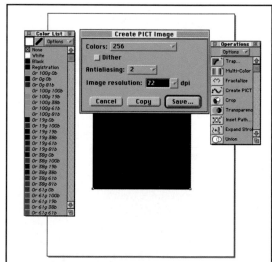

Step 1: Open the Color List Palette. Under Options, choose Import. Locate the clut.bcs file, within the CLUT folder on the *Coloring Web Graphics* CD-ROM.

Step 2: Double-click on the file name clut.bcs and this window will appear. Hold the Shift key down to select all the color chips within the set, and click OK.

Step 3: If you use these colors to paint with, you can save them as a PICT file for conversion to GIF in another program. Highlight the artwork, and select Create PICT in the Operations palette. Make sure that Dither is left unchecked in the Save window. This will ensure that the browser-safe color selection will be preserved.

Working with Color Picker-Based Applications

Certain programs don't let you mix colors by percentages or RGB values. A few such programs include Adobe PageMill, Claris Homepage, and BBEdit, which all rely on the Apple Color Picker to choose custom colors.

Pantone has come to the rescue with a product called ColorWeb ■ http://www.pantone.com. This Internet-safe color picking system includes two components: a printed swatch set and a System Color Picker that displays the 216 safe colors inside the Apple Color Picker dialog box.

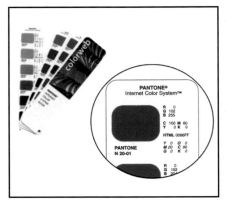

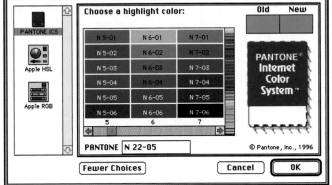

The Pantone Internet Color Guide looks like a typical Pantone color swatch book, only it has a Web-color spin. It presents and organizes the 216 browser-safe colors in chromatic order, and lists the values for RGB, CMYK, Hexadecimal, and Hexachrome (their proprietary color format for picking printing ink colors).

If you install Pantone's ColorWeb software, it will add another entry into the Apple Color Picker choices, called Pantone ICS, that will enable you to pick from the 216 browser-safe colors.

It should be noted that there is no perfectly accurate way to convert CMYK values to RGB. The numbers that the Pantone Internet Color Guide cites for CMYK Internet-safe values are ballpark approximations intended for print only, and do not yield browser-safe colors when converted to RGB. The two color spaces—RGB and CMYK—do not share common colors consistently. Some RGB colors are outside of the CMYK color gamut, and there is nothing anyone can adjust to create a reliable conversion method.

The ColorWeb software is an excellent (Mac-only) tool that offers the capability to pick browser-safe colors in programs that do not support RGB decimal or RGB percentage-based values. Pricing and order information is available at the Pantone Web site.

Custom Palettes for Shockwave Documents

Macromedia Director is an interactive authoring tool that has a huge installed user base. With the announcement of Shockwave, a plug-in that makes Director projects viewable from the Web, Director-based projects are situated to become a common file type on the Web.

It's possible to assign custom palettes to Director documents. Information on this process is available from ■ http://www.macromedia.com/support/technotes/shockwave/developer/shocktechnotes/palettes/colpalette.html. Director 5.0 even ships with a 216-color palette, which is located under the Xtras pull-down menu. The file is called PALETTES on Macintoshes and Palettes.cst on Windows.

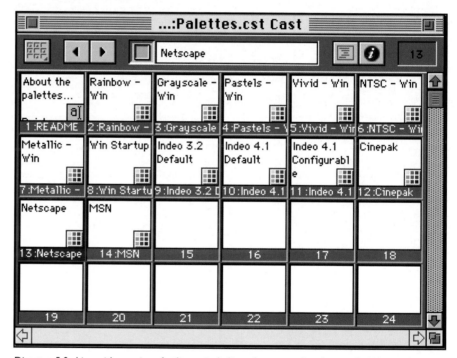

Director 5.0 ships with a series of palettes, including a broswer-safe palette called Netscape.

Hybrid Color Background Tile Creation in Photoshop

You can extend the 216-color limit by creating or using hybrid color tiles, as we described in Chapter 2, "Browser-Safe Color." By checkerboarding or alternating color pixels, you can mix new colors that create the illusion of colors found outside the 216 limit. There are tens of thousands of browser-safe color combinations possible. We show hundreds of examples in the context of suggested color families in Chapter 6, "Color Groupings/Swatches/Directory," and offer those for your use as electronic files on the *Coloring Web Graphics* CD-ROM.

Let's say you want to make your own hybrid color combinations, though. It's possible to make them in any paint program. Unfortunately, with the exception of Photoshop, most paint programs don't let you preview the results until you've created an HTML document and look at the results in a Web browser.

The object is to make a repeating pattern of pixels. There are two types of patterns that work the best: horizontal lines and checkerboards. The reason for this is at a 1:1 ratio, these patterns are the least obvious. We supply templates of these two types of files in black and white on the *Coloring Web Graphics* CD-ROM—they are called ckrbd.gif and lines.gif, and are located in the CLIPART\BRUCEH\TILES folder.

   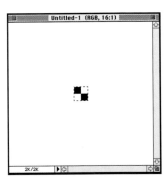

Close-up views of the two types of patterns used for hybrid tile creation.

Creating the pattern for the hybrid tiles can be created with two or four selected pixels, and then defining a pattern based on these selections.

In Photoshop, creating these patterns can be done with a few simple pixels.

Step 1: Using the smallest Pencil Tool, inside a magnified document, create the base art for the pattern tile. Use the Marquee Selection Tool to select either two or four pixels.

Step 2: Under the Edit menu, choose Define Pattern.

Step 3: Create a larger document. Make sure it's an even number of pixels so that the tile will repeat properly in a browser without any erroneous lines or glitches. Under the Edit menu, choose Fill. In the Fill dialog box, select Fill with Pattern.

Tip: You'll get the best looking results if you choose colors that are close in value. This creates the best optical mixture, which tricks the eye into seeing one mixed color as opposed to two distinct mixed colors.

Coloring Hybrid Tiles in Photoshop

Once you have black-and-white color tiles (or any other color combination), you can recolor the tile easily.

Step 1: Set the Magic Wand Tool to a tolerance of 1. This ensures that it will select only one color. Select a single pixel of either black or white. If the tile is two colors other than black and white, select one of those colors.

Step 2: Under the Select Menu, choose Select Similar. This selects everything in the image that has the same color you originally chose. It's now easy to fill this selection with any color you want, using the Edit, Fill menu. To fill the opposite color, choose Select, Inverse, which reverses the selection, and then proceed to fill with another color.

■ tip

Photoshop Shortcuts

A shortcut for filling a selection is to select a color so that it appears in your foreground color toolbar. On Macs, Use Option-Delete, and Alt-Delete on PCs.

A shortcut for filling with a pattern is Shift-Delete on the Mac and on the PC.

Coloring Pattern Tiles in Photoshop

The process for coloring pattern tiles is the same for filling hybrid tiles.

To recolor any of the tiles on the CD, make your selection with the Magic Wand Tool set to a Tolerance of 1. Under the Select Menu, choose Select Similar. It's now easy to fill this selection with any color you want, using the Edit, Fill menu. To fill the opposite color, choose Select, Inverse, which reverses the selection, and proceed to fill with another color.

To recolor any of the tiles on the CD, make your selection with the Magic Wand Tool set to a Tolerance of 1. Under the Select Menu, choose Select Similar. It's now easy to fill this selection with any color you want, using the Edit, Fill menu. To fill the opposite color, choose Select, Inverse, which reverses the selection, and proceed to fill with another color.

Previsualizing Tiles in Photoshop

Working with the Fill with Pattern feature in Photoshop, it's possible to previsualize tileable patterns before sending them to the Web browser for the world to see. We'll work with Don Barnett's artwork (shmancy.gif, available inside the folder CLIPART\DONB\TILES) to show how this is done.

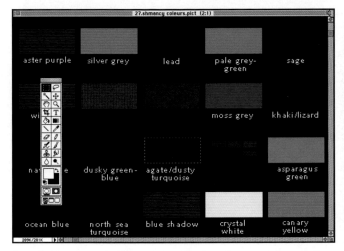

Step 1: Zoom into the file to accurately select the rectangular swatch. Under the File menu, choose Define Pattern.

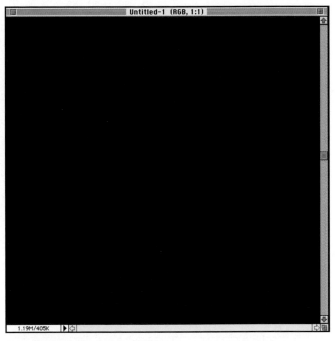

Step 2: Open a blank Photoshop document that will represent your Web page. Select All and choose Edit, Fill. In the Fill dialog box, choose Fill with Pattern.

How to Create Your Own Seamless Tile in Photoshop

We've shown you how to make your own hybrid and recolor existing tiles from the CD, but how are those seamless tiles created to begin with? The following step-by-step tutorial follows Bruce Heavin's process, using Photoshop, the offset filter, and browser-safe colors.

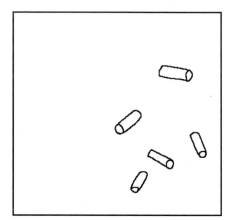

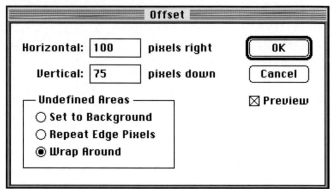

Step 1: Bruce begins drawing intentionally at one side of a 400 x 400 pixel, 72 dpi document. The dimensions of this computer file does not matter, except that its size dictates the number of repeats once the image is tiled in a browser. A small pattern will repeat more times than a large pattern. The size limit in most browsers is 1200 x 1200 pixels, which would almost fill a 21" monitor.

Step 2: Bruce uses the Offset Filter (Filter, Other, Offset) and enters an arbitrary amount of distance. Be sure to check the Wrap Around feature. The offset filter moves the artwork by whatever value you insert into the horizontal and vertical move boxes. When Wrap Around is selected, it moves the artwork and shows the edge mirrored on its opposite side whenever the artwork is moved beyond the edge of the computer file. This helps you see where the seams are and allows you to fix any problems with the image's edges that might cause a repeated pattern's seams to show.

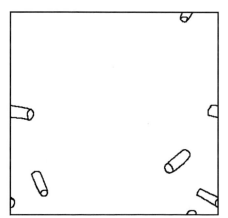

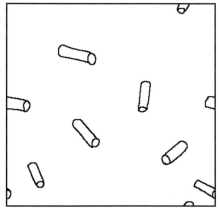

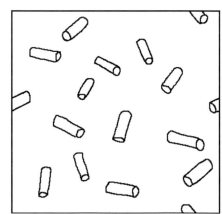

Step 3: Here are the results of the offset. Notice how his artwork has shifted and is mirrored on the opposite sides of the shift. This allows Bruce to work on the edges of this image, making sure that there are no obvious seams in his artwork.

Step 4: Bruce starts to fill in the areas that the Offset Filter show as blank.

Step 5: He repeats the Offset Filter, and continues to add artwork where he sees gaps.

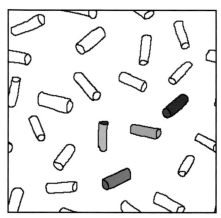

Step 6: He is finished drawing the outlines only after the Offset Filter no longer shows any gaps. He then paints in the outlines, using browser-safe colors (of course!).

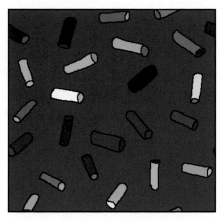

Step 7: Here's the finished 400 x 400 tile.

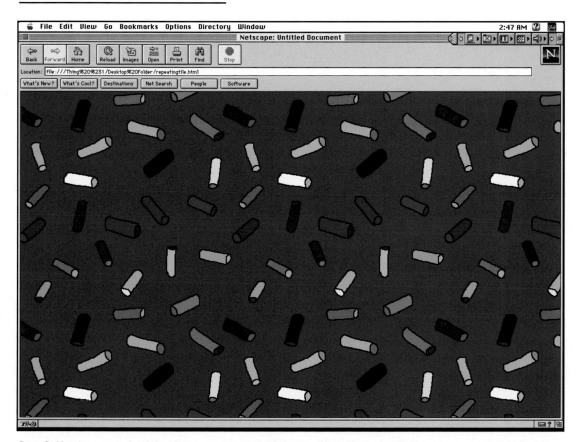

Step 8: Here's an example of the tile in use on a sample Web page. Notice how it's difficult to see any repeats in the artwork? That's the result of creating the artwork using the Offset Filter in Photoshop.

Using a Logo for a Tiled Background

Custom illustrations are great for background tiles, but aren't always appropriate for the job at hand. Many companies like to have their logos repeated as a background image. Here's a simple example of how to use the Photoshop Offset Filter for this task.

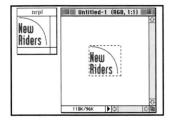

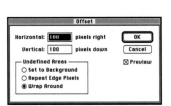

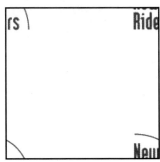

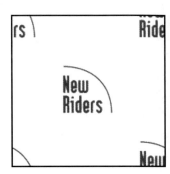

Step 1: In this example, Lynda took the New Riders Publishing logo and copied it into the center of a 200 x 200 pixel, 72 dpi blank Photoshop document.

Step 2: Because she wanted a more uniform alignment than Bruce in his example, she chose to offset the image by half its dimensions (100 x 100).

Step 3: With the Wrap Around feature checked, this offset repositioned the logo into the four corners of the image.

Step 4: She pasted the logo into the center again.

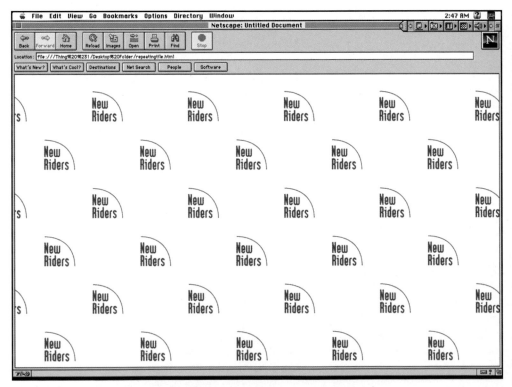

Step 5: Here's the finished example of what this looks like in a browser window.

Previsualizing Web Pages in Photoshop

Most designers would never dream of publishing their work without trying out a few different versions first. We have supplied a template of Don Barnett's Xray.psd file (located in the SWATCH\ODDBALL folder on the *Coloring Web Graphics* CD-ROM) for precisely this purpose. It has the different elements of a Web page separated onto transparent layers that can be filled and changed with ease.

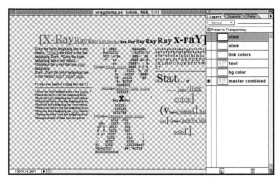

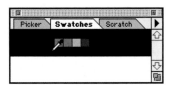

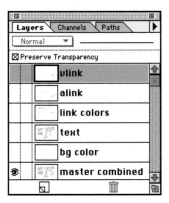

Step 1: Open the Xray.psd file. Try switching different eyes on and off. You'll see how the different elements such as text, links, visited links, active links, and background color are all separated onto distinct layers.

Step 2: Using the Swatches Palette, open a suggested color family file that you like from the CD. Use the Eyedropper and select a color that you wish to fill with.

Step 3: By checking Preserve Transparency, you can fill the parts of the layer that have an image on them, and it masks out the rest. In the case of the vlink layer, it would only fill the text with the color you choose. Without Preserve Transparency checked, you would instead fill the entire image, obliterating your file!

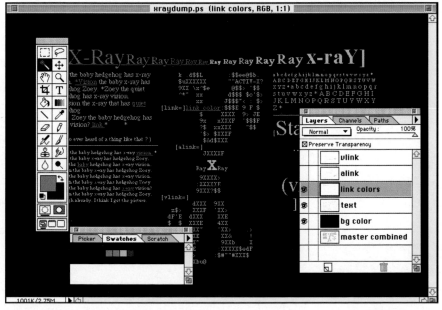

Step 4: You can try out different color combinations to your heart's content. Use Chapter 6, "Color Groupings/Swatches/Directory," or the browser-safe color charts to find the hex conversions to include in your HTML page. Instructions for creating HTML with hex are found in Chapter 2, "Browser-Safe Color."

Color Groupings / Swatches / Directory

How This Chapter Works

This chapter serves as a guide to the electronic files found on the *Coloring Web Graphics* CD-ROM. You (or your clients) can choose colors from the printed charts of suggested color groupings. These suggested groupings can be used exactly as you see them, or as a starting point for your own color explorations. The principle behind this chapter is that the 216 colors can form appealing color schemes when selected from choices that form color relationships.

The cross-platform *Coloring Web Graphics* CD-ROM is organized using three main folders: CLUTS, SWATCHES, and CLIPART. All of the file names on the CD were limited to eight characters or less so that users with older Windows or DOS systems could access the files too.

REMEMBER: This book was printed in CMYK and the files are all stored electronically in RGB. The two color spaces are very different, and the printed book is not an accurate reference to the colors contained within the electronic files.

You'll find file names printed alongside images in this chapter. You can use the CD-ROM guide on the next pages to locate where files are stored on the CD, or use standard search or find file software to search by the file's name.

THE FOLDER MARKED CLUTS: THE MATERIAL CONTAINED IN THIS FOLDER MAY NOT BE USED IN ANY MANNER WHATSOEVER OTHER THAN TO VIEW THE SAME ON YOUR COMPUTER AND MAY BE USED IN YOUR DESIGN OR OTHER WORK ON YOUR COMPUTER ONLY BUT NOT OTHERWISE. THIS MATERIAL IS SUBJECT TO ALL OF THE RESTRICTION PROVISIONS OF THE ACCOMPANYING SOFTWARE LICENSE. SPECIFICALLY BUT NOT IN LIMITATION OF THESE RESTRICTIONS, YOU MAY NOT DISTRIBUTE OR TRANSFER THIS PART OF THE SOFTWARE DESIGNATED AS "CLUTS" NOR ANY OF YOUR DESIGN OR OTHER WORK CONTAINING ANY OF THE SOFTWARE DESIGNATED AS "CLUTS" NOR ANY OF YOUR DESIGN OR OTHER WORK CONTAINING ANY SUCH "CLUTS," ALL AS MORE PARTICULARLY RESTRICTED IN THE ACCOMPANYING SOFTWARE LICENSE.

THE FOLDER MARKED CLIPART\LICENSOR: THE MATERIAL CONTAINED IN THIS FOLDER MAY BE USED ONLY ON YOUR PERSONAL, NON-COMMERCIAL WEB SITE BUT NOT OTHERWISE. YOU MAY NOT OTHERWISE DISTRIBUTE OR TRANSFER IT.

THE FOLDER MARKED SWATCHES: THE MATERIAL CONTAINED IN THIS FOLDER MAY NOT BE USED IN ANY MANNER WHATSOEVER OTHER THAN TO VIEW THE SAME ON YOUR COMPUTER AND MAY BE USED IN YOUR DESIGN OR OTHER WORK ON YOUR COMPUTER ONLY BUT NOT OTHERWISE. THIS MATERIAL IS SUBJECT TO ALL OF THE RESTRICTION PROVISIONS OF THE ACCOMPANYING SOFTWARE LICENSE. SPECIFICALLY BUT NOT IN LIMITATION OF THESE RESTRICTIONS, YOU MAY NOT DISTRIBUTE OR TRANSFER THIS PART OF THE SOFTWARE DESIGNATED AS "SWATCHES" NOR ANY OF YOUR DESIGN OR OTHER WORK CONTAINING ANY OF THE SOFTWARE DESIGNATED AS "SWATCHES" NOR ANY OF YOUR DESIGN OR OTHER WORK CONTAINING ANY SUCH "SWATCHES," ALL AS MORE PARTICULARLY RESTRICTED IN THE ACCOMPANYING SOFTWARE LICENSE.

THE FOLDER MARKED CLIPART\3RDPARTY: THE MATERIAL CONTAINED IN THIS FOLDER MAY BE USED ONLY IN ACCORDANCE WITH ALL OF THE PROVISIONS OF ANY THIRD PARTY LICENSES CONTAINED IN THIS SOFTWARE AND FOLDER. READ ALL FILES PROVIDED, INCLUDING BUT NOT LIMITED TO "READ ME" FILES FOR SUCH RESTRICTIONS. NOTHING CONTAINED IN THIS LICENSE AGREEMENT SHALL BE DEEMED TO GRANT TO YOU ANY PERMISSION OR RIGHTS OF ANY NATURE WHATSOEVER WITH REGARD TO SUCH MATERIALS CONTROLLED BY THIRD PARTIES.

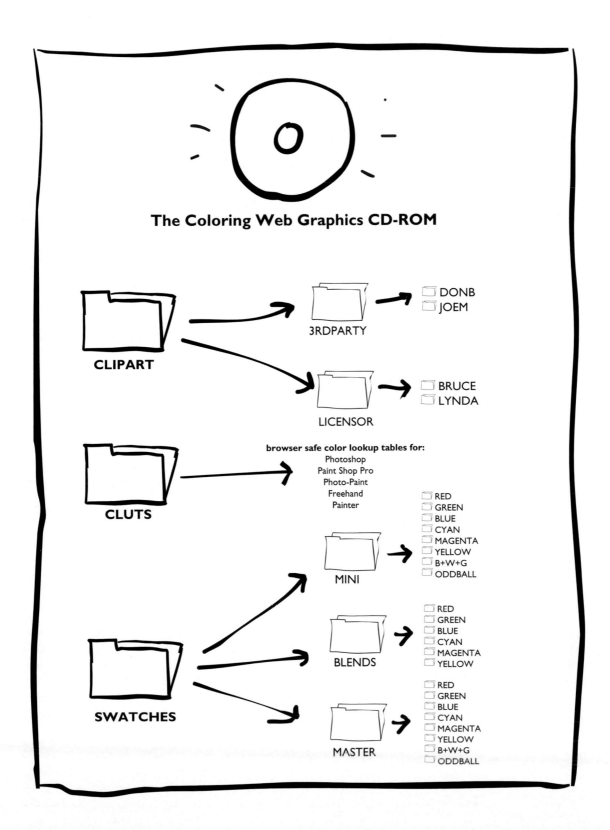

The Coloring Web Graphics CD-ROM

File Organization

In this chapter, you'll find a directory to the thousands of images contained on the cross-platform compatible *Coloring Web Graphics* CD-ROM. This introduction outlines how the files are organized, and the meanings behind some of the legends and naming conventions.

text	link	vlink	alink	bgcolor
CC9999	FF9933	990000	FFCC66	330000
R.204	R.255	R.153	R.255	R.51
G.153	G.153	G.0	G.204	G.0
B.153	B.51	B.0	B.102	B.0

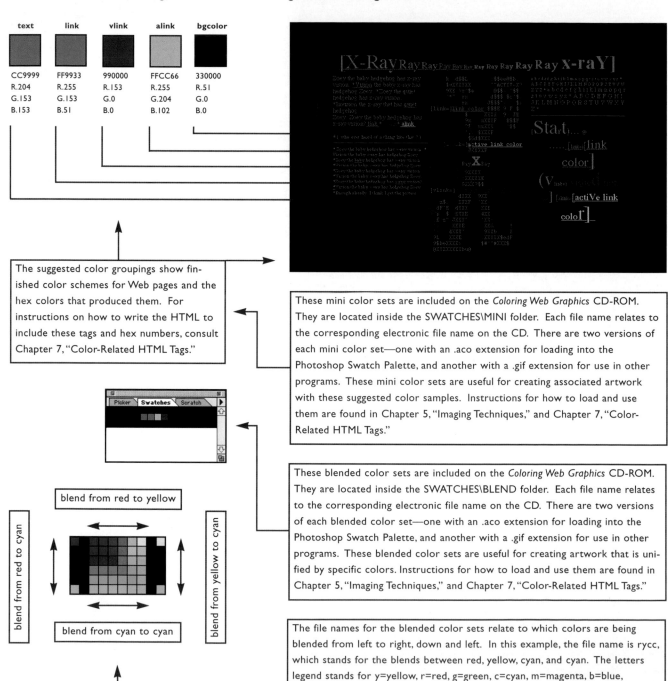

The suggested color groupings show finished color schemes for Web pages and the hex colors that produced them. For instructions on how to write the HTML to include these tags and hex numbers, consult Chapter 7, "Color-Related HTML Tags."

These mini color sets are included on the *Coloring Web Graphics* CD-ROM. They are located inside the SWATCHES\MINI folder. Each file name relates to the corresponding electronic file name on the CD. There are two versions of each mini color set—one with an .aco extension for loading into the Photoshop Swatch Palette, and another with a .gif extension for use in other programs. These mini color sets are useful for creating associated artwork with these suggested color samples. Instructions for how to load and use them are found in Chapter 5, "Imaging Techniques," and Chapter 7, "Color-Related HTML Tags."

These blended color sets are included on the *Coloring Web Graphics* CD-ROM. They are located inside the SWATCHES\BLEND folder. Each file name relates to the corresponding electronic file name on the CD. There are two versions of each blended color set—one with an .aco extension for loading into the Photoshop Swatch Palette, and another with a .gif extension for use in other programs. These blended color sets are useful for creating artwork that is unified by specific colors. Instructions for how to load and use them are found in Chapter 5, "Imaging Techniques," and Chapter 7, "Color-Related HTML Tags."

blend from red to yellow

blend from red to cyan

blend from yellow to cyan

blend from cyan to cyan

rycc

The file names for the blended color sets relate to which colors are being blended from left to right, down and left. In this example, the file name is rycc, which stands for the blends between red, yellow, cyan, and cyan. The letters legend stands for y=yellow, r=red, g=green, c=cyan, m=magenta, b=blue, k=black, and w=white.

The Master Color Palettes are located inside the SWATCHES\MASTER folder on the *Coloring Web Graphics* CD-ROM. Each file name relates to the corresponding electronic file name on the CD. There are two versions of each master color set—one with an .aco extension for loading into the Photoshop Swatch Palette, and another with a .gif extension for use in other programs. These master color palettes are useful for working with colors organized by all the possible variations of a master color in relationship to the other colors. Instructions for how to load and use these swatch-based color families are found in Chapter 5, "Imaging Techniques," and Chapter 7, "Color-Related HTML Tags."

At the front of each of the sections in this chapter, you'll find master color palettes for each color. This example is the master palette for the color red. You can tell the palette's master color by the nine squares in the upper left corner.

bruce10.gif

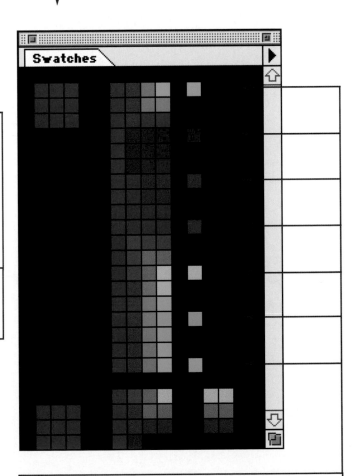

The CLIPART section of the CD-ROM contains artwork organized by artist. This file, for example would be found inside the CLIPART\LICENSOR\BRUCE folder.

The color square at the ends represents the key primary and secondary colors of the 216-color spectrum, which are: cyan, blue, magenta, red, yellow, and green. The master color palette shows all the blended steps from its color (in this example, red) to all the other colors. This can offer an extremely useful organization for artwork that is custom-tailored for the color red.

RED

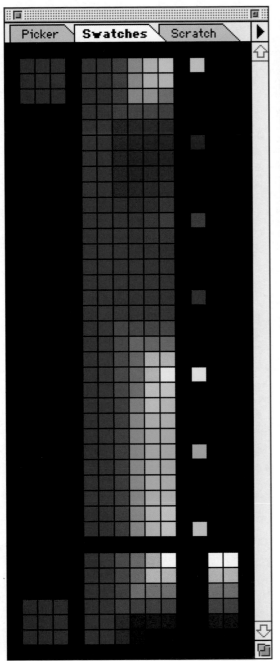

mrs

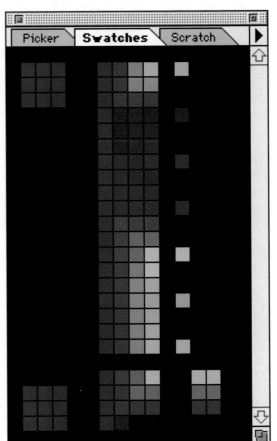

mrd

text	link	vlink	alink	bgcolor
660033	FF0066	CC9999	FF0000	FFCCCC
R. 10	R. 255	R. 204	R. 255	R. 255
G. 0	G. 0	G. 153	G. 0	G. 204
B. 51	B. 102	B. 153	B. 0	B. 204

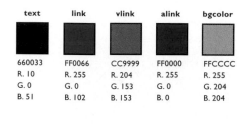

rs01sw

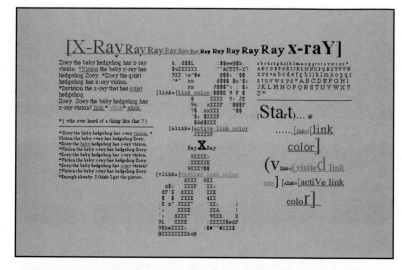

text	link	vlink	alink	tile colors	
663300	FF0000	996666	FF9900	FFCCCC	FFCC99
R. 102	R. 255	R. 153	R. 255	R. 255	R. 255
G. 51	G. 0	G. 102	G. 153	G. 204	G. 204
B. 0	B. 0	B. 102	B. 0	B. 204	B. 153

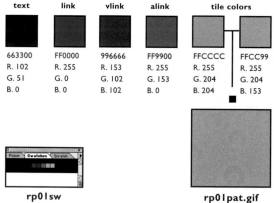

rp01sw

rp01pat.gif

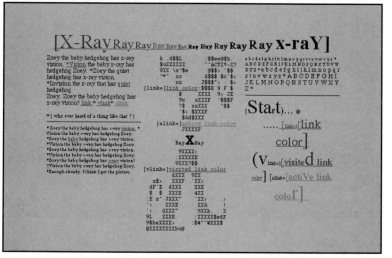

text	link	vlink	alink	hybrid colors	
660000	FF3300	FF6666	FFFFFF	FFCCCC	FFCC99
R. 102	R. 255	R. 255	R. 255	R. 255	R. 255
G. 0	G. 51	G. 102	G. 255	G. 204	G. 204
B. 0	B. 0	B. 102	B. 255	B. 204	B. 153

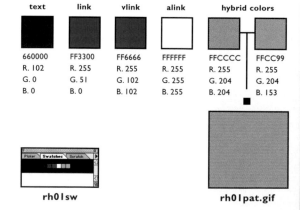

rh01sw

rh01pat.gif

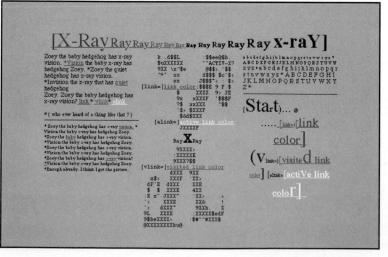

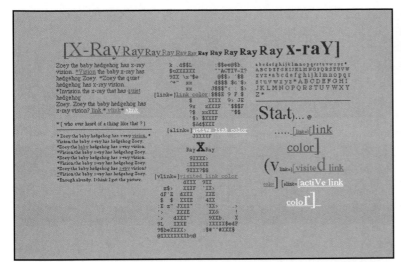

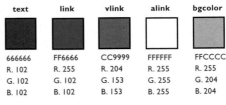

text	link	vlink	alink	bgcolor
666666	FF6666	CC9999	FFFFFF	FFCCCC
R. 102	R. 255	R. 204	R. 255	R. 255
G. 102	G. 102	G. 153	G. 255	G. 204
B. 102	B. 102	B. 153	B. 255	B. 204

rs02sw

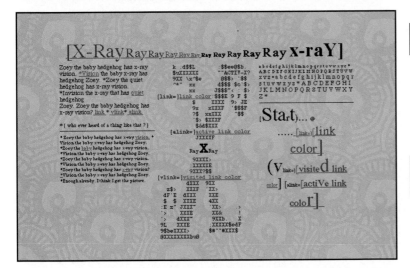

text	link	vlink	alink	tile colors	
333333	FF0000	996666	CC3399	FFCCCC	CCCCCC
R. 51	R. 255	R. 153	R. 204	R. 255	R. 204
G. 51	G. 0	G. 102	G. 51	G. 204	G. 204
B. 51	B. 0	B. 102	B. 153	B. 204	B. 204

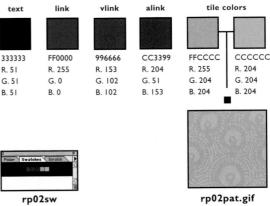

rp02sw

rp02pat.gif

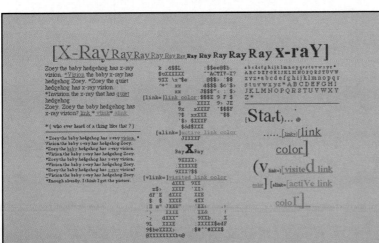

text	link	vlink	alink	hybrid colors	
666666	FF6666	999999	999900	FFCCCC	CCCCCC
R. 102	R. 255	R. 153	R. 153	R. 255	R. 204
G. 102	G. 102	G. 153	G. 153	G. 204	G. 204
B. 102	B. 102	B. 153	B. 0	B. 204	B. 204

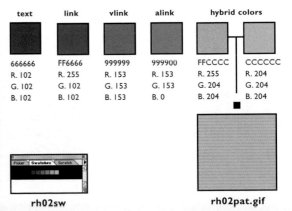

rh02sw

rh02pat.gif

text	link	vlink	alink	bgcolor
330033	CC0033	663366	FF3333	FF6666
R. 51	R. 204	R. 102	R. 255	R. 255
G. 0	G. 0	G. 51	G. 51	G. 102
B. 51	B. 51	B. 102	B. 51	B. 102

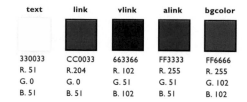

rs03sw

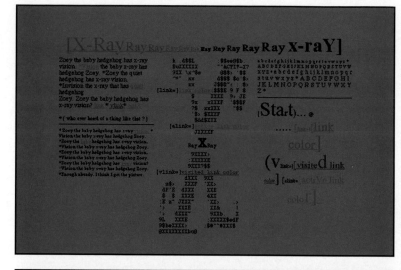

text	link	vlink	alink	tile colors	
330000	CC0033	FF9966	CCCC33	FF6666	FF6633
R. 51	R. 204	R. 255	R. 204	R. 255	R. 255
G. 0	G. 0	G. 153	G. 204	G. 102	G. 102
B. 0	B. 51	B. 102	B. 51	B. 102	B. 51

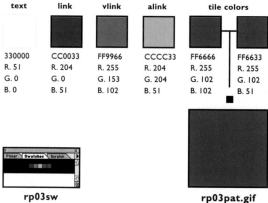

rp03sw

rp03pat.gif

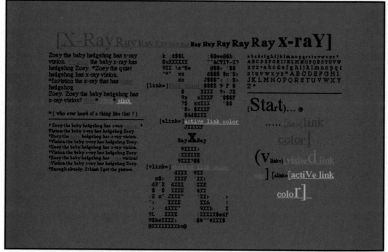

text	link	vlink	alink	hybrid colors	
333333	FF0000	CC9999	FF9900	FF6666	FF6633
R. 51	R. 255	R. 204	R. 255	R. 255	R. 255
G. 51	G. 0	G. 153	G. 153	G. 102	G. 102
B. 51	B. 0	B. 153	B. 0	B. 102	B. 51

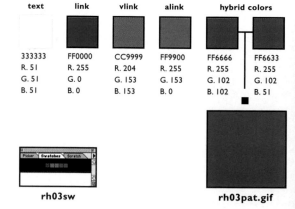

rh03sw

rh03pat.gif

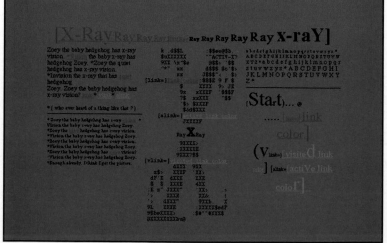

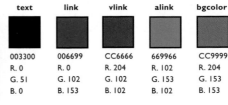

text	link	vlink	alink	bgcolor
003300	006699	CC6666	669966	CC9999
R. 0	R. 0	R. 204	R. 102	R. 204
G. 51	G. 102	G. 102	G. 153	G. 153
B. 0	B. 153	B. 102	B. 102	B. 153

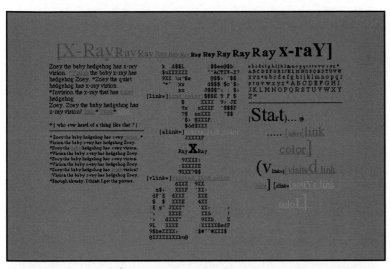

rs04sw

text	link	vlink	alink	tile colors	
003333	000099	9900CC	CCCCFF	CC9999	999999
R. 0	R. 0	R. 153	R. 204	R. 204	R. 153
G. 51	G. 0	G. 0	G. 204	G. 153	G. 153
B. 51	B. 153	B. 204	B. 255	B. 153	B. 153

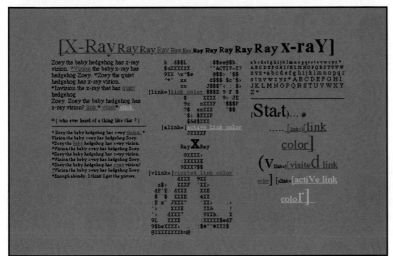

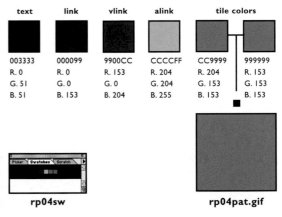

rp04sw

rp04pat.gif

text	link	vlink	alink	hybrid colors	
663333	FF0000	CC6666	CCCCFF	CC9999	999999
R. 102	R. 255	R. 204	R. 204	R. 204	R. 153
G. 51	G. 0	G. 102	G. 204	G. 153	G. 153
B. 51	B. 0	B. 102	B. 255	B. 153	B. 153

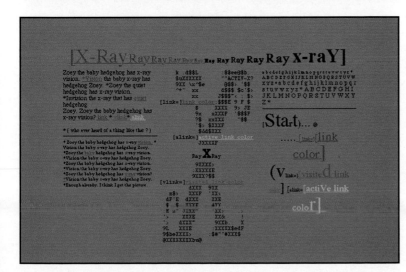

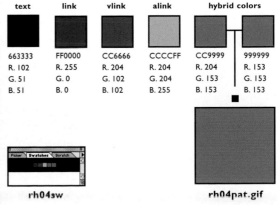

rh04sw

rh04pat.gif

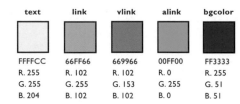

text	link	vlink	alink	bgcolor
FFFFCC	66FF66	669966	00FF00	FF3333
R. 255	R. 102	R. 102	R. 0	R. 255
G. 255	G. 255	G. 153	G. 255	G. 51
B. 204	B. 102	B. 102	B. 0	B. 51

rs05sw

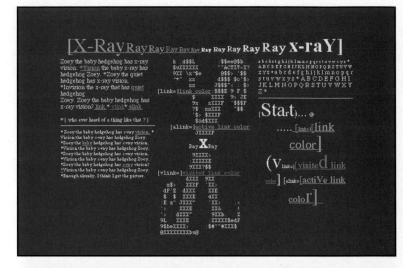

text	link	vlink	alink	tile colors	
FFFFCC	FFFF33	CCCC99	990000	FF3333	CC3333
R. 255	R. 255	R. 204	R. 153	R. 255	R. 204
G. 255	G. 255	G. 204	G. 0	G. 51	G. 51
B. 205	B. 51	B. 153	B. 0	B. 51	B. 51

rp05sw

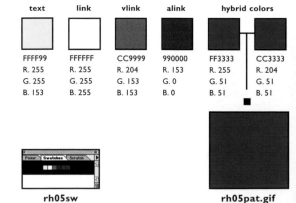

rp05pat.gif

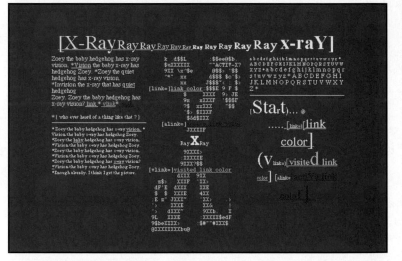

text	link	vlink	alink	hybrid colors	
FFFF99	FFFFFF	CC9999	990000	FF3333	CC3333
R. 255	R. 255	R. 204	R. 153	R. 255	R. 204
G. 255	G. 255	G. 153	G. 0	G. 51	G. 51
B. 153	B. 255	B. 153	B. 0	B. 51	B. 51

rh05sw

rh05pat.gif

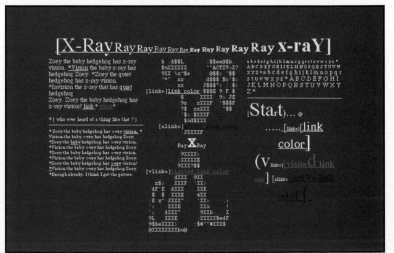

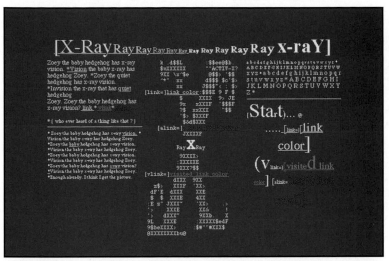

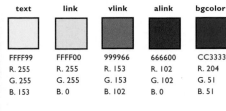

text	link	vlink	alink	bgcolor
FFFF99	FFFF00	999966	666600	CC3333
R. 255	R. 255	R. 153	R. 102	R. 204
G. 255	G. 255	G. 153	G. 102	G. 51
B. 153	B. 0	B. 102	B. 0	B. 51

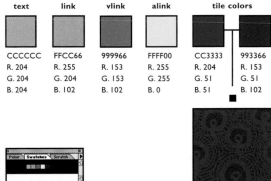

rs06sw

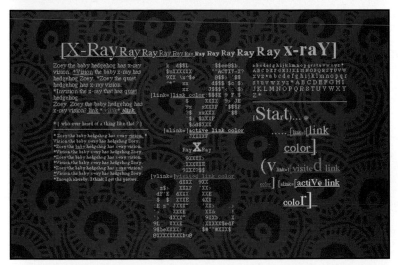

text	link	vlink	alink	tile colors	
CCCCCC	FFCC66	999966	FFFF00	CC3333	993366
R. 204	R. 255	R. 153	R. 255	R. 204	R. 153
G. 204	G. 204	G. 153	G. 255	G. 51	G. 51
B. 204	B. 102	B. 102	B. 0	B. 51	B. 102

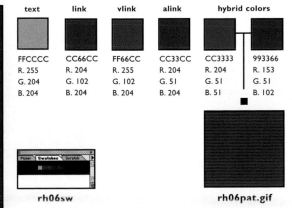

rp06sw

rp06pat.gif

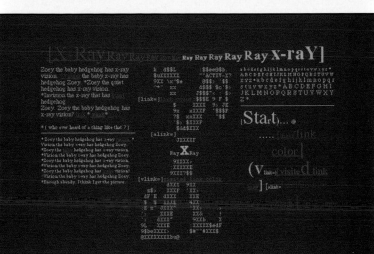

text	link	vlink	alink	hybrid colors	
FFCCCC	CC66CC	FF66CC	CC33CC	CC3333	993366
R. 255	R. 204	R. 255	R. 204	R. 204	R. 153
G. 204	G. 102	G. 102	G. 51	G. 51	G. 51
B. 204	B. 204	B. 204	B. 204	B. 51	B. 102

rh06sw

rh06pat.gif

text	link	vlink	alink	bgcolor

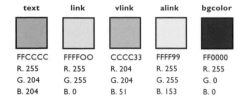

FFCCCC	FFFFOO	CCCC33	FFFF99	FF0000
R. 255	R. 255	R. 204	R. 255	R. 255
G. 204	G. 255	G. 204	G. 255	G. 0
B. 204	B. 0	B. 51	B. 153	B. 0

rs07sw

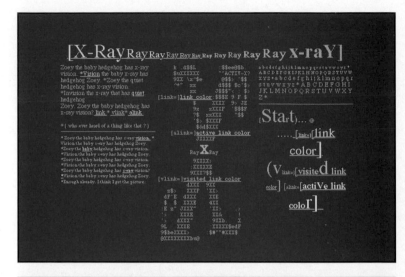

text	link	vlink	alink	tile colors	

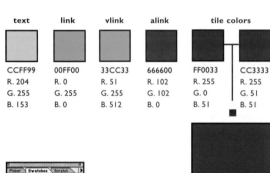

CCFF99	00FF00	33CC33	666600	FF0033	CC3333
R. 204	R. 0	R. 51	R. 102	R. 255	R. 255
G. 255	G. 255	G. 255	G. 102	G. 0	G. 51
B. 153	B. 0	B. 512	B. 0	B. 51	B. 51

rp07sw

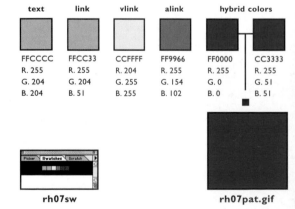

rp07pat.gif

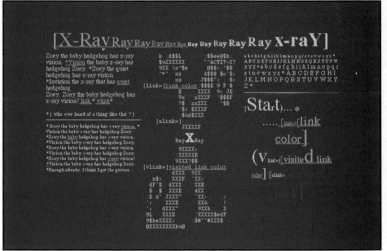

text	link	vlink	alink	hybrid colors	

FFCCCC	FFCC33	CCFFFF	FF9966	FF0000	CC3333
R. 255	R. 255	R. 204	R. 255	R. 255	R. 255
G. 204	G. 204	G. 255	G. 154	G. 0	G. 51
B. 204	B. 51	B. 255	B. 102	B. 0	B. 51

rh07sw

rh07pat.gif

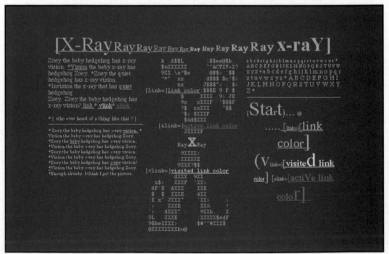

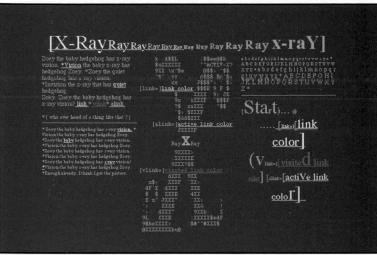

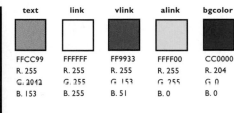

text	link	vlink	alink	bgcolor
FFCC99	FFFFFF	FF9933	FFFF00	CC0000
R. 255	R. 255	R. 255	R. 255	R. 204
G. 204	G. 255	G. 153	G. 255	G. 0
B. 153	B. 255	B. 51	B. 0	B. 0

rs08sw

text	link	vlink	alink	tile colors	
FFCCCC	FFFF99	FFCC33	330000	CC0000	993300
R. 255	R. 255	R. 255	R. 51	R. 204	R. 153
G. 204	G. 255	G. 204	G. 0	G. 0	G. 51
B. 204	B. 153	B. 51	B. 0	B. 0	B. 0

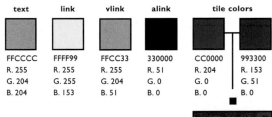

rp08sw

rp08pat.gif

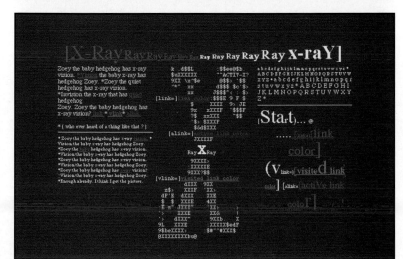

text	link	vlink	alink	hybrid colors	
FFFFCC	FF66FF	999966	FF6666	CC0000	993300
R. 255	R. 255	R. 153	R. 255	R. 204	R. 153
G. 255	G. 102	G. 153	G. 102	G. 0	G. 51
B. 204	B. 255	B. 102	B. 102	B. 0	B. 0

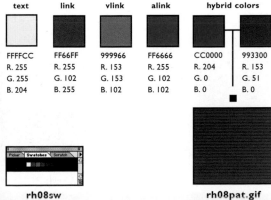

rh08sw

rh08pat.gif

text	link	vlink	alink	bgcolor
FFCCFF	FFFF00	CCCC33	CCCC99	993300
R. 255	R. 255	R. 204	R. 204	R. 153
G. 204	G. 255	G. 204	G. 204	G. 51
B. 255	B. 0	B. 51	B. 153	B. 0

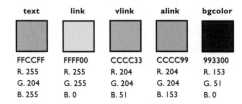

rs09sw

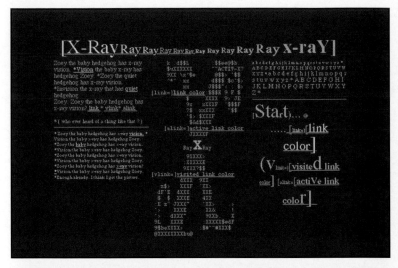

text	link	vlink	alink	tile colors	
CCFFFF	6666FF	9999CC	666666	993300	333333
R. 204	R. 102	R. 153	R. 102	R. 153	R. 51
G. 255	G. 102	G. 153	G. 102	G. 51	G. 51
B. 255	B. 255	B. 204	B. 102	B. 0	B. 51

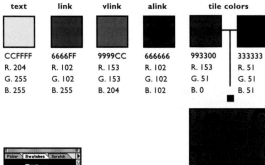

rp09sw

rp09pat.gif

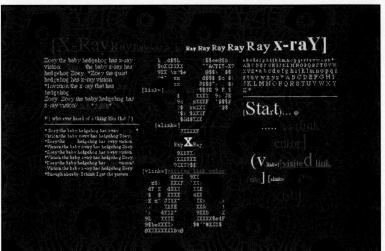

text	link	vlink	alink	hybrid colors	
FFCCFF	CCCC33	CCCC99	999999	993300	333333
R. 255	R. 204	R. 204	R. 153	R. 153	R. 51
G. 204	G. 204	G. 204	G. 153	G. 51	G. 51
B. 255	B. 51	B. 153	B. 153	B. 0	B. 51

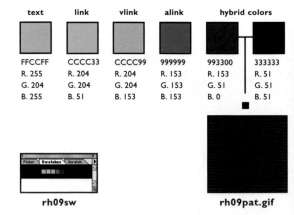

rh09sw

rh09pat.gif

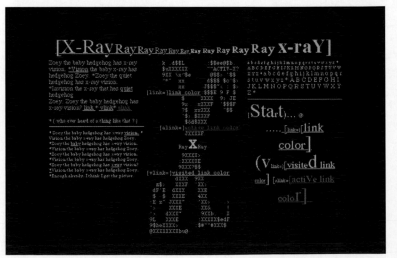

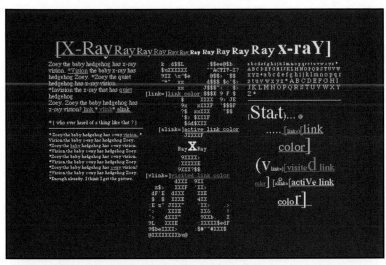

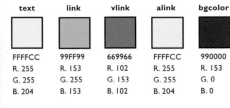

text	link	vlink	alink	bgcolor
FFFFCC	99FF99	669966	FFFFCC	990000
R. 255	R. 153	R. 102	R. 255	R. 153
G. 255	G. 255	G. 153	G. 255	G. 0
B. 204	B. 153	B. 102	B. 204	B. 0

rs10sw

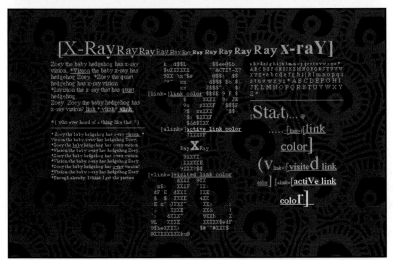

text	link	vlink	alink	tile colors	
FFCCCC	FFCC00	FFCC66	FFFFFF	990000	660033
R. 255	R. 255	R. 255	R. 255	R. 153	R. 102
G. 204	G. 204	G. 204	G. 255	G. 0	G. 0
B. 204	B. 0	B. 102	B. 255	B. 0	B. 51

rp10sw

rp10pat.gif

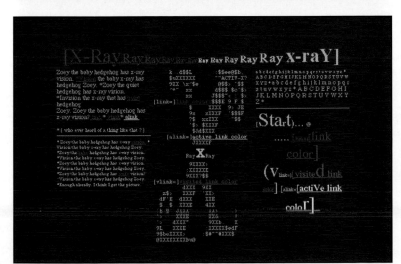

text	link	vlink	alink	hybrid colors	
FFCCFF	9966FF	FF66FF	FFFFCC	990000	660033
R. 255	R. 153	R. 255	R. 255	R. 153	R. 102
G. 204	G. 102	G. 102	G. 255	G. 0	G. 0
B. 255	B. 255	B. 255	B. 204	B. 0	B. 51

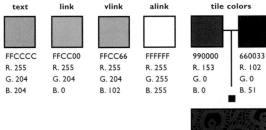

rh10sw

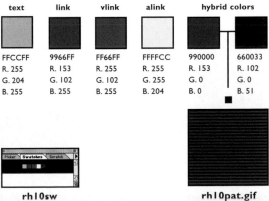

rh10pat.gif

text	link	vlink	alink	bgcolor
FFCC99	FF3300	996666	CC6666	660000
R. 255	R. 255	R. 153	R. 204	R. 102
G. 204	G. 51	G. 102	G. 102	G. 0
B. 153	B. 0	B. 102	B. 102	B. 0

rs11sw

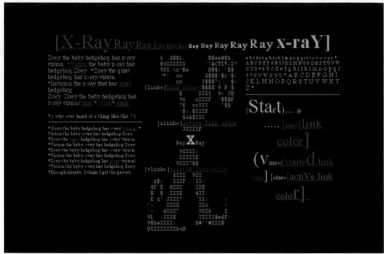

text	link	vlink	alink	tile colors	
CCCC99	66CCFF	CCCC33	CCCCCC	660033	660000
R. 204	R. 102	R. 204	R. 204	R. 102	R. 102
G. 204	G. 204	G. 204	G. 204	G. 0	G. 0
B. 153	B. 255	B. 51	B. 204	B. 51	B. 0

rp11sw

rp11pat.gif

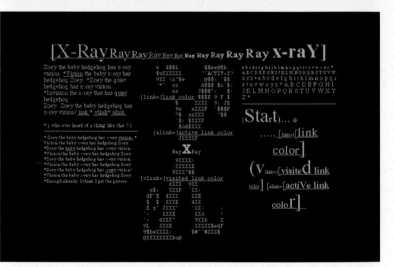

text	link	vlink	alink	hybrid colors	
FF9999	FF3333	996666	CCCCCC	660033	660000
R. 255	R. 255	R. 153	R. 204	R. 102	R. 102
G. 153	G. 51	G. 102	G. 204	G. 0	G. 0
B. 153	B. 51	B. 102	B. 204	B. 51	B. 0

rh11sw

rh11pat.gif

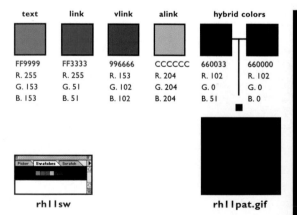

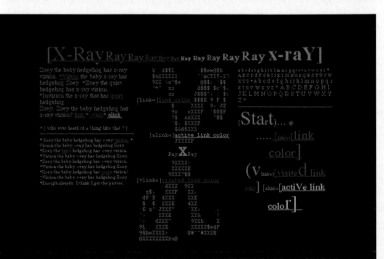

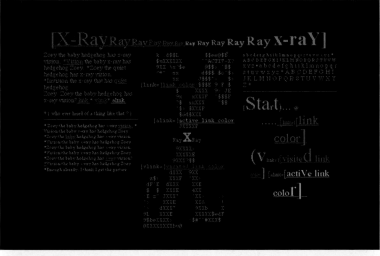

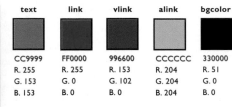

text	link	vlink	alink	bgcolor
CC9999	FF0000	996600	CCCCCC	330000
R. 255	R. 255	R. 153	R. 204	R. 51
G. 153	G. 0	G. 102	G. 204	G. 0
B. 153	B. 0	B. 0	B. 204	B. 0

rs12sw

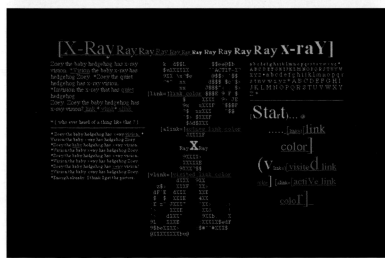

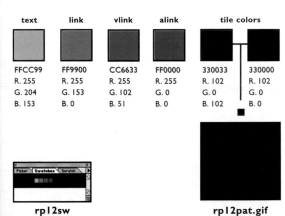

text	link	vlink	alink	tile colors	
FFCC99	FF9900	CC6633	FF0000	330033	330000
R. 255	R. 255	R. 255	R. 255	R. 102	R. 102
G. 204	G. 153	G. 102	G. 0	G. 0	G. 0
B. 153	B. 0	B. 51	B. 0	B. 102	B. 0

rp12sw **rp12pat.gif**

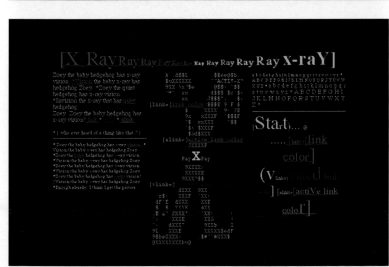

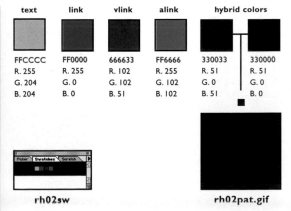

text	link	vlink	alink	hybrid colors	
FFCCCC	FF0000	666633	FF6666	330033	330000
R. 255	R. 255	R. 102	R. 255	R. 51	R. 51
G. 204	G. 0	G. 102	G. 102	G. 0	G. 0
B. 204	B. 0	B. 51	B. 102	B. 51	B. 0

rh02sw **rh02pat.gif**

Row 1

text	link	vlink	alink	bgcolor
FFCCCC	FFFF66	FFCC99	CCCCCC	663333
R. 255	R. 255	R. 255	R. 204	R. 102
G. 204	G. 255	G. 204	G. 204	G. 51
B. 204	B. 102	B. 153	B. 204	B. 51

rs13sw

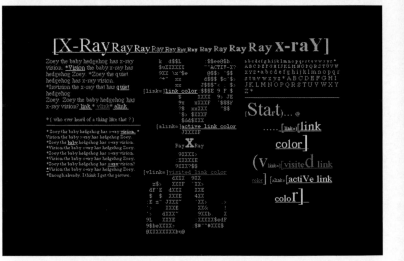

Row 2

text	link	vlink	alink	tile colors	
FFCC99	FFFF66	999966	FFFF00	333300	663333
R. 255	R. 255	R. 153	R. 255	R. 51	R. 102
G. 204	G. 255	G. 153	G. 255	G. 51	G. 51
B. 153	B. 102	B. 102	B. 0	B. 0	B. 51

rp13sw

rp13pat.gif

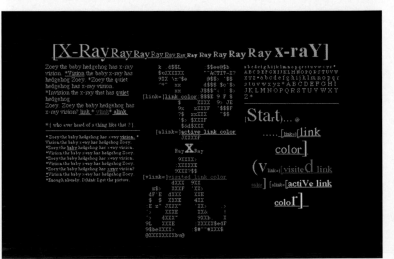

Row 3

text	link	vlink	alink	hybrid colors	
FFCC99	CCCC33	999966	FFFF99	333300	663333
R. 255	R. 204	R. 153	R. 255	R. 51	R. 102
G. 204	G. 204	G. 153	G. 255	G. 51	G. 51
B. 153	B. 51	B. 102	B. 153	B. 0	B. 51

rh13sw

rh13pat.gif

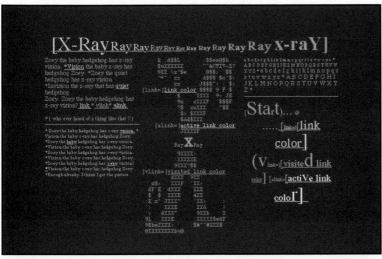

text	link	vlink	alink	bgcolor
FFCC99	FFFF00	FFCC33	FFFFFF	996666
R. 255	R. 255	R. 255	R. 255	R. 153
G. 204	G. 255	G. 204	G. 255	G. 102
B. 153	B. 0	B. 51	B. 255	B. 102

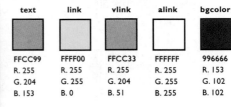

rs14sw

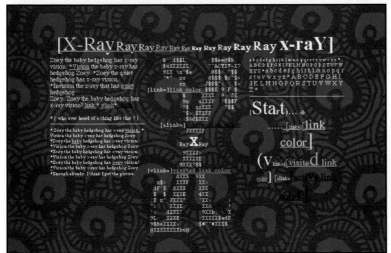

text	link	vlink	alink	tile colors	
FFFFFF	FFFF99	CCCC99	663333	FF6666	996666
R. 255	R. 255	R. 204	R. 102	R. 255	R. 153
G. 255	G. 255	G. 204	G. 51	G. 102	G. 102
B. 255	B. 153	B. 153	B. 51	B. 102	B. 102

rp14sw

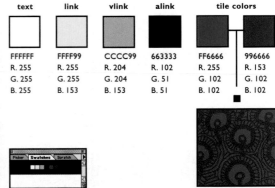

rp14pat.gif

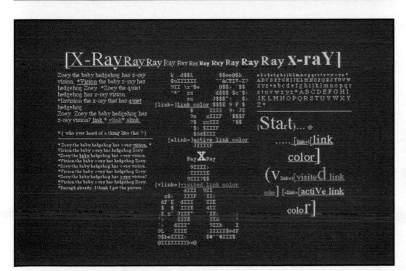

text	link	vlink	alink	hybrid colors	
CCFFCC	FFFF66	66CC66	FFFF00	FF6666	996666
R. 204	R. 255	R. 102	R. 255	R. 255	R. 153
G. 255	G. 255	G. 204	G. 255	G. 102	G. 102
B. 204	B. 102	B. 102	B. 0	B. 102	B. 102

rh14sw

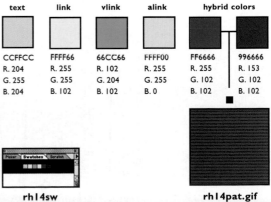

rh14pat.gif

text	link	vlink	alink	bgcolor
660000	FF0000	663333	FF6666	CC9999
R. 102	R. 255	R. 102	R. 255	R. 204
G. 0	G. 0	G. 51	G. 102	G. 153
B. 0	B. 0	B. 51	B. 102	B. 153

rs15sw

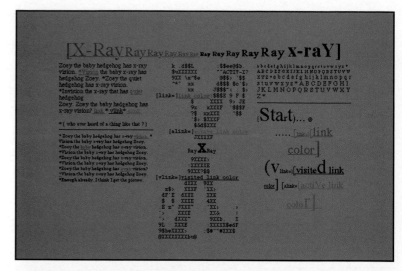

text	link	vlink	alink	tile colors	
663333	993300	666633	333333	CC9999	CC9966
R. 102	R. 153	R. 102	R. 51	R. 204	R. 204
G. 51	G. 51	G. 102	G. 51	G. 153	G. 153
B. 51	B. 0	B. 51	B. 51	B. 153	B. 102

rp15sw

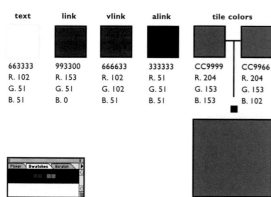

rp15pat.gif

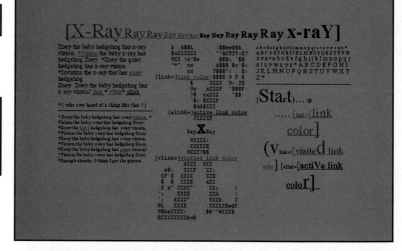

text	link	vlink	alink	hybrid colors	
663333	FFFF99	CCCCCC	FFFF00	CC9999	CC9966
R. 102	R. 255	R. 204	R. 255	R. 204	R. 204
G. 51	G. 255	G. 204	G. 255	G. 153	G. 153
B. 51	B. 153	B. 204	B. 0	B. 153	B. 102

rh15sw

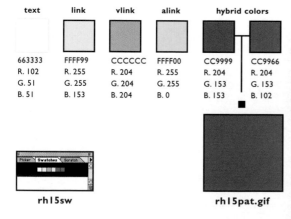

rh15pat.gif

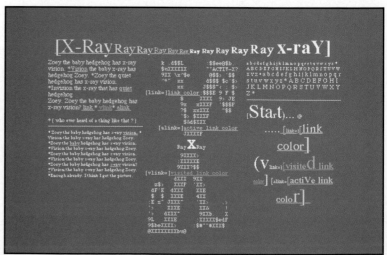

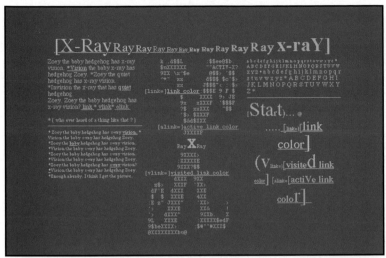

text	link	vlink	alink	bgcolor
FFCC99	99FF99	CCCCCC	00FF00	CC6666
R. 255	R. 153	R. 204	R. 0	R. 204
G. 204	G. 255	G. 204	G. 255	G. 102
B. 153	B. 153	B. 204	B. 0	B. 102

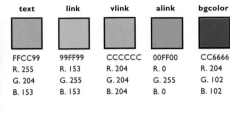

rs16sw

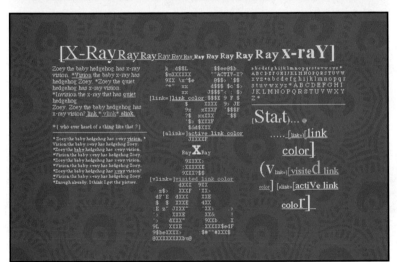

text	link	vlink	alink	tile colors	
FFFF00	FFFF99	CCCC99	FFFFCC	FF6666	CC6666
R. 255	R. 255	R. 204	R. 255	R. 255	R. 204
G. 255	G. 255	G. 204	G. 255	G. 102	G. 102
B. 0	B. 153	B. 153	B. 204	B. 102	B. 102

rp16sw

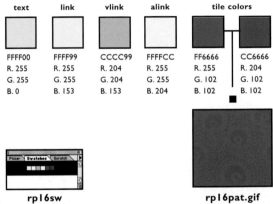

rp16pat.gif

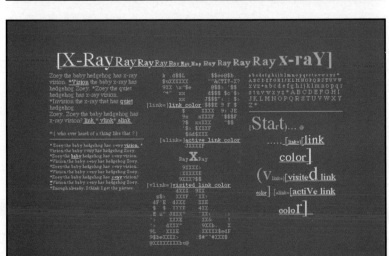

text	link	vlink	alink	hybrid colors	
FFCC33	FFFF99	CCFFCC	FFFF00	FF6666	CC6666
R. 255	R. 255	R. 204	R. 255	R. 255	R. 204
G. 204	G. 255	G. 255	G. 255	G. 102	G. 102
B. 51	B. 153	B. 204	B. 0	B. 102	B. 102

rh16sw

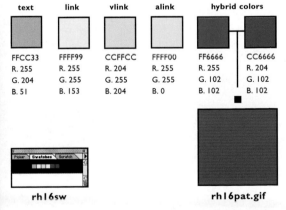

rh16pat.gif

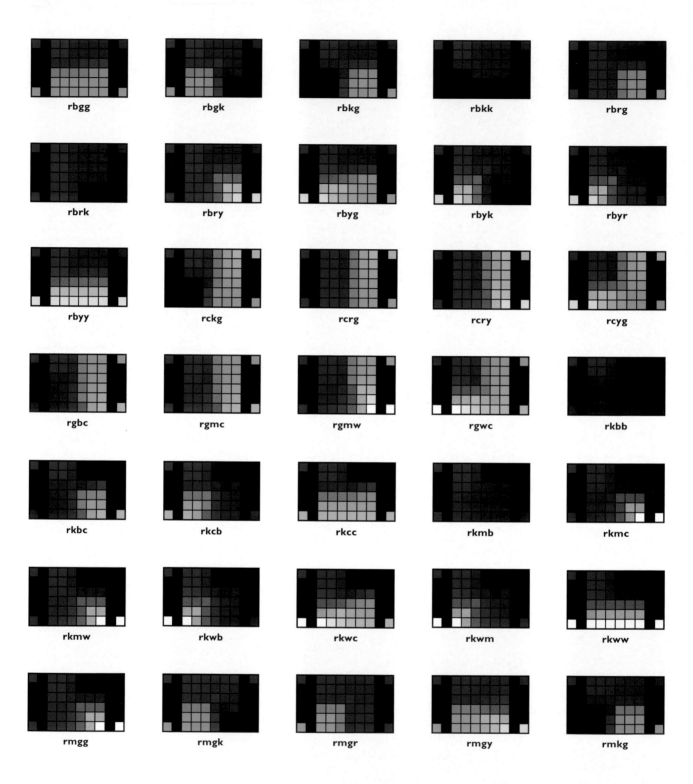

rbgg	rbgk	rbkg	rbkk	rbrg
rbrk	rbry	rbyg	rbyk	rbyr
rbyy	rckg	rcrg	rcry	rcyg
rgbc	rgmc	rgmw	rgwc	rkbb
rkbc	rkcb	rkcc	rkmb	rkmc
rkmw	rkwb	rkwc	rkwm	rkww
rmgg	rmgk	rmgr	rmgy	rmkg

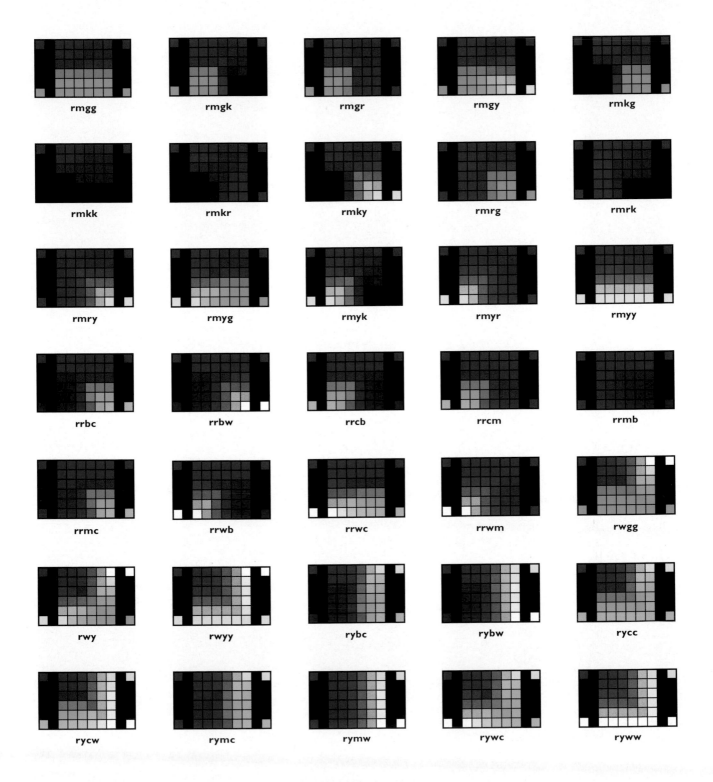

rmgg rmgk rmgr rmgy rmkg

rmkk rmkr rmky rmrg rmrk

rmry rmyg rmyk rmyr rmyy

rrbc rrbw rrcb rrcm rrmb

rrmc rrwb rrwc rrwm rwgg

rwy rwyy rybc rybw rycc

rycw rymc rymw rywc ryww

GREEN

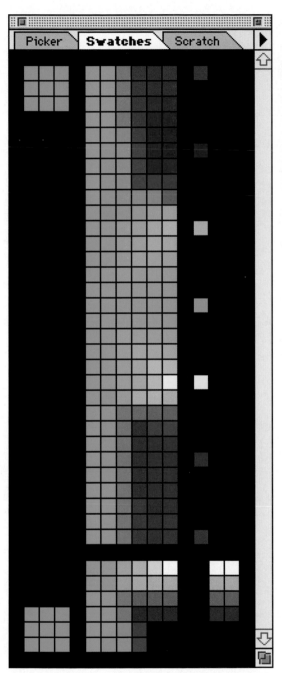

rgsw.aco

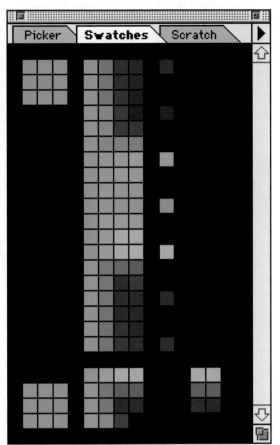

mgd

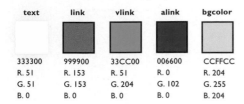

text	link	vlink	alink	bgcolor
333300	999900	33CC00	006600	CCFFCC
R. 51	R. 153	R. 51	R. 0	R. 204
G. 51	G. 153	G. 204	G. 102	G. 255
B. 0	B. 0	B. 0	B. 0	B. 204

gs01sw

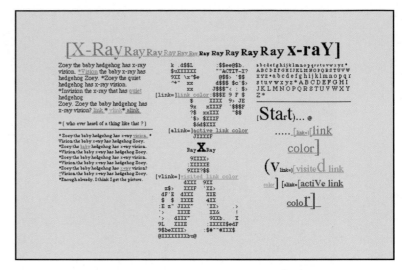

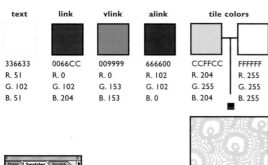

text	link	vlink	alink	tile colors	
336633	0066CC	009999	666600	CCFFCC	FFFFFF
R. 51	R. 0	R. 0	R. 102	R. 204	R. 255
G. 102	G. 102	G. 153	G. 102	G. 255	G. 255
B. 51	B. 204	B. 153	B. 0	B. 204	B. 255

gp01sw

gp01pat.gif

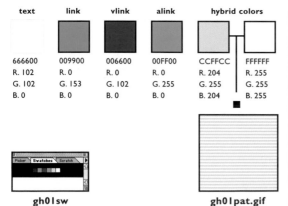

text	link	vlink	alink	hybrid colors	
666600	009900	006600	00FF00	CCFFCC	FFFFFF
R. 102	R. 0	R. 0	R. 0	R. 204	R. 255
G. 102	G. 153	G. 102	G. 255	G. 255	G. 255
B. 0	B. 0	B. 0	B. 0	B. 204	B. 255

gh01sw

gh01pat.gif

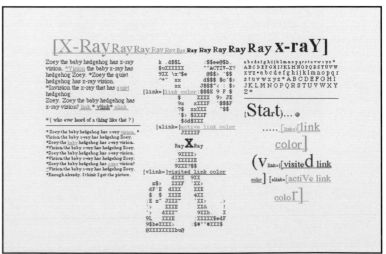

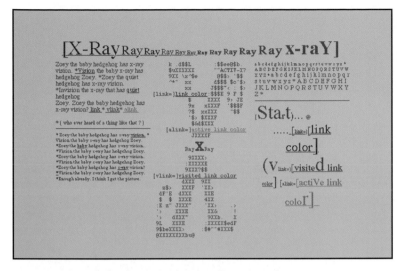

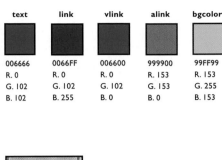

text	link	vlink	alink	bgcolor
006666	0066FF	006600	999900	99FF99
R. 0	R. 0	R. 0	R. 153	R. 153
G. 102	G. 102	G. 102	G. 153	G. 255
B. 102	B. 255	B. 0	B. 0	B. 153

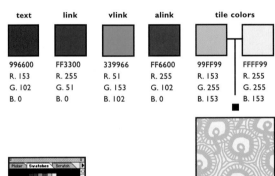

gs02sw

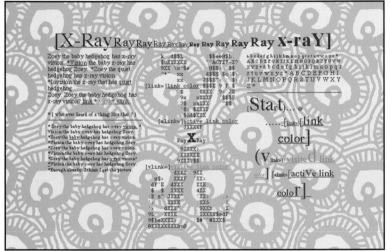

text	link	vlink	alink	tile colors	
996600	FF3300	339966	FF6600	99FF99	FFFF99
R. 153	R. 255	R. 51	R. 255	R. 153	R. 255
G. 102	G. 51	G. 153	G. 102	G. 255	G. 255
B. 0	B. 0	B. 102	B. 0	B. 153	B. 153

gp02sw

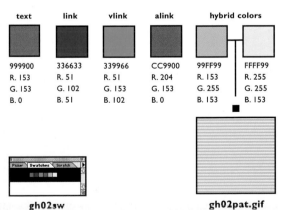

gp02pat.gif

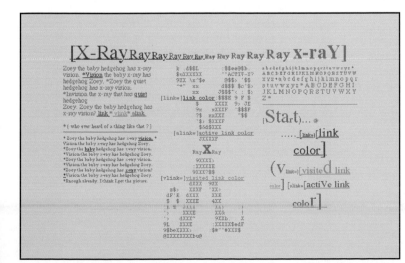

text	link	vlink	alink	hybrid colors	
999900	336633	339966	CC9900	99FF99	FFFF99
R. 153	R. 51	R. 51	R. 204	R. 153	R. 255
G. 153	G. 102	G. 153	G. 153	G. 255	G. 255
B. 0	B. 51	B. 102	B. 0	B. 153	B. 153

gh02sw

gh02pat.gif

First group

text	link	vlink	alink	bgcolor
336666	999900	339900	009999	CCFF99
R. 51	R. 153	R. 51	R. 0	R. 204
G. 102	G. 153	G. 153	G. 153	G. 255
B. 102	B. 0	B. 0	B. 153	B. 153

gs03sw

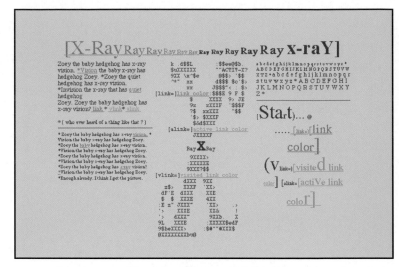

Second group

text	link	vlink	alink	tile colors	
333366	3399FF	0000FF	999900	CCFF99	FFFF99
R. 51	R. 51	R. 0	R. 153	R. 204	R. 255
G. 51	G. 153	G. 0	G. 153	G. 255	G. 255
B. 102	B. 255	B. 255	B. 0	B. 153	B. 153

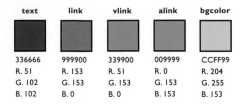

gp03sw

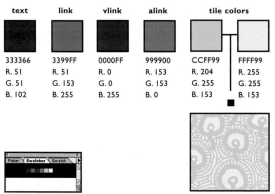

gp03pat.gif

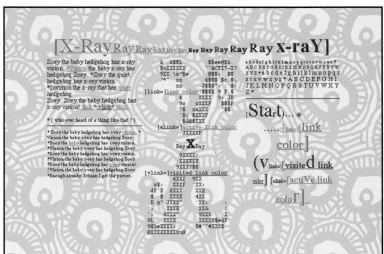

Third group

text	link	vlink	alink	hybrid colors	
336633	00CC00	996600	009999	CCFF99	FFFF99
R. 51	R. 0	R. 153	R. 0	R. 204	R. 255
G. 102	G. 204	G. 102	G. 153	G. 255	G. 255
B. 51	B. 0	B. 0	B. 153	B. 153	B. 153

gh03sw

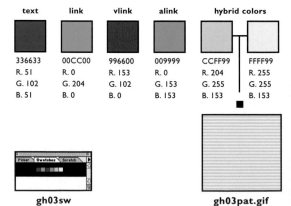

gh03pat.gif

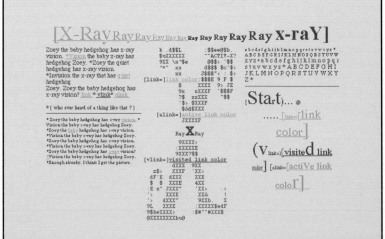

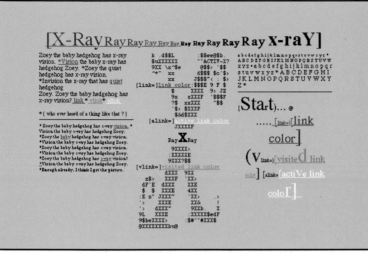

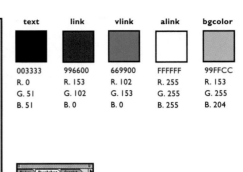

text
003333
R. 0
G. 51
B. 51

link
996600
R. 153
G. 102
B. 0

vlink
669900
R. 102
G. 153
B. 0

alink
FFFFFF
R. 255
G. 255
B. 255

bgcolor
99FFCC
R. 153
G. 255
B. 204

gs04sw

text
006633
R. 0
G. 102
B. 51

link
996600
R. 153
G. 102
B. 0

vlink
669900
R. 102
G. 153
B. 0

alink
FF3300
R. 255
G. 51
B. 0

tile colors
99FFCC
R. 153
G. 255
B. 204

FFFF99
R. 255
G. 255
B. 153

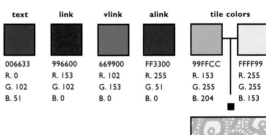

gp04w

gp04pat.gif

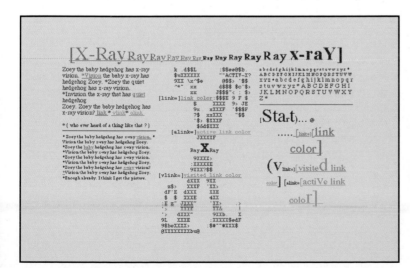

text
336666
R. 51
G. 102
B. 102

link
999900
R. 153
G. 153
B. 0

vlink
339900
R. 51
G. 153
B. 0

alink
009999
R. 0
G. 153
B. 153

hybrid colors
99FFCC
R. 153
G. 255
B. 204

FFFF99
R. 255
G. 255
B. 153

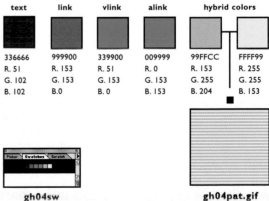

gh04sw

gh04pat.gif

text	link	vlink	alink	bgcolor
006699	336600	666600	003300	66FF66
R. 0	R. 51	R. 102	R. 0	R. 102
G. 102	G. 102	G. 102	G. 51	G. 255
B. 153	B. 0	B. 0	B. 0	B. 102

gs05sw

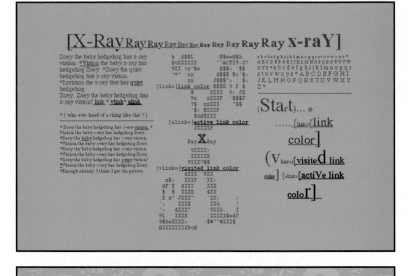

text	link	vlink	alink	tile colors	
336633	0099CC	669900	003366	66FF66	66FFCC
R. 51	R. 0	R. 102	R. 0	R. 102	R. 102
G. 102	G. 153	G. 153	G. 51	G. 255	G. 255
B. 51	B. 204	B. 0	B. 102	B. 102	B. 204

gp05sw

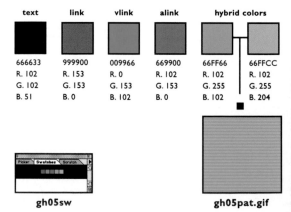

gp05pat.gif

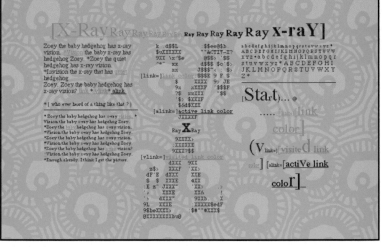

text	link	vlink	alink	hybrid colors	
666633	999900	009966	669900	66FF66	66FFCC
R. 102	R. 153	R. 0	R. 102	R. 102	R. 102
G. 102	G. 153	G. 153	G. 153	G. 255	G. 255
B. 51	B. 0	B. 102	B. 0	B. 102	B. 204

gh05sw

gh05pat.gif

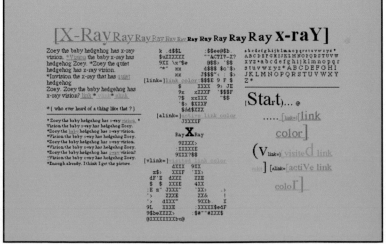

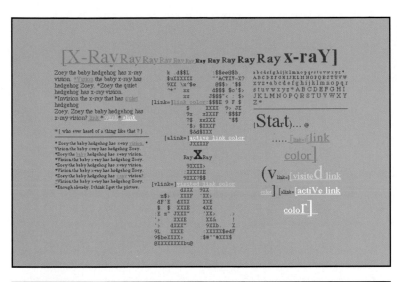

text	link	vlink	alink	bgcolor
336633	669900	CCFFCC	FFFFFF	99CC99
R. 51	R. 102	R. 204	R. 255	R. 153
G. 102	G. 153	G. 255	G. 255	G. 204
B. 51	B. 0	B. 204	B. 255	B. 153

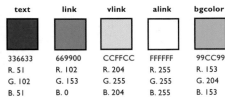

gs06sw

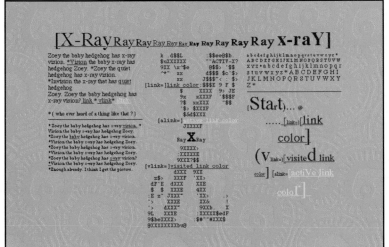

text	link	vlink	alink	tile colors	
333366	666600	666666	CCFFCC	99CC99	CCCCCC
R. 51	R. 102	R. 102	R. 204	R. 153	R. 204
G. 51	G. 102	G. 102	G. 255	G. 204	G. 204
B. 102	B. 0	B. 102	B. 204	B. 153	B. 204

gp06sw

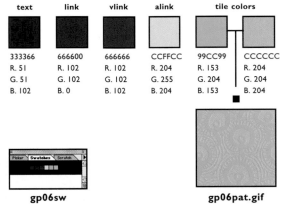

gp06pat.gif

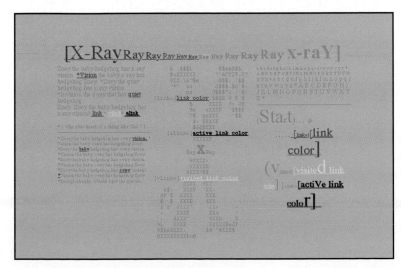

text	link	vlink	alink	hybrid colors	
009900	336633	CCFFCC	000000	99CC99	CCCCCC
R. 0	R. 51	R. 204	R. 0	R. 153	R. 204
G. 153	G. 102	G. 255	G. 0	G. 204	G. 204
B. 0	B. 51	B. 204	B. 0	B. 153	B. 204

gh06sw

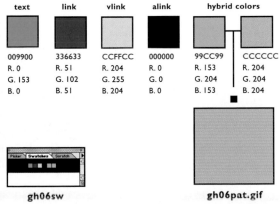

gh06pat.gif

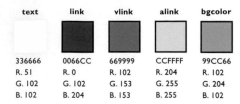

text	link	vlink	alink	bgcolor
336666	0066CC	669999	CCFFFF	99CC66
R. 51	R. 0	R. 102	R. 204	R. 102
G. 102	G. 102	G. 153	G. 255	G. 204
B. 102	B. 204	B. 153	B. 255	B. 102

gs07sw

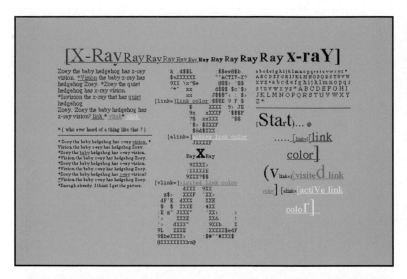

text	link	vlink	alink	tile colors	
003300	CC6600	666600	999900	99CC66	CCCC99
R. 0	R. 204	R. 102	R. 153	R. 153	R. 204
G. 51	G. 102	G. 102	G. 153	G. 204	G. 204
B. 0	B. 0	B. 0	B. 0	B. 102	B. 153

gp07sw

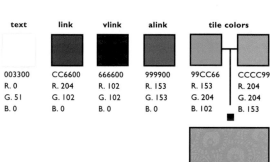

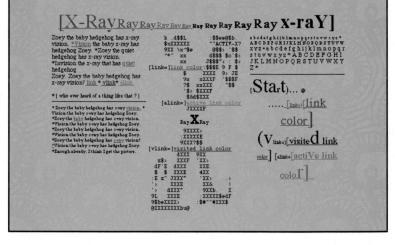

gp07pat.gif

text	link	vlink	alink	hybrid colors	
663333	FFFF00	FF6666	996666	99CC66	CCCC99
R. 102	R. 255	R. 255	R. 153	R. 153	R. 204
G. 51	G. 255	G. 102	G. 102	G. 204	G. 204
B. 51	B. 0	B. 102	B. 102	B. 102	B. 153

gh07sw

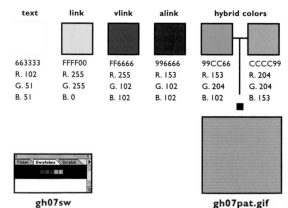

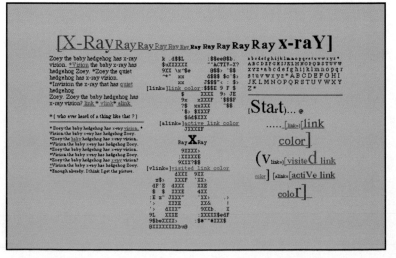

gh07pat.gif

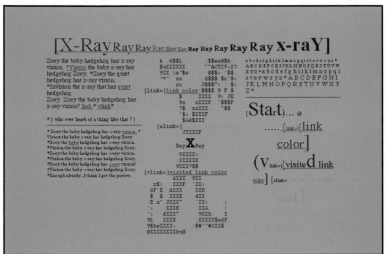

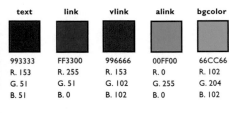

text	link	vlink	alink	bgcolor
993333	FF3300	996666	00FF00	66CC66
R. 153	R. 255	R. 153	R. 0	R. 102
G. 51	G. 51	G. 102	G. 255	G. 204
B. 51	B. 0	B. 102	B. 0	B. 102

gs08sw

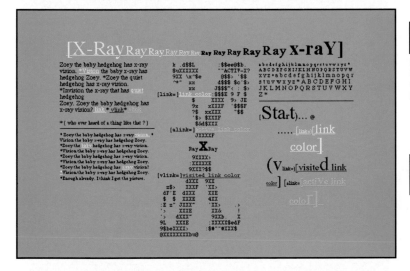

text	link	vlink	alink	tile colors	
003300	FFFF99	666600	CCCC99	66CC66	33CCCC
R. 0	R. 255	R. 102	R. 204	R. 102	R. 51
G. 51	G. 255	G. 102	G. 204	G. 204	G. 204
B. 0	B. 153	B. 0	B. 153	B. 102	B. 204

gp08sw

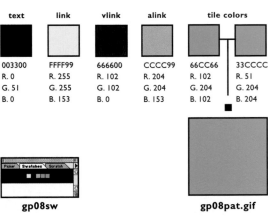

gp08pat.gif

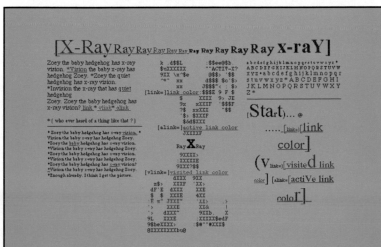

text	link	vlink	alink	hybrid colors	
660066	CC33CC	CC6666	FF0000	66CC66	33CCCC
R. 102	R. 255	R. 153	R. 153	R. 255	R. 204
G. 102	G. 102	G. 153	G. 153	G. 204	G. 204
B. 102	B. 102	B. 153	B. 0	B. 204	B. 204

gh08sw

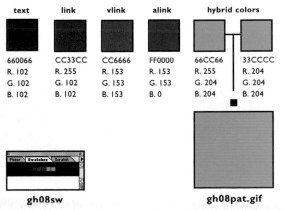

gh08pat.gif

text	link	vlink	alink	bgcolor
336633	0066FF	6666CC	CCFFFF	33FF00
R. 51	R. 0	R. 102	R. 204	R. 51
G. 102	G. 102	G. 102	G. 255	G. 255
B. 51	B. 255	B. 204	B. 255	B. 0

gs09sw

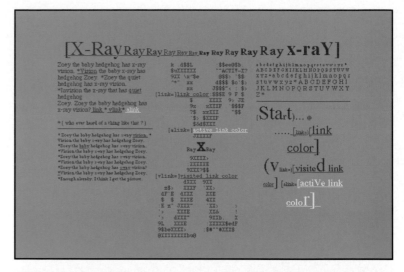

text	link	vlink	alink	tile colors	
666600	FF6600	CC6633	999900	66FF66	33FF00
R. 102	R. 255	R. 204	R. 153	R. 102	R. 51
G. 102	G. 102	G. 102	G. 153	G. 255	G. 255
B. 0	B. 0	B. 51	B. 0	B. 102	B. 0

gp09sw

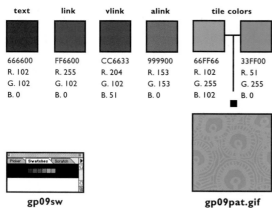

gp09pat.gif

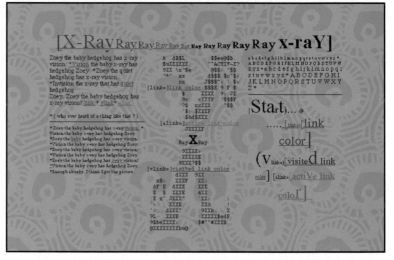

text	link	vlink	alink	hybrid colors	
006633	0066CC	669966	CCFFFF	33FF00	66FF66
R. 0	R. 0	R. 102	R. 204	R. 51	R. 102
G.102	G. 102	G. 153	G. 255	G. 255	G. 255
B. 51	B. 204	B. 102	B. 255	B. 0	B. 102

gh09sw

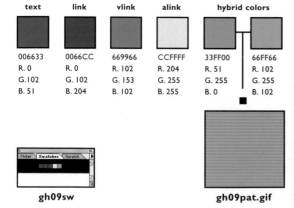

gh09pat.gif

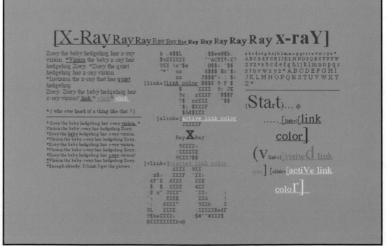

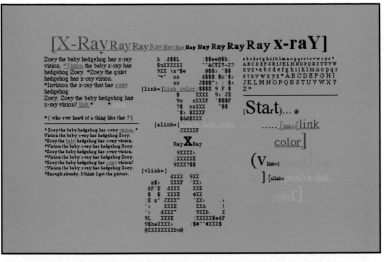

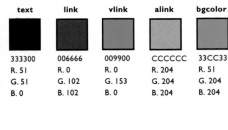

text
333300
R. 51
G. 51
B. 0

link
006666
R. 0
G. 102
B. 102

vlink
009900
R. 0
G. 153
B. 0

alink
CCCCCC
R. 204
G. 204
B. 204

bgcolor
33CC33
R. 51
G. 204
B. 204

gs010sw

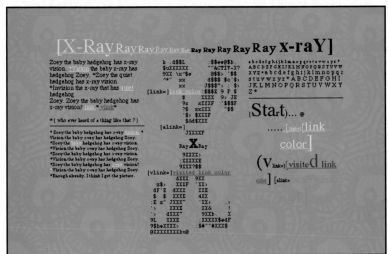

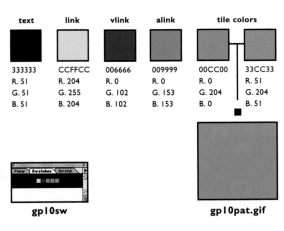

text
333333
R. 51
G. 51
B. 51

link
CCFFCC
R. 204
G. 255
B. 204

vlink
006666
R. 0
G. 102
B. 102

alink
009999
R. 0
G. 153
B. 153

tile colors
00CC00
R. 0
G. 204
B. 0

33CC33
R. 51
G. 204
B. 51

gp10sw

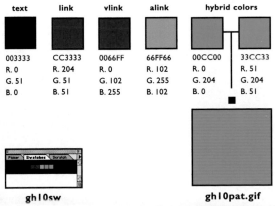

gp10pat.gif

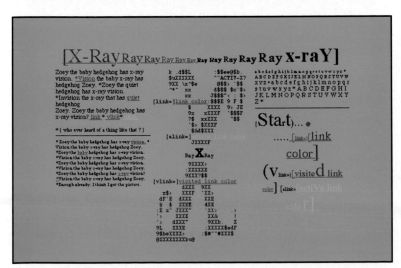

text
003333
R. 0
G. 51
B. 0

link
CC3333
R. 204
G. 51
B. 51

vlink
0066FF
R. 0
G. 102
B. 255

alink
66FF66
R. 102
G. 255
B. 102

hybrid colors
00CC00
R. 0
G. 204
B. 0

33CC33
R. 51
G. 204
B. 51

gh10sw

gh10pat.gif

text	link	vlink	alink	bgcolor
333300	993333	66CC66	000000	339933
R. 51	R. 153	R. 102	R. 0	R. 51
G. 51	G. 51	G. 204	G. 0	G. 153
B. 0	B. 51	B. 102	B. 0	B. 51

gs11sw

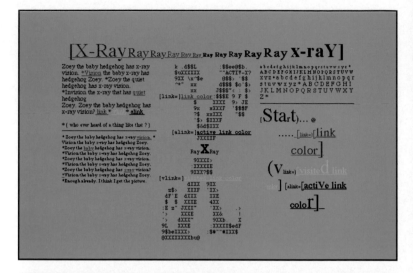

text	link	vlink	alink	tile colors	
99FF99	FFFF00	CCCC99	CCCCCC	339933	009900
R. 153	R. 255	R. 204	R. 204	R. 51	R. 0
G. 255	G. 255	G. 204	G. 204	G. 153	G. 153
B. 153	B. 0	B. 153	B. 204	B. 51	B. 0

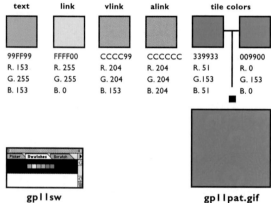

gp11sw   **gp11pat.gif**

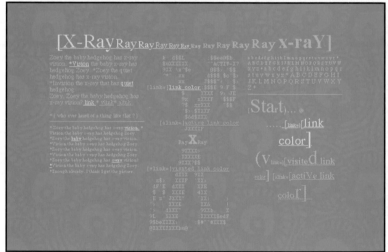

text	link	vlink	alink	hybrid colors	
FFFF99	FFCC00	CCCCCC	336633	009900	339933
R. 255	R. 255	R. 204	R. 51	R. 0	R. 51
G. 255	G. 204	G. 204	G. 102	G. 153	G.153
B. 153	B. 0	B. 204	B. 51	B. 0	B. 51

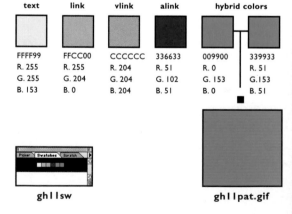

gh11sw   **gh11pat.gif**

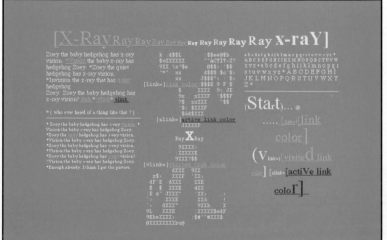

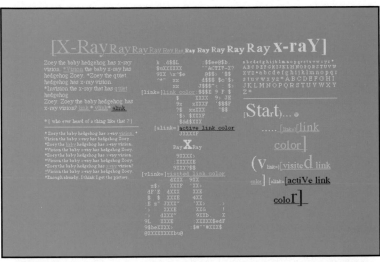

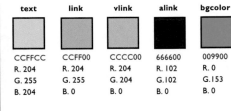

text	link	vlink	alink	bgcolor
CCFFCC	CCFF00	CCCC00	666600	009900
R. 204	R. 204	R. 204	R. 102	R. 0
G. 255	G. 255	G. 204	G.102	G.153
B. 204	B. 0	B. 0	B. 0	B. 0

gs12sw

text	link	vlink	alink	tile colors	
FFFFCC	FFFF00	66CC66	333300	009900	669900
R. 255	R. 255	R. 102	R. 51	R. 0	R. 102
G. 255	G. 255	G. 204	G. 51	G. 153	G. 153
B. 204	B. 0	B. 102	B. 0	B. 0	B. 0

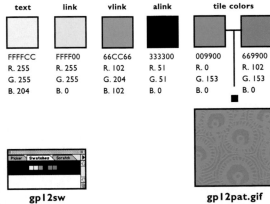

gp12sw

gp12pat.gif

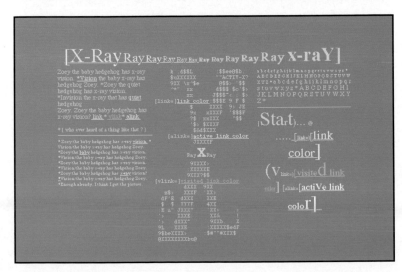

text	link	vlink	alink	hybrid colors	
CCFFCC	FFFF66	CCCC99	FFFFFF	009900	669900
R. 204	R. 255	R. 204	R. 255	R. 0	R. 102
G. 255	G. 255	G. 204	G. 255	G. 153	G. 153
B. 204	B. 102	B. 153	B. 255	B. 0	B. 0

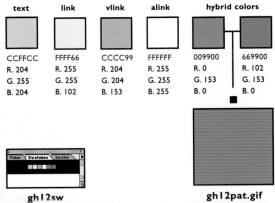

gh12sw

gh12pat.gif

text	link	vlink	alink	bgcolor
CCCC99	99FF99	33CC33	669966	006600
R. 204	R. 153	R. 51	R. 102	R. 0
G. 204	G. 255	G. 204	G.153	G. 102
B.153	B. 153	B. 51	B. 102	B. 0

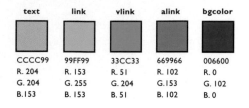

gs13sw

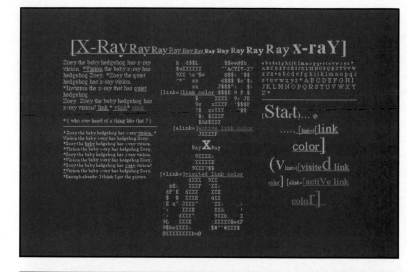

text	link	vlink	alink	tile colors	
CCCC99	6699FF	9999CC	33CCCC	006633	006600
R. 204	R. 102	R. 153	R. 51	R. 0	R. 0
G. 204	G.153	G. 153	G. 204	G. 102	G. 102
B.153	B. 255	B. 204	B. 204	B. 51	B. 0

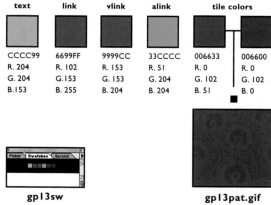

gp13sw

gp13pat.gif

text	link	vlink	alink	hybrid colors	
FFFFCC	FFCC66	CC9999	FF6600	006600	006633
R. 255	R. 255	R. 204	R. 255	R. 0	R. 0
G. 255	G. 204	G. 153	G. 102	G. 102	G. 102
B. 204	B. 102	B. 153	B. 0	B. 0	B. 51

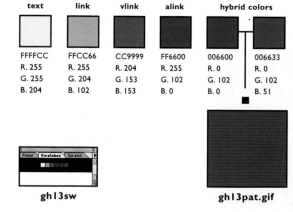

gh13sw

gh13pat.gif

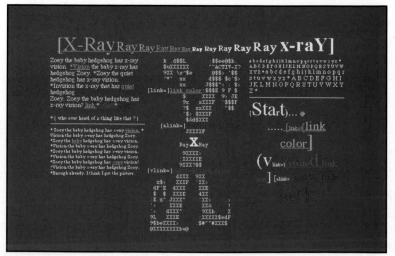

coloring

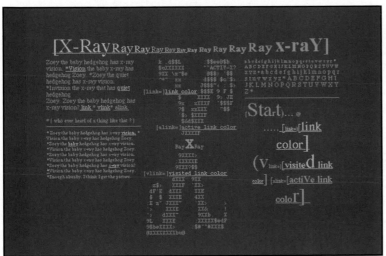

text	link	vlink	alink	bgcolor
00CC00	CCFF00	CCCC99	00FF00	336600
R. 0	R. 204	R. 204	R. 0	R. 51
G. 204	G. 255	G. 204	G. 255	G. 102
B. 0	B. 0	B. 153	B. 0	B. 0

gs14sw

text	link	vlink	alink	tile colors	
CCCC99	FFFF00	CCCC33	FFFFCC	336600	666600
R. 204	R. 255	R. 204	R. 255	R. 51	R. 102
G. 204	G. 255	G. 204	G. 255	G. 102	G. 102
B. 153	B. 0	B. 51	B. 204	B. 0	B. 0

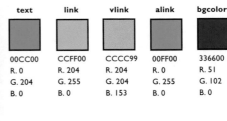

gp14sw

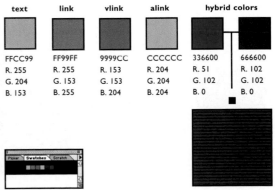

gp14pat.gif

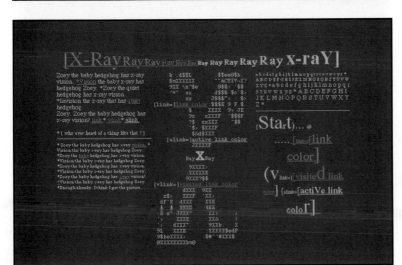

text	link	vlink	alink	hybrid colors	
FFCC99	FF99FF	9999CC	CCCCCC	336600	666600
R. 255	R. 255	R. 153	R. 204	R. 51	R. 102
G. 204	G. 153	G. 153	G. 204	G. 102	G. 102
B. 153	B. 255	B. 204	B. 204	B. 0	B. 0

gh14sw

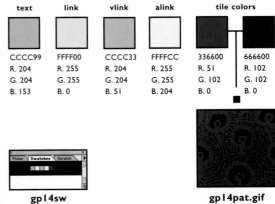

gh14pat.gif

text	link	vlink	alink	bgcolor
999999	CCCC33	996600	FFFFCC	003300
R. 153	R. 204	R. 204	R. 255	R. 0
G. 153	G. 204	G. 102	G. 255	G. 51
B. 153	B. 51	B. 0	B. 204	B. 0

gs15sw

text	link	vlink	alink	tile colors	
33CC99	CCCC33	996600	99CC99	003333	003300
R. 51	R. 204	R. 153	R. 153	R. 0	R. 0
G. 204	G. 204	G. 102	G. 204	G. 51	G. 51
B. 153	B. 51	B. 0	B. 153	B. 51	B. 0

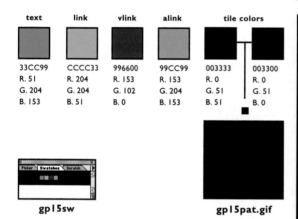

gp15sw

gp15pat.gif

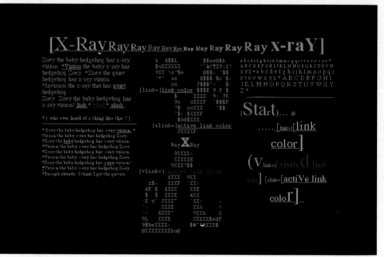

text	link	vlink	alink	hybrid colors	
33CC99	999933	666633	99CC99	003300	003333
R. 51	R. 153	R. 102	R. 153	R. 0	R. 0
G. 204	G. 153	G. 102	G. 204	G. 51	G. 51
B. 153	B. 51	B. 51	B. 153	B. 0	B. 51

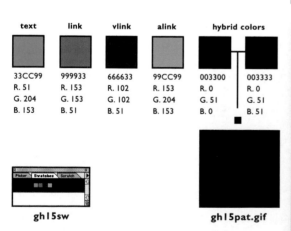

gh15sw

gh15pat.gif

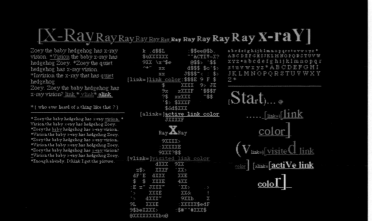

text	link	vlink	alink	bgcolor
CCCC99	33CC33	999900	FFFFFF	003300
R. 204	R. 51	R. 153	R. 255	R. 0
G. 204	G. 204	G. 153	G. 255	G. 51
B. 153	B. 51	B. 0	B. 255	B. 0

gs16sw

text	link	vlink	alink	tile colors	
FFCCFF	CC33CC	9966CC	336633	003300	333333
R. 255	R. 204	R. 153	R. 51	R. 0	R. 51
G. 204	G. 51	G. 102	G. 102	G. 51	G. 51
B. 255	B. 204	B. 204	B. 51	B. 51	B. 51

gp16sw

gp16pat.gif

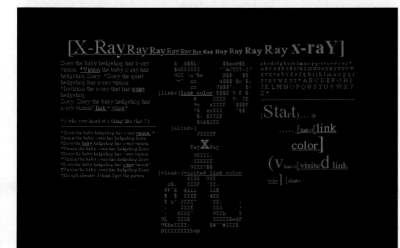

text	link	vlink	alink	hybrid colors	
999966	009933	999900	000000	003300	333333
R. 153	R. 0	R. 153	R. 0	R. 0	R. 51
G. 153	G. 153	G. 153	G. 0	G. 51	G. 51
B. 102	B. 51	B. 0	B. 0	B. 0	B. 51

gh16sw

gh02pat.gif

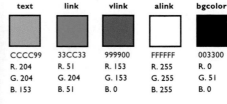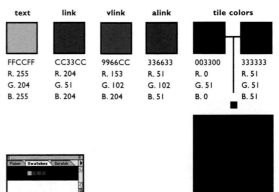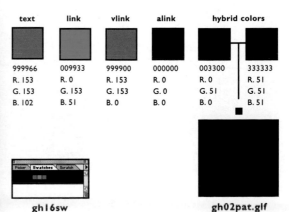

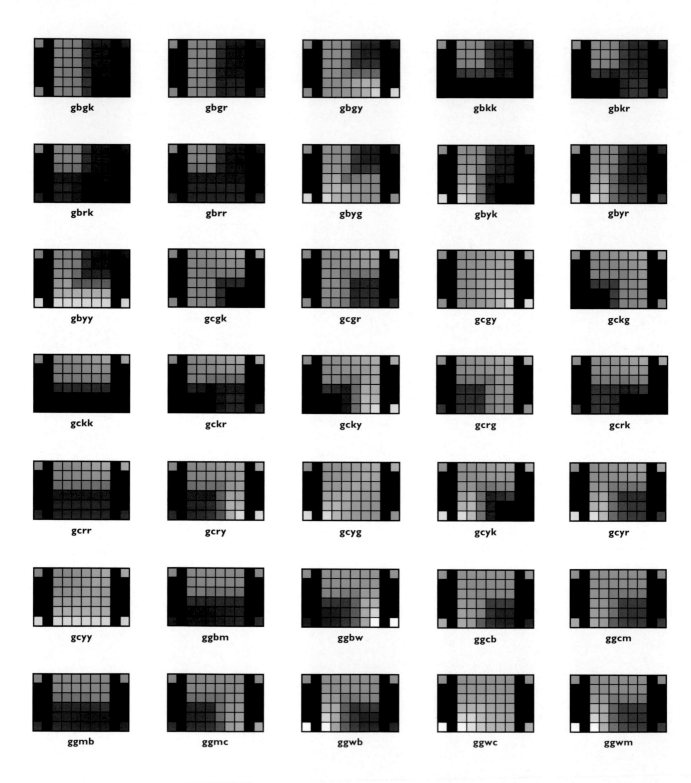

gbgk gbgr gbgy gbkk gbkr

gbrk gbrr gbyg gbyk gbyr

gbyy gcgk gcgr gcgy gckg

gckk gckr gcky gcrg gcrk

gcrr gcry gcyg gcyk gcyr

gcyy ggbm ggbw ggcb ggcm

ggmb ggmc ggwb ggwc ggwm

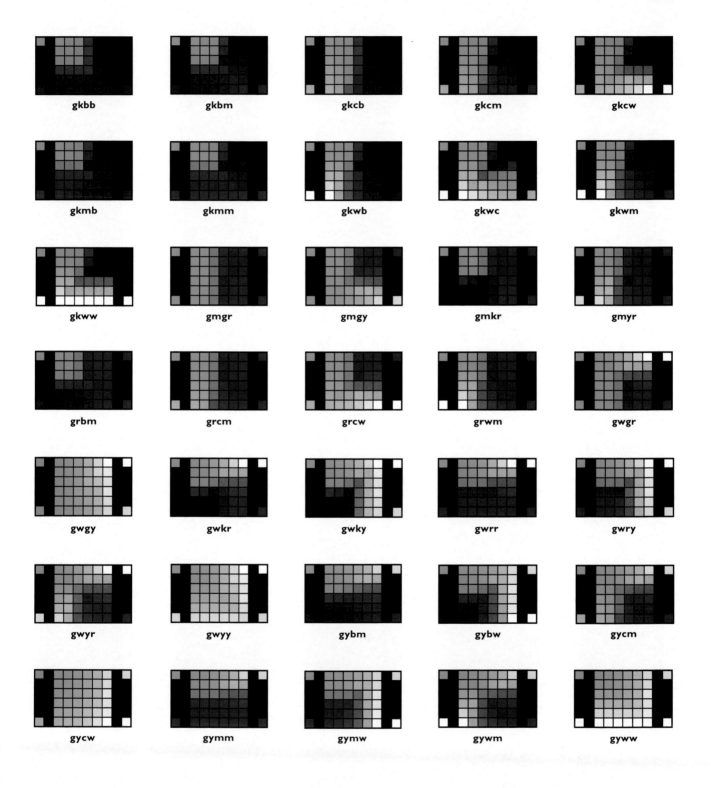

gkbb gkbm gkcb gkcm gkcw

gkmb gkmm gkwb gkwc gkwm

gkww gmgr gmgy gmkr gmyr

grbm grcm grcw grwm gwgr

gwgy gwkr gwky gwrr gwry

gwyr gwyy gybm gybw gycm

gycw gymm gymw gywm gyww

BLUE

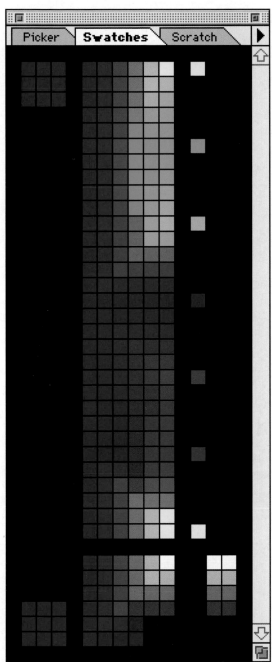

mbs

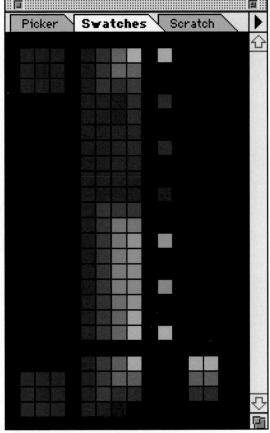

mbd

First grouping

text	link	vlink	alink	bgcolor
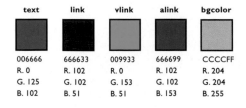				
006666	666633	009933	666699	CCCCFF
R. 0	R. 102	R. 0	R. 102	R. 204
G. 125	G. 102	G. 153	G. 102	G. 204
B. 102	B. 51	B. 51	B. 153	B. 255

bs01sw

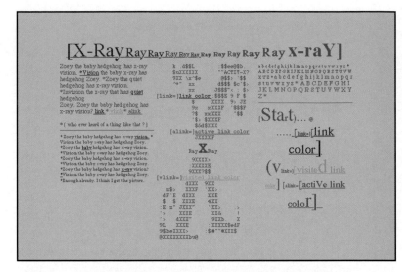

Second grouping

text	link	vlink	alink	tile colors	
333366	3333CC	996600	FFFFFF	CCCCCC	CCCCFF
R. 51	R. 51	R. 153	R. 255	R. 204	R. 204
G. 51	G. 51	G. 102	G. 255	G. 204	G. 204
B. 102	B. 204	B. 0	B. 255	B. 204	B. 255

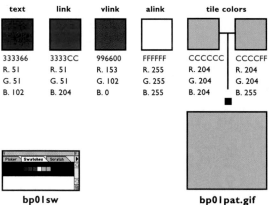

bp01sw

bp01pat.gif

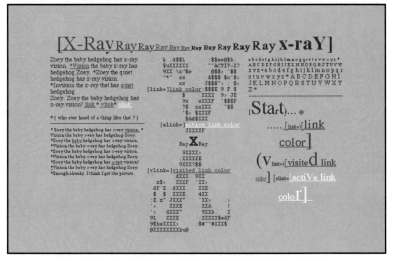

Third grouping

text	link	vlink	alink	hybrid colors	
666699	CC33CC	996699	FF00CC	CCCCCC	CCCCFF
R. 102	R. 204	R. 153	R. 255	R. 204	R. 204
G. 102	G. 51	G. 102	G. 0	G. 204	G. 204
B. 153	B. 204	B. 153	B. 204	B. 204	B. 255

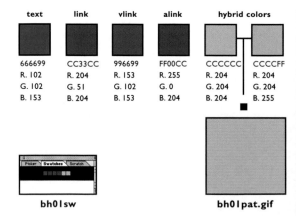

bh01sw

bh01pat.gif

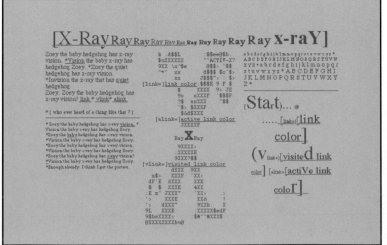

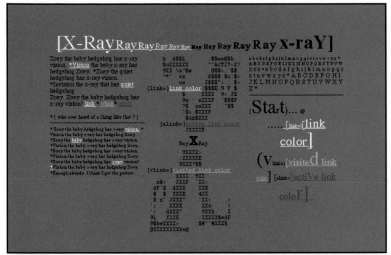

text	link	vlink	alink	bgcolor
333300	FFFFFF	CCFFFF	6666FF	9999FF
R. 51	R. 255	R. 204	R. 102	R. 153
G. 51	G. 255	G. 255	G. 102	G. 153
B. 0	B. 255	B. 255	B. 255	B. 255

bs02sw

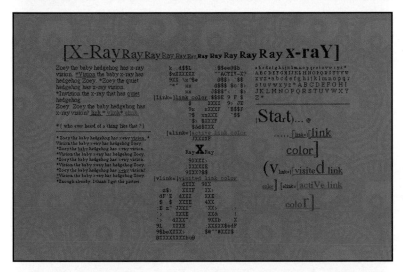

text	link	vlink	alink	tile colors	
333366	0000FF	666666	FF00FF	CC99FF	99FFFF
R. 51	R. 0	R. 102	R. 255	R. 204	R. 153
G. 51	G. 0	G. 102	G. 0	G. 153	G. 255
B. 102	B. 255	B. 102	B. 255	B. 255	B. 255

bp02sw

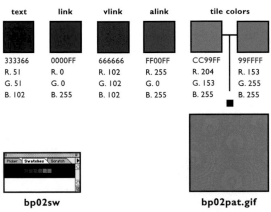

bp02pat.gif

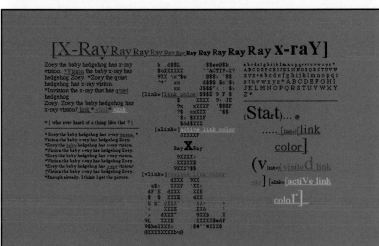

text	link	vlink	alink	hybrid colors	
333300	0000FF	006699	CCCCCC	CC99FF	9999FF
R. 51	R. 0	R. 0	R. 204	R. 204	R. 153
G. 51	G. 0	G. 102	G. 204	G. 153	G. 153
B. 0	B. 255	B. 153	B. 204	B. 255	B. 255

bh02sw

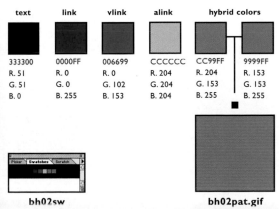

bh02pat.gif

text	link	vlink	alink	bgcolor
333366	CC00CC	9900CC	FF0000	9999CC
R. 51	R. 204	R. 153	R. 255	R. 153
G. 51	G. 0	G. 0	G. 0	G. 153
B. 102	B. 204	B. 204	B. 0	B. 204

bs03sw

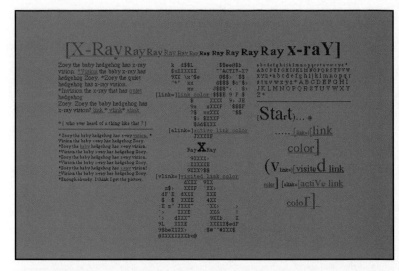

text	link	vlink	alink	tile colors	
663333	FF0000	CC3333	CC6666	CC99FF	9999CC
R. 102	R. 255	R. 204	R. 204	R. 204	R. 153
G. 51	G. 0	G. 51	G. 102	G. 153	G. 153
B. 51	B. 0	B. 51	B. 102	B. 255	B. 204

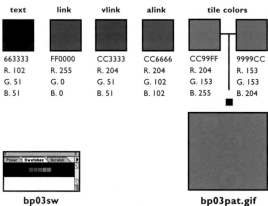

bp03sw

bp03pat.gif

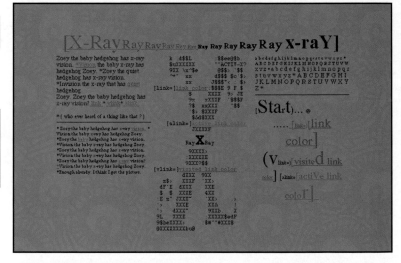

text	link	vlink	alink	hybrid colors	
333333	0033FF	6666CC	CCCCCC	CC99FF	9999CC
R. 51	R. 0	R. 102	R. 204	R. 204	R. 153
G. 51	G. 51	G. 102	G. 204	G. 153	G. 153
B. 51	B. 255	B. 204	B. 204	B. 255	B. 204

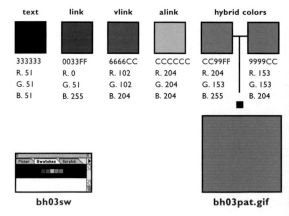

bh03sw

bh03pat.gif

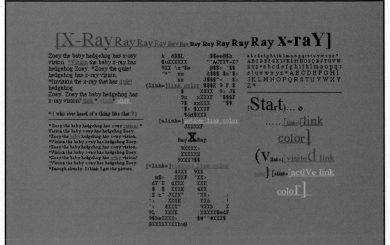

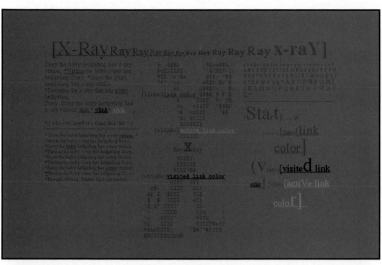

text	link	vlink	alink	bgcolor
003399	0000CC	333333	9999FF	6666FF
R. 0	R. 0	R. 51	R. 153	R. 102
G. 51	G. 0	G. 51	G. 153	G. 102
B. 153	B. 204	B. 51	B. 255	B. 255

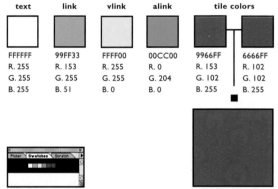

bs04sw

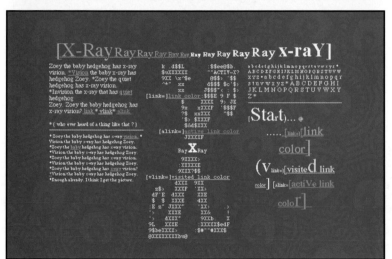

text	link	vlink	alink	tile colors	
FFFFFF	99FF33	FFFF00	00CC00	9966FF	6666FF
R. 255	R. 153	R. 255	R. 0	R. 153	R. 102
G. 255	G. 255	G. 255	G. 204	G. 102	G. 102
B. 255	B. 51	B. 0	B. 0	B. 255	B. 255

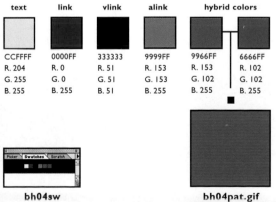

bp04sw

bp04pat.gif

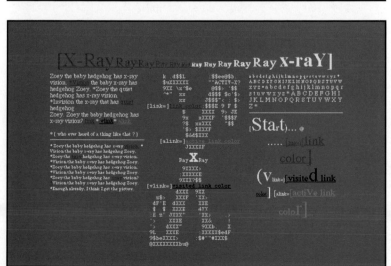

text	link	vlink	alink	hybrid colors	
CCFFFF	0000FF	333333	9999FF	9966FF	6666FF
R. 204	R. 0	R. 51	R. 153	R. 153	R. 102
G. 255	G. 0	G. 51	G. 153	G. 102	G. 102
B. 255	B. 255	B. 51	B. 255	B. 255	B. 255

bh04sw

bh04pat.gif

text	link	vlink	alink	bgcolor
99CC99	00FF00	339933	FFFFFF	3333FF
R. 153	R. 0	R. 51	R. 255	R. 51
G. 204	G. 255	G. 153	G. 255	G. 51
B. 153	B. 0	B. 51	B. 255	B. 255

bs05sw

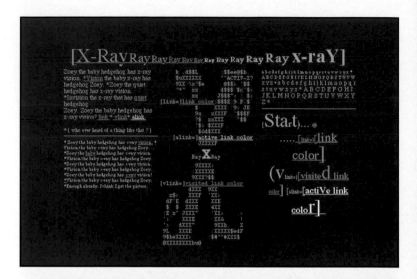

text	link	vlink	alink	tile colors	
CCCCFF	FFCC33	999999	FFFFFF	6633FF	3333FF
R. 204	R. 255	R. 153	R. 255	R. 102	R. 51
G. 204	G. 204	G. 153	G. 255	G. 51	G. 51
B. 204	B. 51	B. 153	B. 255	B. 255	B. 255

bp05sw

bp05pat.gif

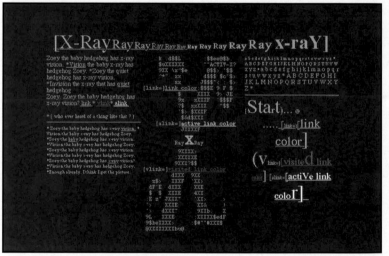

text	link	vlink	alink	hybrid colors	
000033	9999FF	0000FF	666699	6633FF	3333FF
R. 0	R. 153	R. 0	R. 102	R. 102	R. 51
G. 0	G. 153	G. 0	G. 102	G. 51	G. 51
B. 51	B. 255	B. 255	B. 153	B. 255	B. 255

bh05sw

bh05pat.gif

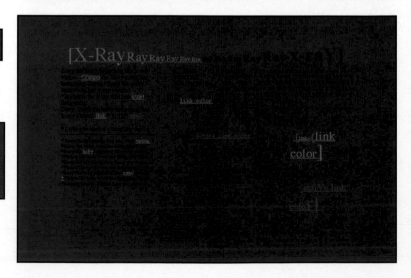

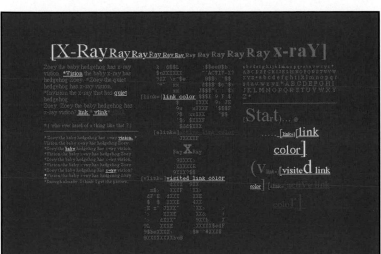

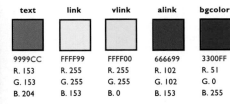

text	link	vlink	alink	bgcolor
9999CC	FFFF99	FFFF00	666699	3300FF
R. 153	R. 255	R. 255	R. 102	R. 51
G. 153	G. 255	G. 255	G. 102	G. 0
B. 204	B. 153	B. 0	B. 153	B. 255

bs06sw

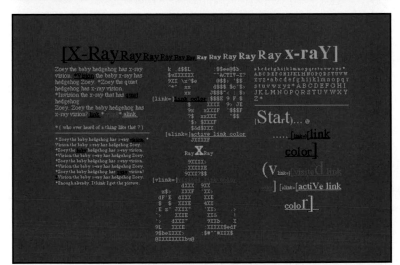

text	link	vlink	alink	tile colors	
33CCCC	0000CC	6666FF	CCCCFF	6600FF	3300FF
R. 51	R. 0	R. 102	R. 204	R. 102	R. 51
G. 204	G. 0	G. 102	G. 204	G. 0	G. 0
B. 204	B. 51	B. 255	B. 255	B. 255	B. 255

bp06sw

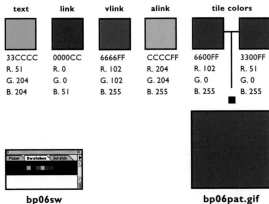

bp06pat.gif

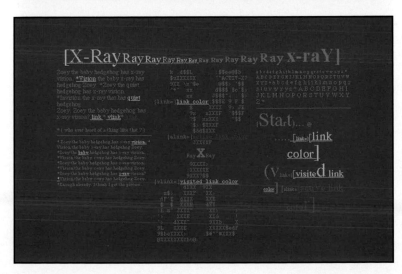

text	link	vlink	alink	hybrid colors	
6699FF	00FFFF	CCCCCC	666699	6600FF	3300FF
R. 51	R. 0	R. 204	R. 102	R. 102	R. 51
G. 153	G. 255	G. 204	G. 102	G. 0	G. 0
B. 255	B. 255	B. 204	B. 153	B. 255	B. 255

bh06sw

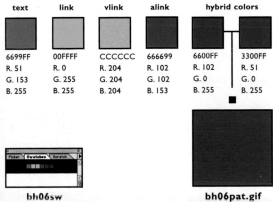

bh06pat.gif

text	link	vlink	alink	bgcolor
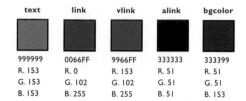
999999	0066FF	9966FF	333333	333399
R. 153	R. 0	R. 153	R. 51	R. 51
G. 153	G. 102	G. 102	G. 51	G. 51
B. 153	B. 255	B. 255	B. 51	B. 153

bs07sw

text	link	vlink	alink	tile colors	
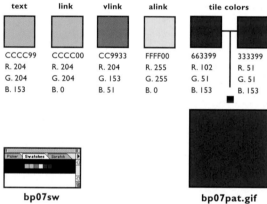
CCCC99	CCCC00	CC9933	FFFF00	663399	333399
R. 204	R. 204	R. 204	R. 255	R. 102	R. 51
G. 204	G. 204	G. 153	G. 255	G. 51	G. 51
B. 153	B. 0	B. 51	B. 0	B. 153	B. 153

bp07sw

bp07pat.gif

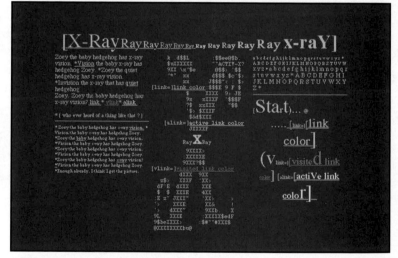

text	link	vlink	alink	hybrid colors	
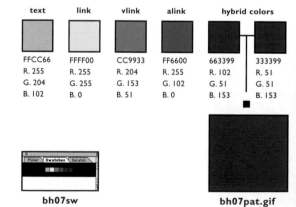
FFCC66	FFFF00	CC9933	FF6600	663399	333399
R. 255	R. 255	R. 204	R. 255	R. 102	R. 51
G. 204	G. 255	G. 153	G. 102	G. 51	G. 51
B. 102	B. 0	B. 51	B. 0	B. 153	B. 153

bh07sw

bh07pat.gif

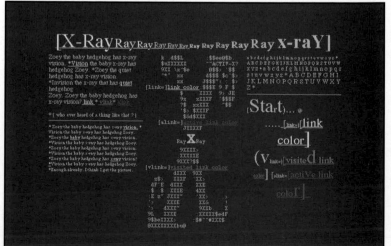

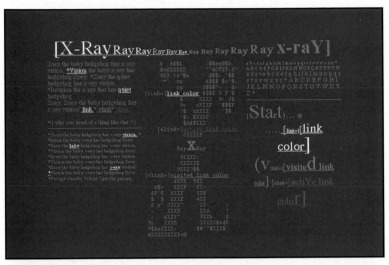

text	link	vlink	alink	bgcolor
9999CC	FFFFFF	999966	CC6633	333399
R. 153	R. 255	R. 153	R. 204	R. 51
G. 153	G. 255	G. 153	G. 102	G. 51
B. 204	B. 255	B. 102	B. 51	B. 153

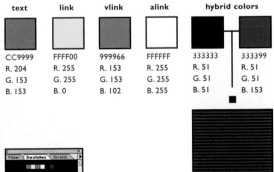

bs08sw

text	link	vlink	alink	tile colors	
FFFFFF	FFCC00	999966	FFFF00	333333	333399
R. 255	R. 255	R. 153	R. 255	R. 51	R. 51
G. 255	G. 204	G. 153	G. 255	G. 51	G. 51
B. 255	B. 0	B. 102	B. 0	B. 51	B. 153

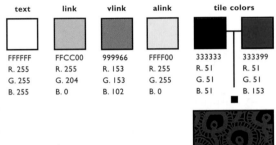

bp08sw

bp08pat.gif

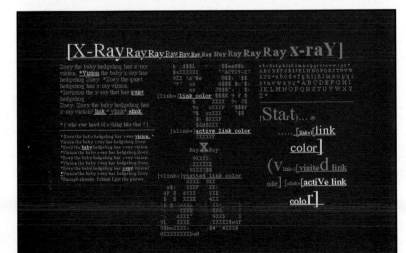

text	link	vlink	alink	hybrid colors	
CC9999	FFFF00	999966	FFFFFF	333333	333399
R. 204	R. 255	R. 153	R. 255	R. 51	R. 51
G. 153	G. 255	G. 153	G. 255	G. 51	G. 51
B. 153	B. 0	B. 102	B. 255	B. 51	B. 153

bh08sw

bh08pat.gif

text	link	vlink	alink	bgcolor
CC99CC	FF33FF	666666	3333CC	333366
R. 204	R. 255	R. 102	R. 51	R. 51
G. 153	G. 51	G. 102	G. 51	G. 51
B. 204	B. 255	B. 102	B. 204	B. 102

bs09sw

text	link	vlink	alink	tile colors	
FF9999	FF3333	9966FF	CC0000	333333	333366
R. 255	R. 255	R. 153	R. 204	R. 51	R. 51
G. 153	G. 51	G. 102	G. 0	G. 51	G. 51
B. 153	B. 51	B. 255	B. 0	B. 51	B. 102

bp09sw

bp09pat.gif

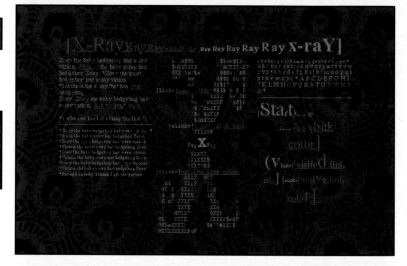

text	link	vlink	alink	hybrid colors	
9999CC	6666FF	666666	3333CC	333333	333366
R. 153	R. 102	R. 102	R. 51	R. 51	R. 51
G. 153	G. 102	G. 102	G. 51	G. 51	G. 51
B. 204	B. 255	B. 102	B. 204	B. 51	B. 102

bh09sw

bh09pat.gif

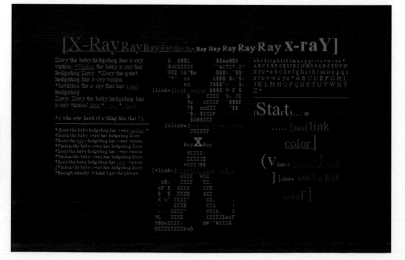

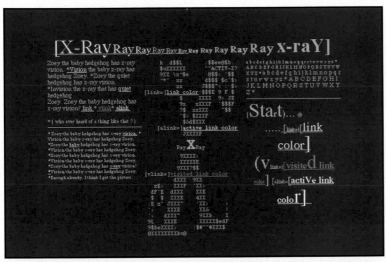

text	link	vlink	alink	bgcolor
99CC99	FFFF00	669900	FFFFFF	0000CC
R. 153	R. 255	R. 51	R. 255	R. 0
G. 204	G. 255	G. 153	G. 255	G. 0
B. 153	B. 0	B. 0	B. 255	B. 204

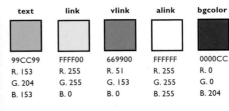

bs10sw

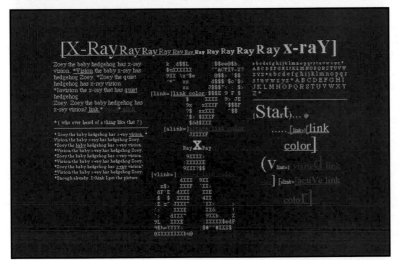

text	link	vlink	alink	tile colors	
CCCCCC	00FFFF	CC33FF	006666	0000CC	3300CC
R. 204	R. 0	R. 204	R. 0	R. 0	R. 51
G. 204	G. 255	G. 51	G. 102	G. 204	G. 0
B. 204	B. 255	B. 255	B. 102	B. 204	B. 204

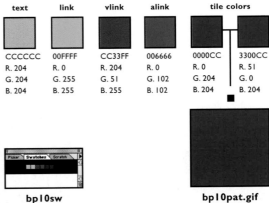

bp10sw

bp10pat.gif

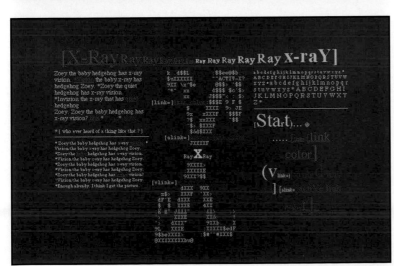

text	link	vlink	alink	hybrid colors	
CCCCCC	CC6666	6633CC	FF0000	0000CC	3300CC
R. 204	R. 204	R. 102	R. 255	R. 0	R. 51
G. 204	G. 102	G. 51	G. 0	G. 0	G. 0
B. 204	B. 102	B. 204	B. 0	B. 204	B. 204

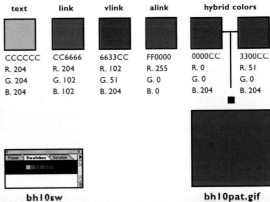

bh10sw

bh10pat.gif

text	link	vlink	alink	bgcolor
6666FF	999966	666600	003333	000099
R. 102	R. 153	R. 102	R. 0	R. 0
G. 102	G. 153	G. 102	G. 51	G. 0
B. 255	B. 100	B. 0	B. 51	B. 153

bs11sw

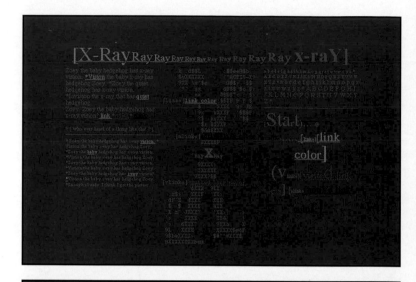

text	link	vlink	alink	tile colors	
9999CC	FFFFFF	009966	3333FF	330099	000099
R. 153	R. 255	R. 0	R. 51	R. 51	R. 0
G. 153	G. 255	G. 153	G. 51	G. 0	G. 0
B. 204	B. 255	B. 102	B. 255	B. 153	B. 153

bp11sw

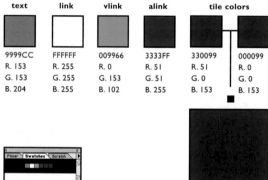

bp11pat.gif

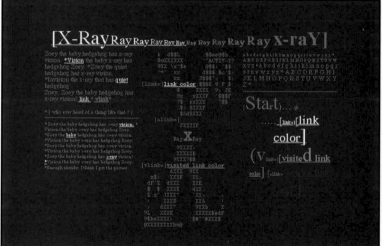

text	link	vlink	alink	hybrid colors	
9999CC	FF6666	009966	669966	330099	000099
R. 153	R. 255	R. 0	R. 102	R. 51	R. 0
G. 153	G. 102	G. 153	G. 153	G. 0	G. 0
B. 204	B. 102	B. 102	B. 102	B. 153	B. 153

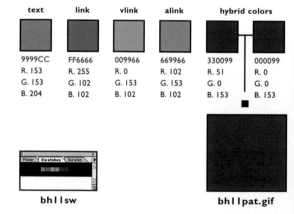

bh11sw

bh11pat.gif

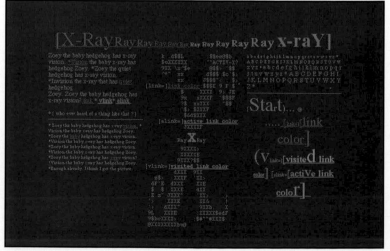

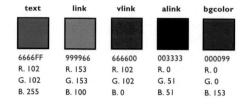

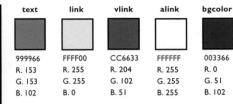

text	link	vlink	alink	bgcolor
999966	FFFF00	CC6633	FFFFFF	003366
R. 153	R. 255	R. 204	R. 255	R. 0
G. 153	G. 255	G. 102	G. 255	G. 51
B. 102	B. 0	B. 51	B. 255	B. 102

bs12sw

text	link	vlink	alink	tile colors	
9999CC	CCCC66	996633	FFFF00	333333	003366
R. 153	R. 255	R. 153	R. 255	R. 51	R. 0
G. 153	G. 255	G. 102	G. 255	G. 51	G. 51
B. 204	B. 102	B. 51	B. 0	B. 51	B. 102

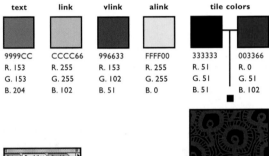

bp12sw

bp12pat.gif

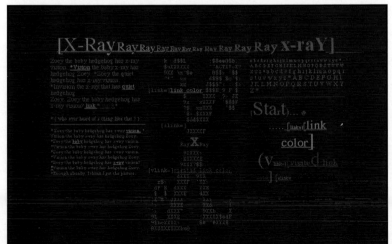

text	link	vlink	alink	hybrid colors	
6666FF	999966	666600	333300	333333	999966
R. 51	R. 153	R. 102	R. 102	R. 51	R. 153
G. 51	G. 153	G. 102	G. 102	G. 51	G. 153
B. 255	B. 102	B. 0	B. 0	B. 51	B. 102

bh12sw

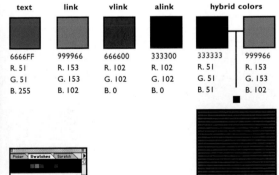

bh12pat.gif

text	link	vlink	alink	bgcolor
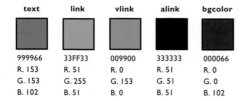				
999966	33FF33	009900	333333	000066
R. 153	R. 51	R. 0	R. 51	R. 0
G. 153	G. 255	G. 153	G. 51	G. 0
B. 102	B. 51	B. 0	B. 51	B. 102

bs13sw

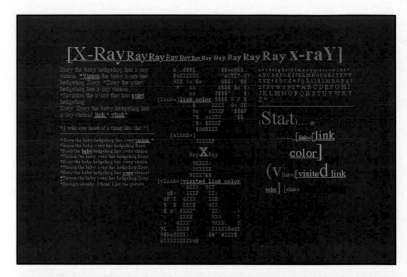

text	link	vlink	alink	tile colors	
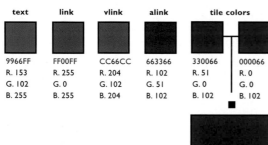					
9966FF	FF00FF	CC66CC	663366	330066	000066
R. 153	R. 255	R. 204	R. 102	R. 51	R. 0
G. 102	G. 0	G. 102	G. 51	G. 0	G. 0
B. 255	B. 255	B. 204	B. 102	B. 102	B. 102

bp13sw

bp13pat.gif

text	link	vlink	alink	hybrid colors	
009999	00CC00	669966	006600	330066	000066
R. 0	R. 0	R. 102	R. 0	R. 51	R. 0
G. 153	G. 204	G. 153	G. 102	G. 0	G. 0
B. 153	B. 0	B. 102	B. 0	B. 102	B. 102

bh13sw

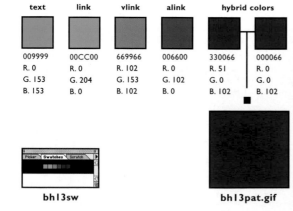

bh13pat.gif

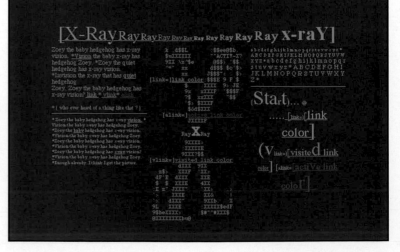

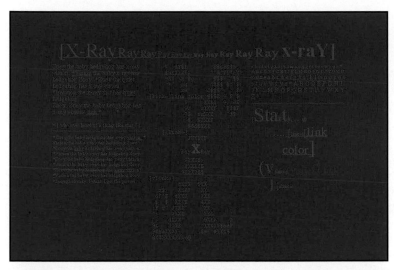

text	link	vlink	alink	bgcolor
996699	6666FF	6600FF	0000FF	000066
R. 153	R. 102	R. 102	R. 0	R. 0
G. 102	G. 102	G. 0	G. 0	G. 0
B. 153	B. 255	B. 255	B. 255	B. 102

bs14sw

text	link	vlink	alink	tile colors	
CC66CC	FF0066	CC3333	990000	330033	000066
R. 204	R. 255	R. 204	R. 153	R. 51	R. 0
G. 102	G. 0	G. 51	G. 0	G. 0	G. 0
B. 204	B. 102	B. 51	B. 0	B. 51	B. 102

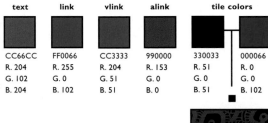

bp14sw

bp14pat.gif

text	link	vlink	alink	hybrid colors	
6666FF	0000FF	9999FF	333366	330033	000066
R. 102	R. 0	R. 153	R. 51	R. 51	R. 0
G. 102	G. 0	G. 153	G. 51	G. 0	G. 0
B. 204	B. 255	B. 255	B. 102	B. 51	B. 102

bh14sw

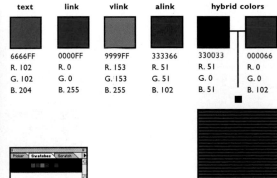

bh14pat.gif

text	link	vlink	alink	bgcolor
666699	9999FF	999999	3333FF	000033
R. 102	R. 153	R. 153	R. 51	R. 0
G. 102	G. 153	G. 153	G. 51	G. 0
B. 153	B. 255	B. 153	B. 255	B. 51

bs15sw

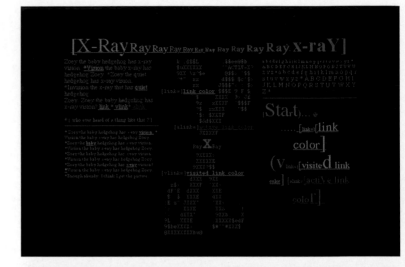

text	link	vlink	alink	tile colors	
9999CC	FFFFFF	666666	CC33CC	330033	000033
R. 153	R. 255	R. 102	R. 204	R. 51	R. 0
G. 153	G. 255	G. 102	G. 51	G. 0	G. 0
B. 204	B. 255	B. 102	B. 204	B. 51	B. 51

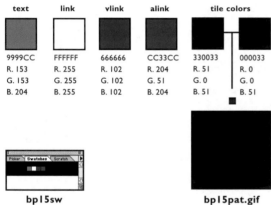

bp15sw

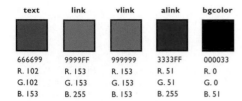

bp15pat.gif

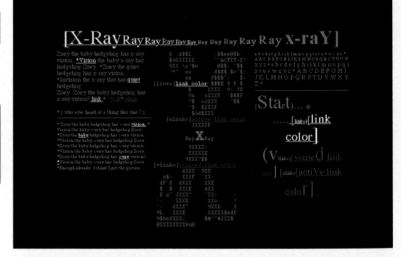

text	link	vlink	alink	hybrid colors	
CC66CC	FF99FF	999999	CC33CC	330033	000033
R. 204	R. 255	R. 153	R. 204	R. 51	R. 0
G. 102	G. 153	G. 153	G. 51	G. 0	G. 0
B. 204	B. 255	B. 153	B. 204	B. 51	B. 51

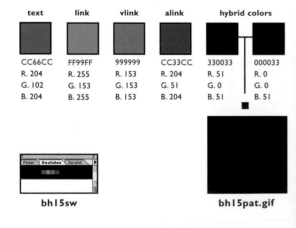

bh15sw

bh15pat.gif

text	link	vlink	alink	bgcolor
996666	FF0000	333333	FFFFFF	000033
R. 153	R. 255	R. 51	R. 255	R. 0
G. 102	G. 0	G. 51	G. 255	G. 0
B. 102	B. 0	B. 51	B. 255	B. 51

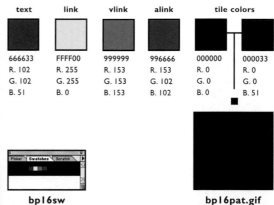

bs16sw

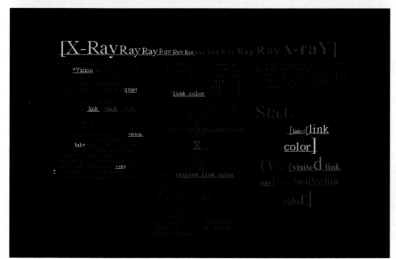

text	link	vlink	alink	tile colors	
666633	FFFF00	999999	996666	000000	000033
R. 102	R. 255	R. 153	R. 153	R. 0	R. 0
G. 102	G. 255	G. 153	G. 102	G. 0	G. 0
B. 51	B. 0	B. 153	B. 102	B. 0	B. 51

bp16sw

bp16pat.gif

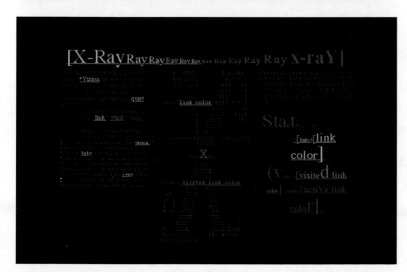

text	link	vlink	alink	hybrid colors	
336666	CCCC99	999999	996666	000000	000033
R. 51	R. 204	R. 153	R. 153	R. 0	R. 0
G. 102	G. 204	G. 153	G. 102	G. 0	G. 0
B. 102	B. 153	B. 153	B. 102	B. 0	B. 51

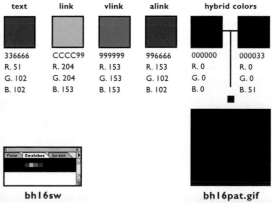

bh16sw

bh16pat.gif

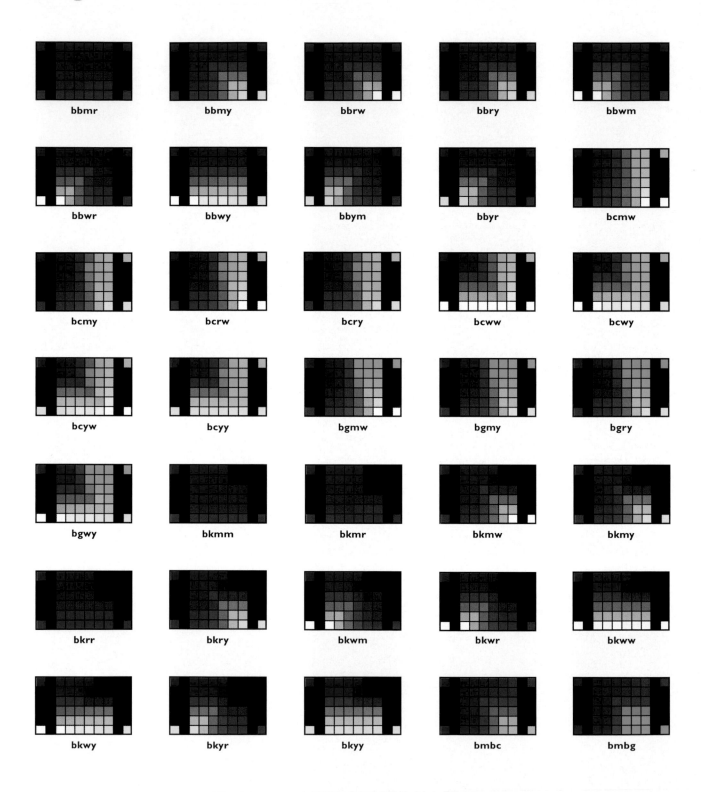

bbmr   bbmy   bbrw   bbry   bbwm

bbwr   bbwy   bbym   bbyr   bcmw

bcmy   bcrw   bcry   bcww   bcwy

bcyw   bcyy   bgmw   bgmy   bgry

bgwy   bkmm   bkmr   bkmw   bkmy

bkrr   bkry   bkwm   bkwr   bkww

bkwy   bkyr   bkyy   bmbc   bmbg

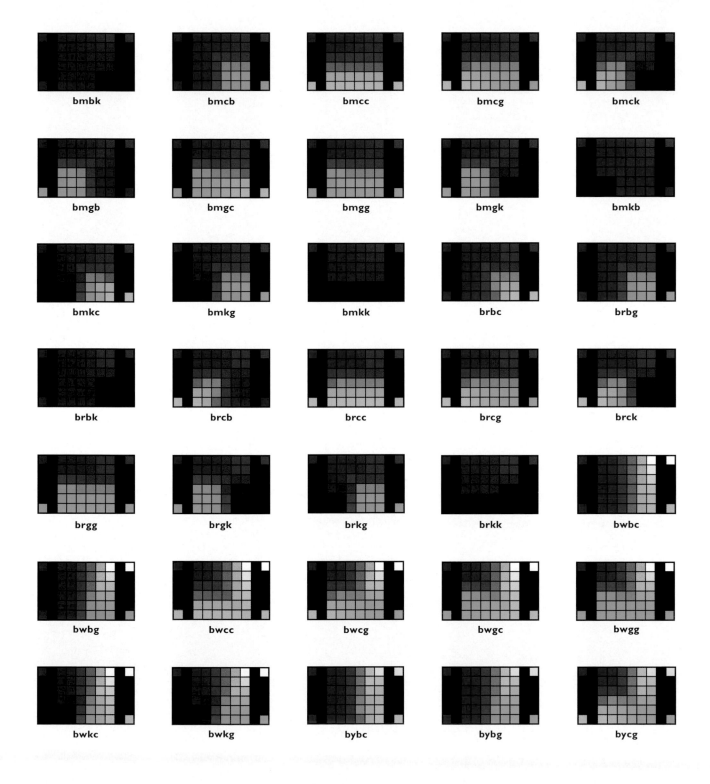

bmbk	bmcb	bmcc	bmcg	bmck
bmgb	bmgc	bmgg	bmgk	bmkb
bmkc	bmkg	bmkk	brbc	brbg
brbk	brcb	brcc	brcg	brck
brgg	brgk	brkg	brkk	bwbc
bwbg	bwcc	bwcg	bwgc	bwgg
bwkc	bwkg	bybc	bybg	bycg

CYAN

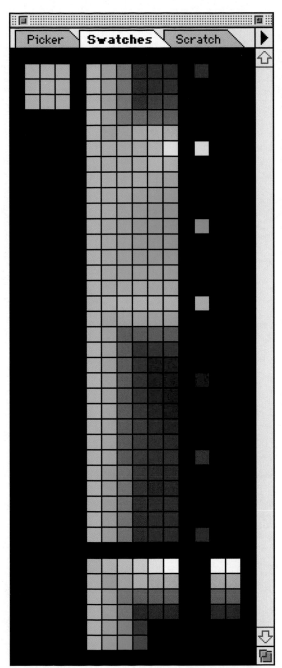

mcs

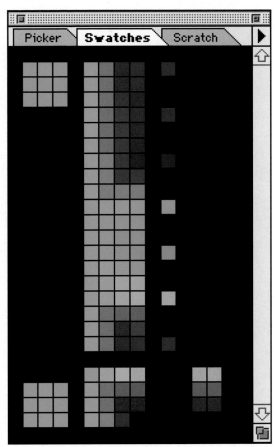

mcd

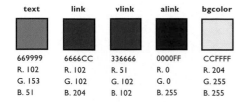

text	link	vlink	alink	bgcolor
669999	6666CC	336666	0000FF	CCFFFF
R. 102	R. 102	R. 51	R. 0	R. 204
G. 153	G. 102	G. 102	G. 0	G. 255
B. 51	B. 204	B. 102	B. 255	B. 255

cs01sw

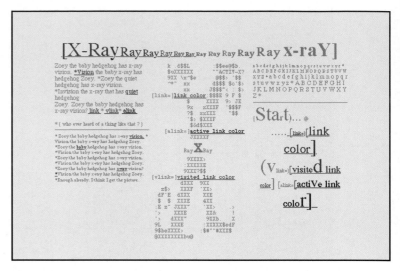

text	link	vlink	alink	tile colors	
666666	999933	CCCC66	CCCCCC	FFFFFF	CCFFFF
R. 102	R. 255	R. 153	R. 255	R. 255	R. 255
G. 51	G. 0	G. 102	G. 153	G. 204	G. 204
B. 0	B. 0	B. 102	B. 0	B. 204	B. 153

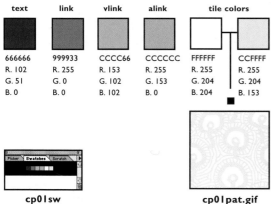

cp01sw

cp01pat.gif

text	link	vlink	alink	hybrid colors	
666699	0000FF	6666CC	CCCCCC	FFFFFF	CCFFFF
R. 102	R. 255	R. 255	R. 255	R. 255	R. 255
G. 0	G. 51	G. 102	G. 255	G. 204	G. 204
B. 0	B. 0	B. 102	B. 255	B. 204	B. 153

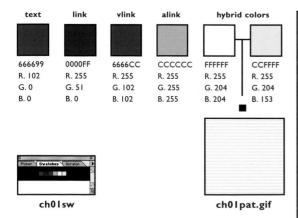

ch01sw

ch01pat.gif

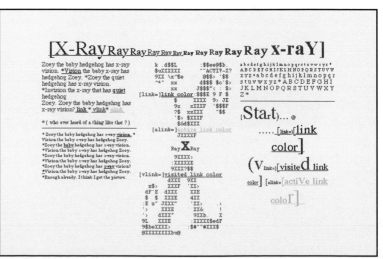

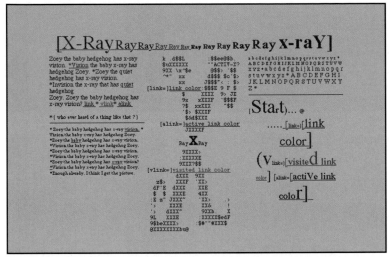

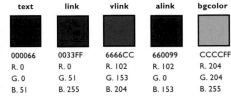

text	link	vlink	alink	bgcolor
000066	0033FF	6666CC	660099	CCCCFF
R. 0	R. 0	R. 102	R. 102	R. 204
G. 0	G. 51	G. 153	G. 0	G. 204
B. 51	B. 255	B. 204	B. 153	B. 255

cs02sw

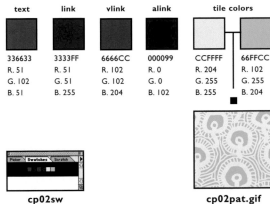

text	link	vlink	alink	tile colors	
336633	3333FF	6666CC	000099	CCFFFF	66FFCC
R. 51	R. 51	R. 102	R. 0	R. 204	R. 102
G. 102	G. 51	G. 102	G. 102	G. 255	G. 255
B. 51	B. 255	B. 204	B. 102	B. 255	B. 204

cp02sw

cp02pat.gif

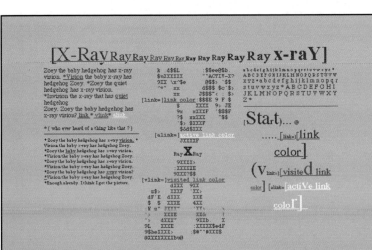

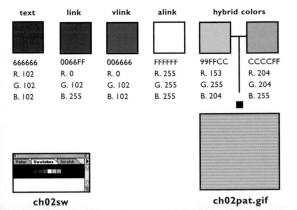

text	link	vlink	alink	hybrid colors	
666666	0066FF	006666	FFFFFF	99FFCC	CCCCFF
R. 102	R. 0	R. 0	R. 255	R. 153	R. 204
G. 102	G. 102	G. 102	G. 255	G. 255	G. 204
B. 102	B. 255	B. 102	B. 255	B. 204	B. 255

ch02sw

ch02pat.gif

cs03sw

text	link	vlink	alink	bgcolor
003333	999900	339999	FFFF00	66FFFF
R. 10	R. 255	R. 204	R. 255	R. 255
G. 0	G. 0	G. 153	G. 0	G. 204
B. 51	B. 102	B. 153	B. 0	B. 204

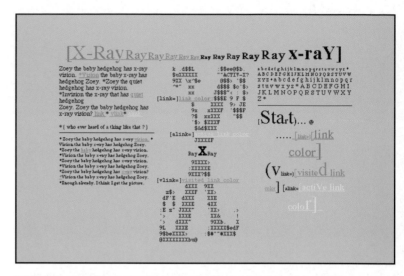

cp03sw / cp03pat.gif

text	link	vlink	alink	tile colors	
336666	0066FF	669999	33CCCC	66FFFF	99FFCC
R. 102	R. 255	R. 153	R. 255	R. 255	R. 255
G. 51	G. 0	G. 102	G. 153	G. 204	G. 204
B. 0	B. 0	B. 102	B. 0	B. 204	B. 153

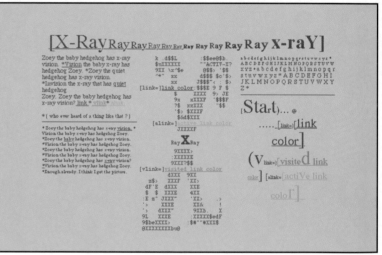
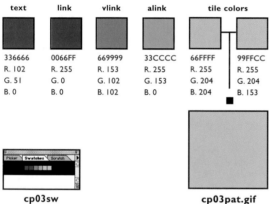

ch03sw / ch03pat.gif

text	link	vlink	alink	hybrid colors	
336633	669900	66CC66	3366CC	66FFFF	99FFCC
R. 51	R. 102	R. 102	R. 51	R. 102	R. 153
G. 102	G. 153	G. 204	G. 102	G. 255	G. 255
B. 51	B. 0	B. 102	B. 204	B. 255	B. 204

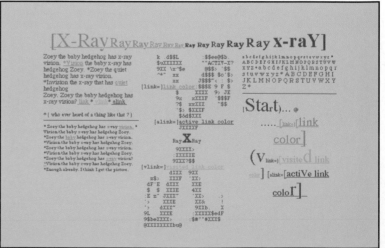
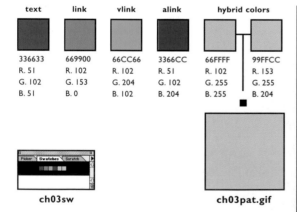

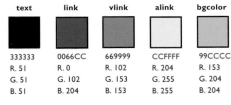

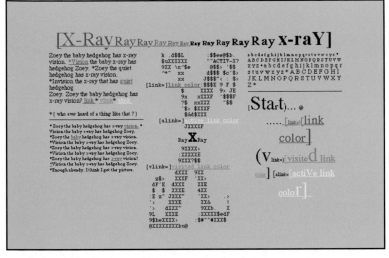

text	link	vlink	alink	bgcolor
333333	0066CC	669999	CCFFFF	99CCCC
R. 51	R. 0	R. 102	R. 204	R. 153
G. 51	G. 102	G. 153	G. 255	G. 204
B. 51	B. 204	B. 153	B. 255	B. 204

cs04sw

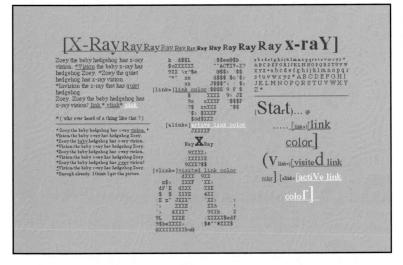

text	link	vlink	alink	tile colors	
336666	0066FF	006699	FFFFFF	CCCCCC	99CCCC
R. 51	R. 0	R. 0	R. 255	R. 204	R. 153
G. 102	G. 102	G. 102	G. 255	G. 204	G. 204
B. 102	B. 255	B. 153	B. 255	B. 204	B. 204

cp04sw

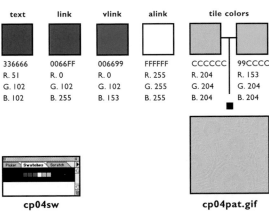

cp04pat.gif

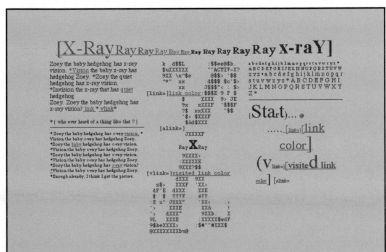

text	link	vlink	alink	hybrid colors	
003366	0066CC	666666	00FFFF	CCCCCC	99CCCC
R. 0	R. 0	R. 102	R. 0	R. 204	R. 153
G. 51	G. 102	G. 102	G. 255	G. 204	G. 204
B. 102	B. 204	B. 102	B. 255	B. 204	B. 204

ch04sw

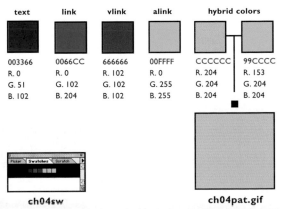

ch04pat.gif

text	link	vlink	alink	bgcolor
003300	FFFF99	CCFFCC	FFFF00	66CCCC
R. 0	R. 255	R. 204	R. 255	R. 102
G. 51	G. 255	G. 255	G. 255	G. 204
B. 0	B. 153	B. 204	B. 0	B. 204

cs05sw

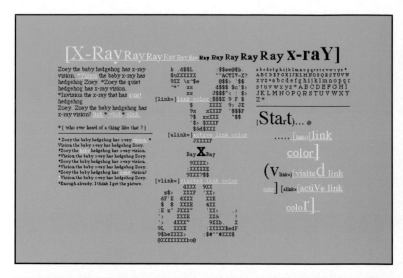

text	link	vlink	alink	tile colors	
663300	FF3300	996666	FF6666	99CCFF	66CCCC
R. 102	R. 255	R. 153	R. 255	R. 153	R. 102
G. 51	G. 51	G. 102	G. 102	G. 204	G. 204
B. 0	B. 0	B. 102	B. 102	B. 255	B. 204

cp05sw

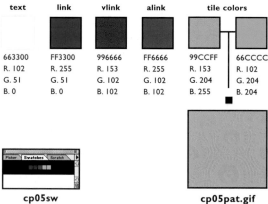

cp05pat.gif

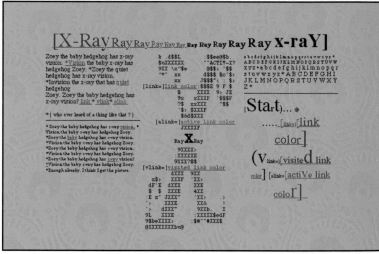

text	link	vlink	alink	hybrid colors	
663300	FF6600	996666	FF0000	99CCFF	66CCCC
R. 102	R. 255	R. 153	R. 255	R. 153	R. 102
G. 51	G. 102	G. 102	G. 0	G. 204	G. 204
B. 0	B. 0	B. 102	B. 0	B. 255	B. 204

ch05sw

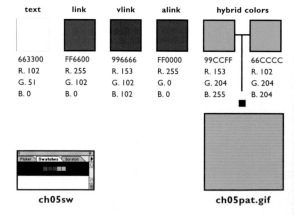

ch05pat.gif

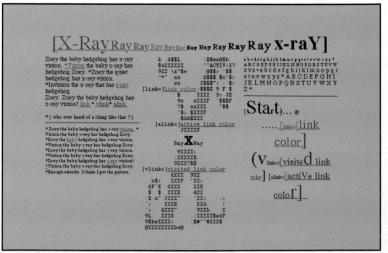

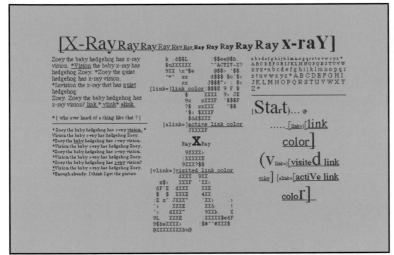

text	link	vlink	alink	bgcolor
666666	CC3333	996666	FF0000	66CCFF
R. 102	R. 204	R. 153	R. 255	R. 102
G. 102	G. 51	G. 102	G. 0	G. 204
B. 102	B. 51	B. 102	B. 0	B. 255

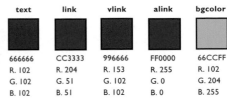

cs06sw

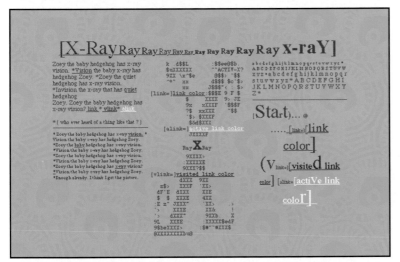

text	link	vlink	alink	tile colors	
336666	0066FF	9933CC	FFFFFF	66CCFF	33CCFF
R. 51	R. 0	R. 153	R. 255	R. 102	R. 51
G. 102	G. 102	G. 51	G. 255	G. 204	G. 204
B. 102	B. 255	B. 204	B. 255	B. 255	B. 255

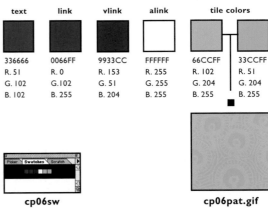

cp06sw

cp06pat.gif

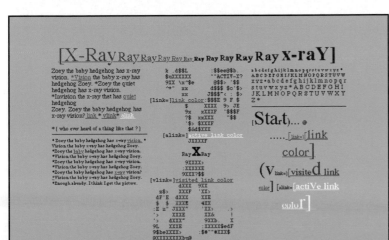

text	link	vlink	alink	hybrid colors	
333366	CC6600	996666	FFFFFF	66CCFF	33CCFF
R. 51	R. 204	R. 153	R. 255	R. 102	R. 51
G. 51	G. 102	G. 102	G. 255	G. 204	G. 204
B. 102	B. 0	B. 102	B. 255	B. 255	B. 255

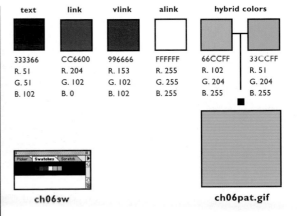

ch06sw

ch06pat.gif

text	link	vlink	alink	bgcolor
333399	CC00CC	663366	330033	00CCFF
R. 51	R. 204	R. 102	R. 51	R. 0
G. 51	G. 0	G. 51	G. 0	G. 204
B. 153	B. 204	B. 102	B. 51	B. 255

cs07sw

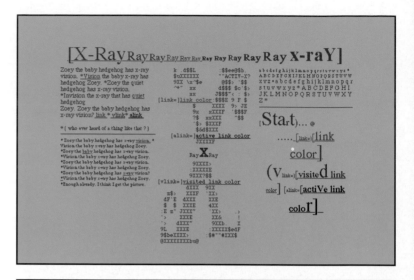

text	link	vlink	alink	tile colors	
003300	FF0000	CC33CC	FF9999	00CCFF	00CC99
R. 0	R. 255	R. 204	R. 255	R. 0	R. 0
G. 51	G. 0	G. 51	G. 153	G. 204	G. 204
B. 0	B. 0	B. 204	B. 153	B. 255	B. 255

cp07sw

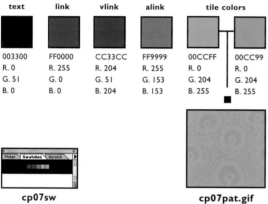

cp07pat.gif

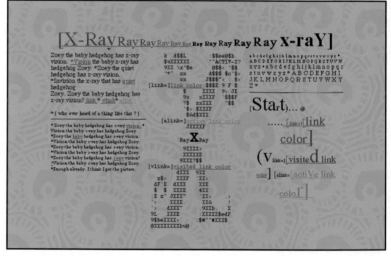

text	link	vlink	alink	hybrid colors	
666666	FFFFFF	FFFF99	FFFF00	00CCFF	00CC99
R. 102	R. 255	R. 255	R. 255	R. 0	R. 0
G. 102	G. 255	G. 255	G. 255	G. 204	G. 204
B. 102	B. 255	B. 153	B. 0	B. 255	B. 153

ch07sw

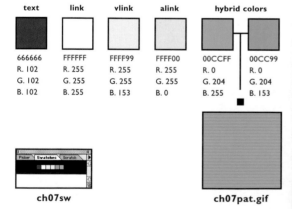

ch07pat.gif

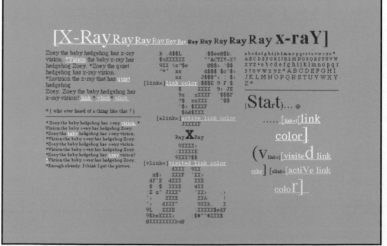

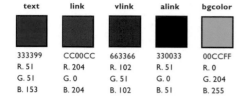

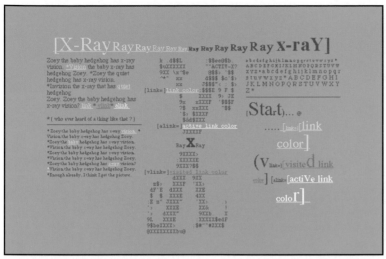

text	link	vlink	alink	bgcolor
006600	CCFFCC	999933	FFFFFF	00CCCC
R. 0	R. 204	R. 153	R. 255	R. 0
G. 102	G. 255	G. 153	G. 255	G. 204
B. 0	B. 204	B. 102	B. 255	B. 204

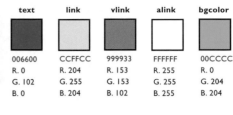

cs08sw

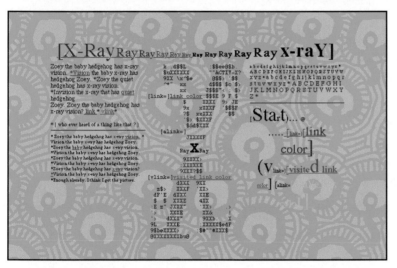

text	link	vlink	alink	tile colors	
003333	0000FF	FF00FF	00FFFF	CCCCCC	00CCCC
R. 0	R. 0	R. 255	R. 0	R. 204	R. 0
G. 51	G. 0	G. 0	G. 255	G. 204	G. 204
B. 51	B. 255	B. 255	B. 255	B. 204	B. 204

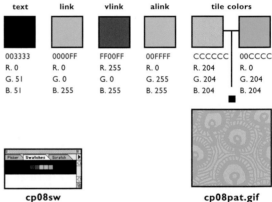

cp08sw

cp08pat.gif

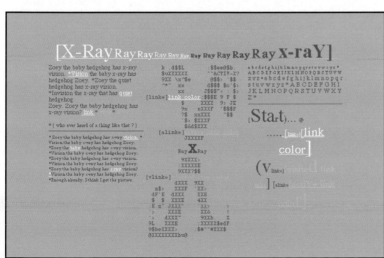

text	link	vlink	alink	hybrid colors	
006699	FFFFFF	99FF99	00FFFF	CCCCCC	00CCCC
R. 0	R. 255	R. 153	R. 0	R. 204	R. 0
G. 102	G. 255	G. 255	G. 255	G. 204	G. 204
B. 153	B. 255	B. 153	B. 255	B. 204	B. 204

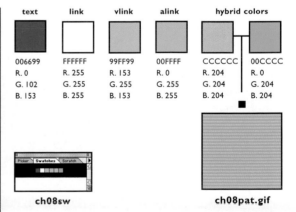

ch08sw

ch08pat.gif

text	link	vlink	alink	bgcolor
FFFFFF	FFFF00	CCCCCC	CCCC33	009900
R. 255	R. 255	R. 204	R. 204	R. 0
G. 255	G. 255	G. 204	G. 204	G. 153
B. 255	B.0	B. 204	B. 51	B. 0

cs09sw

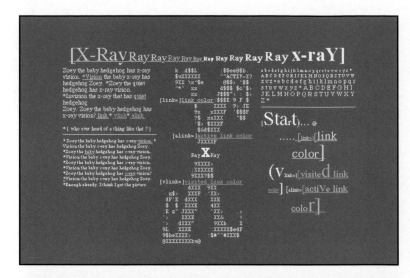

text	link	vlink	alink	tile colors	
99FFFF	00FFFF	99CCCC	FFFFFF	0099FF	3399CC
R. 153	R. 0	R. 153	R. 255	R. 0	R. 51
G. 255	G. 255	G. 204	G. 255	G. 153	G. 153
B. 255	B. 255	B. 204	B. 255	B. 255	B. 204

cp09sw

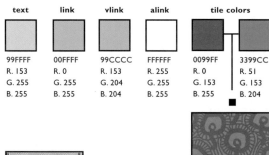

cp09pat.gif

text	link	vlink	alink	hybrid colors	
333333	0000FF	99CCCC	FFFFFF	0099FF	3399CC
R. 0	R. 0	R. 153	R. 255	R. 0	R. 51
G. 51	G. 0	G. 204	G. 255	G. 153	G. 153
B. 51	B. 255	B. 204	B. 255	B. 255	B. 204

ch09sw

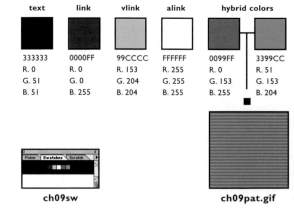

ch09pat.gif

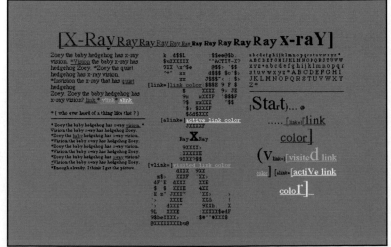

coloring

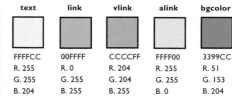
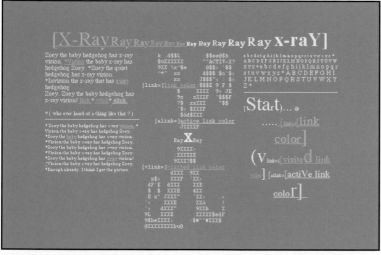

text	link	vlink	alink	bgcolor
FFFFCC	00FFFF	CCCCFF	FFFF00	3399CC
R. 255	R. 0	R. 204	R. 255	R. 51
G. 255	G. 255	G. 204	G. 255	G. 153
B. 204	B. 255	B. 255	B. 0	B. 204

cs10sw

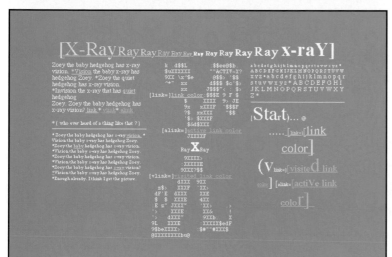

text	link	vlink	alink	tile colors	
FFFFFF	FFFF00	CCCC99	CCCC33	0099CC	009999
R. 255	R. 255	R. 204	R. 204	R. 0	R. 0
G. 255	G. 255	G. 204	G. 204	G. 153	G. 153
B. 255	B. 0	B. 153	B. 51	B. 204	B. 153

cp10sw

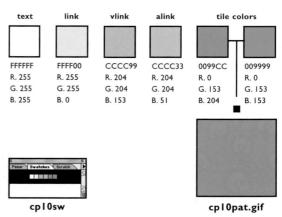

cp10pat.gif

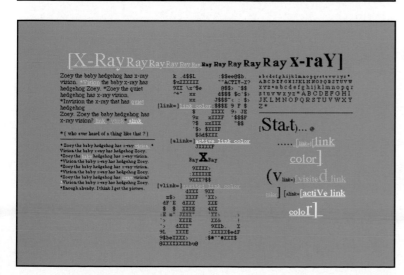

text	link	vlink	alink	hybrid colors	
003333	99FFFF	CCCCCC	FFFFFF	0099CC	009999
R. 0	R. 153	R. 204	R. 255	R. 0	R. 0
G. 51	G. 255	G. 204	G. 255	G. 153	G. 153
B. 51	B. 255	B. 204	B. 255	B. 204	B. 153

ch10sw

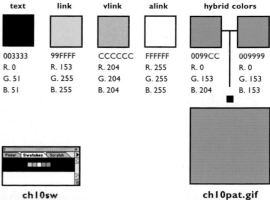

ch10pat.gif

text	link	vlink	alink	bgcolor
99FFFF	33CCFF	CCCCCC	336666	339999
R. 153	R. 51	R. 204	R. 51	R. 51
G. 255	G. 204	G. 204	G. 102	G. 153
B. 255	B. 255	B. 204	B. 102	B. 153

cs11sw

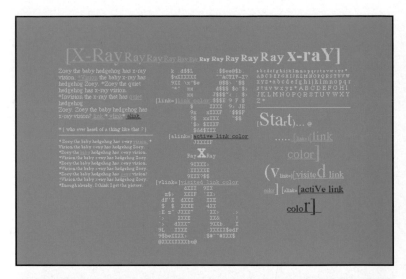

text	link	vlink	alink	tile colors	
FFFFFF	FFFF00	66FF00	666600	999999	339999
R. 255	R. 255	R. 102	R. 102	R. 153	R. 51
G. 255	G. 255	G. 255	G. 102	G. 153	G. 153
B. 255	B. 0	B. 0	B. 0	B. 153	B. 153

cp11sw

cp11pat.gif

text	link	vlink	alink	hybrid colors	
CCFFCC	66CC66	CCCCCC	CCCC00	999999	339999
R. 204	R. 102	R. 204	R. 204	R. 153	R. 51
G. 255	G. 204	G. 204	G. 204	G. 153	G. 153
B. 204	B. 102	B. 204	B. 0	B. 153	B. 153

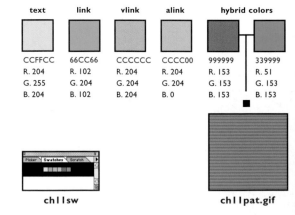

ch11sw

ch11pat.gif

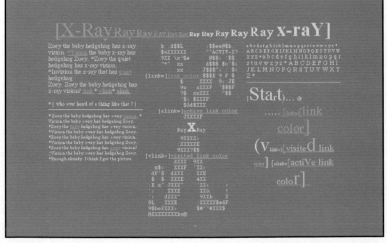

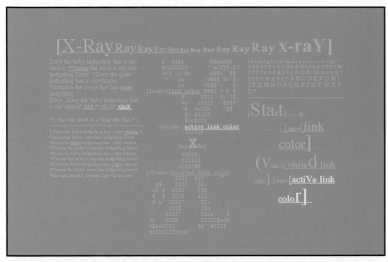

text	link	vlink	alink	bgcolor
99CCCC	66FFFF	99CC99	FFFFFF	009999
R. 153	R. 102	R. 153	R. 255	R. 0
G. 204	G. 255	G. 204	G. 255	G. 153
B. 204	B. 255	B. 153	B. 255	B. 153

cs12sw

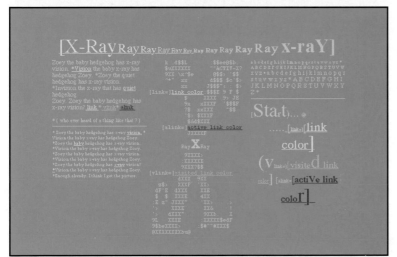

text	link	vlink	alink	tile colors	
CCFF99	FFFF00	CCCCCC	336666	009999	339966
R. 204	R. 255	R. 204	R. 204	R. 0	R. 51
G. 255	G. 255	G. 204	G. 51	G. 153	G. 153
B. 153	B. 0	B. 204	B. 153	B. 153	B. 102

cp12sw

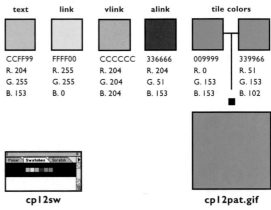

cp12pat.gif

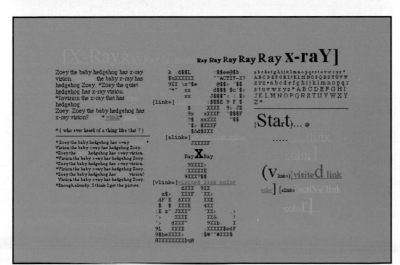

text	link	vlink	alink	hybrid colors	
333333	33CC33	006600	00CCFF	009999	339966
R. 51	R. 51	R. 0	R. 0	R. 0	R. 51
G. 51	G. 204	G. 102	G. 204	G. 153	G. 153
B. 51	B. 51	B. 0	B. 255	B. 153	B. 102

ch12sw

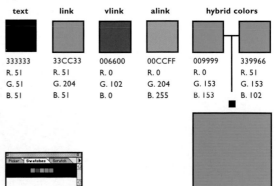

ch12pat.gif

text	link	vlink	alink	bgcolor
99CC99	33CC33	999900	00FF00	336666
R. 153	R. 51	R. 153	R. 0	R. 51
G. 204	G. 204	G. 153	G. 204	G. 102
B. 153	B. 51	B. 0	B. 0	B. 102

cs13sw

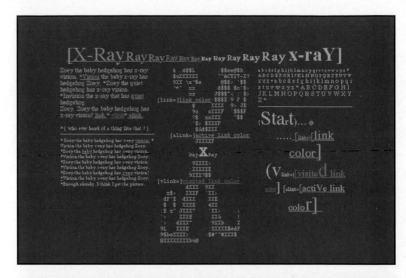

text	link	vlink	alink	tile colors	
CCCCCC	33CCCC	33CC33	99CCCC	666666	336666
R. 204	R. 51	R. 51	R. 153	R. 102	R. 51
G. 204	G. 204	G. 204	G. 204	G. 102	G. 102
B. 204	B. 204	B. 51	B. 204	B. 102	B. 102

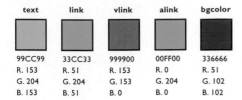

cp13sw

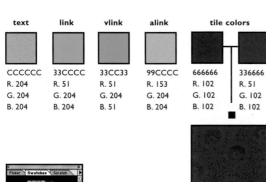

cp13pat.gif

text	link	vlink	alink	hybrid colors	
CC9966	FFCC66	999900	FFFF00	666666	336666
R. 204	R. 255	R. 153	R. 255	R. 102	R. 51
G. 153	G. 204	G. 153	G. 255	G. 102	G. 102
B. 102	B. 102	B. 0	B. 102	B. 102	B. 102

ch13sw

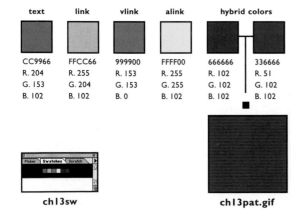

ch13pat.gif

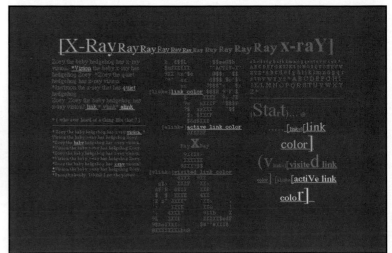

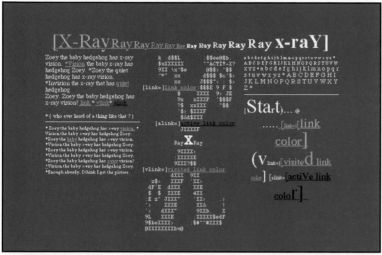

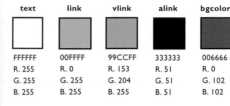

text	link	vlink	alink	bgcolor
FFFFFF	00FFFF	99CCFF	333333	006666
R. 255	R. 0	R. 153	R. 51	R. 0
G. 255	G. 255	G. 204	G. 51	G. 102
B. 255	B. 255	B. 255	B. 51	B. 102

cs14sw

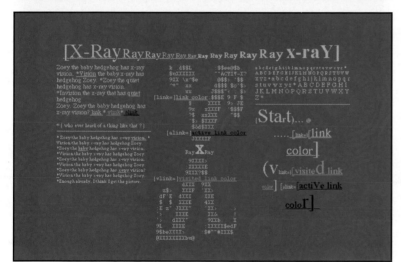

text	link	vlink	alink	tile colors	
CCCCCC	99CC33	339933	333333	006666	006633
R. 204	R. 153	R. 51	R. 51	R. 0	R. 0
G. 204	G. 204	G. 153	G. 51	G. 102	G. 102
B. 204	B. 51	B. 51	B. 51	B. 102	B. 51

cp14sw

cp14pat.gif

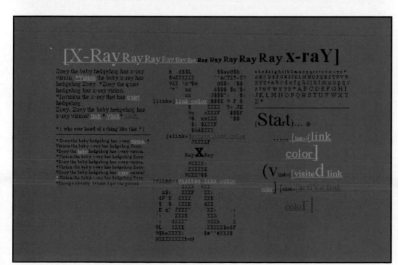

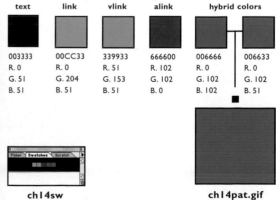

text	link	vlink	alink	hybrid colors	
003333	00CC33	339933	666600	006666	006633
R. 0	R. 0	R. 51	R. 102	R. 0	R. 0
G. 51	G. 204	G. 153	G. 102	G. 102	G. 102
B. 51	B. 51	B. 51	B. 0	B. 102	B. 51

ch14sw

ch14pat.gif

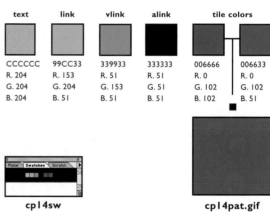

text	link	vlink	alink	bgcolor
FF9999	FF3333	FF6633	666699	003366
R. 255	R. 255	R. 255	R. 102	R. 0
G. 153	G. 51	G. 102	G. 102	G. 51
B. 153	B. 51	B. 51	B. 153	B. 102

cs15sw

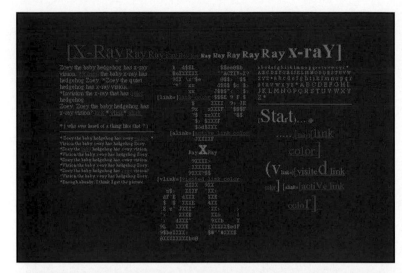

text	link	vlink	alink	tile colors	
6666CC	CC3333	CC6666	000033	003366	003333
R. 102	R. 204	R. 204	R. 0	R. 0	R. 0
G. 102	G. 51	G. 102	G. 0	G. 51	G. 51
B. 204	B. 51	B. 102	B. 51	B. 102	B. 51

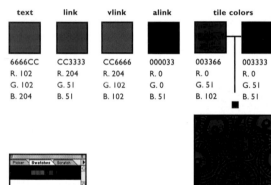

cp15sw

cp15pat.gif

text	link	vlink	alink	hybrid colors	
9999CC	3399CC	6666FF	666666	003366	003333
R. 153	R. 51	R. 102	R. 102	R. 0	R. 0
G. 153	G. 153	G. 102	G. 102	G. 51	G. 51
B. 204	B. 204	B. 255	B. 102	B. 102	B. 51

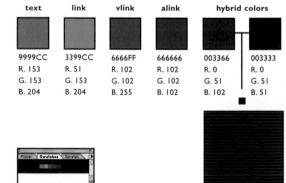

ch15sw

ch15pat.gif

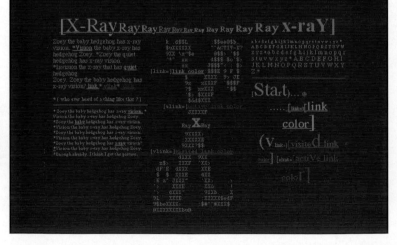

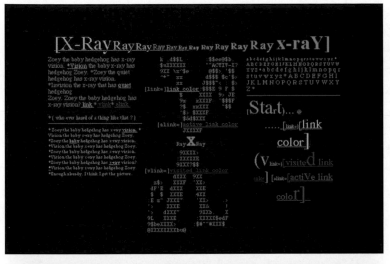

text	link	vlink	alink	bgcolor
339999	00FFFF	666666	6666FF	003333
R. 51	R. 0	R. 102	R. 102	R. 0
G. 153	G. 255	G. 102	G. 102	G. 51
B. 153	B. 255	B. 102	B. 255	B. 51

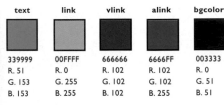

cs16sw

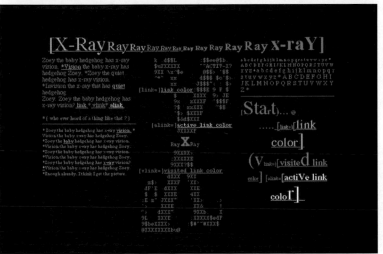

text	link	vlink	alink	tile colors	
669999	00FFFF	339999	FFFFFF	333333	003333
R. 102	R. 0	R. 51	R. 255	R. 51	R. 0
G. 153	G. 255	G. 153	G. 255	G. 51	G. 51
B. 153	B. 255	B. 153	B. 255	B. 51	B. 51

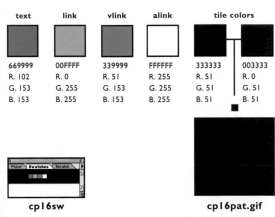

cp16sw

cp16pat.gif

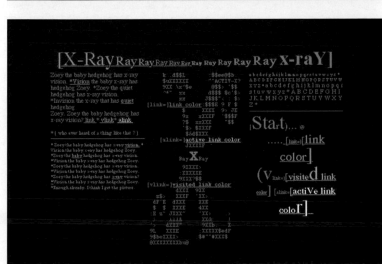

text	link	vlink	alink	hybrid colors	
669966	33FF00	00FFFF	FFFFFF	333333	003333
R. 102	R. 51	R. 0	R. 255	R. 51	R. 0
G. 153	G. 255	G. 255	G. 255	G. 51	G. 51
B. 102	B. 0	B. 255	B. 255	B. 51	B. 51

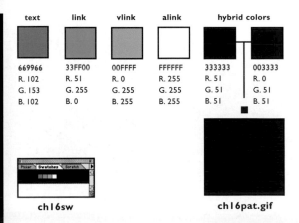

ch16sw

ch16pat.gif

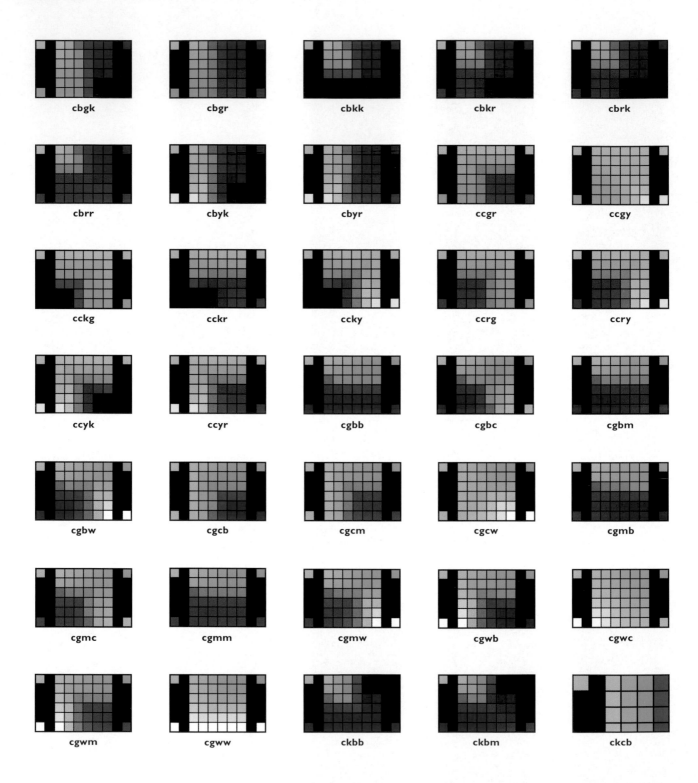

cbgk	cbgr	cbkk	cbkr	cbrk
cbrr	cbyk	cbyr	ccgr	ccgy
cckg	cckr	ccky	ccrg	ccry
ccyk	ccyr	cgbb	cgbc	cgbm
cgbw	cgcb	cgcm	cgcw	cgmb
cgmc	cgmm	cgmw	cgwb	cgwc
cgwm	cgww	ckbb	ckbm	ckcb

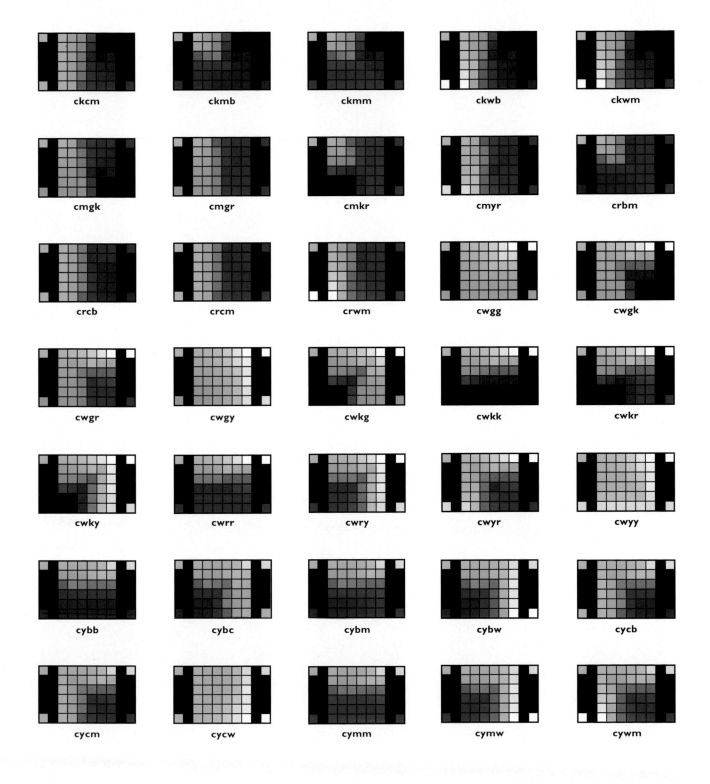

ckcm ckmb ckmm ckwb ckwm

cmgk cmgr cmkr cmyr crbm

crcb crcm crwm cwgg cwgk

cwgr cwgy cwkg cwkk cwkr

cwky cwrr cwry cwyr cwyy

cybb cybc cybm cybw cycb

cycm cycw cymm cymw cywm

MAGENTA

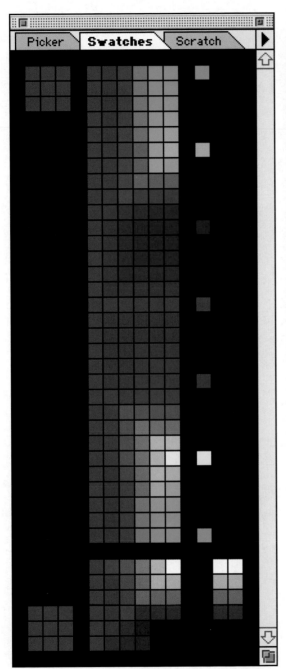

mms

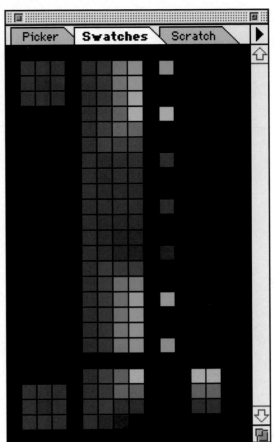

mmd

Group 1

text	link	vlink	alink	bgcolor
6666CC	0000FF	CC33CC	9999CC	FFCCFF
R. 102	R. 0	R. 204	R. 153	R. 255
G. 102	G. 0	G. 102	G. 153	G. 204
B. 204	B. 255	B. 204	B. 204	B. 255

ms01sw

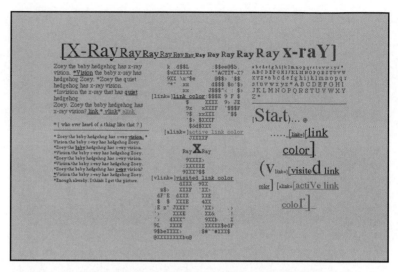

Group 2

text	link	vlink	alink	tile colors	
666666	FF00000	FF00FF	FF9999	FFCCFF	CCCCFF
R. 102	R. 255	R. 255	R. 255	R. 255	R. 204
G. 102	G. 0	G. 0	G. 153	G. 204	G. 204
B. 102	B. 0	B. 255	B. 153	B. 255	B. 255

mp01sw

mp01pat.gif

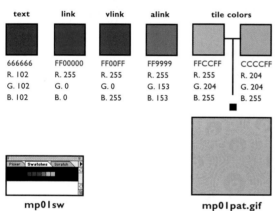

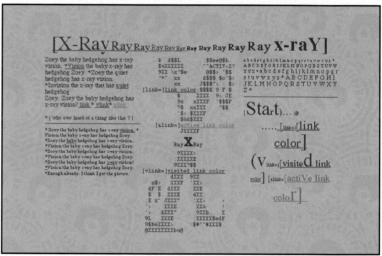

Group 3

text	link	vlink	alink	hybrid colors	
996699	FF00FF	993399	FFFFFF	CCCCFF	FFCCFF
R. 153	R. 255	R. 153	R. 255	R. 204	R. 255
G. 102	G. 0	G. 51	G. 255	G. 204	G. 204
B. 153	B. 255	B. 153	B. 255	B. 255	B. 255

mh01sw

mh01pat.gif

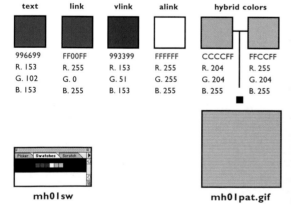

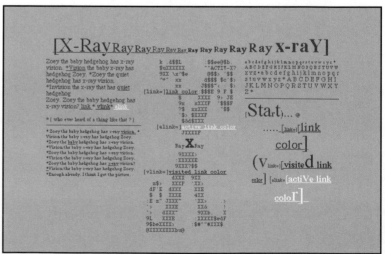

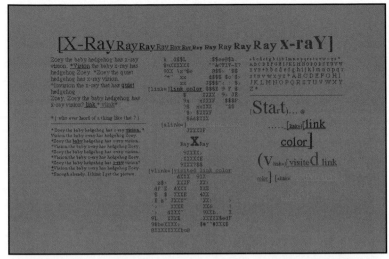

	text	link	vlink	alink	bgcolor
	666666	0000FF	6666CC	999966	FF99FF
	R. 102	R. 0	R. 102	R. 153	R. 255
	G. 102	G. 0	G. 102	G. 153	G. 153
	B. 102	B. 255	B. 204	B. 102	B. 255

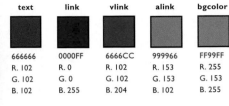

ms02sw

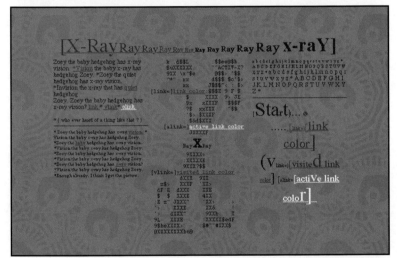

	text	link	vlink	alink	tile colors	
	663366	FF0099	CC33CC	FFFFFF	FF99FF	FF99CC
	R. 102	R. 255	R. 204	R. 255	R. 255	R. 255
	G. 51	G. 0	G. 51	G. 255	G. 153	G. 153
	B. 102	B. 153	B. 204	B. 255	B. 255	B. 204

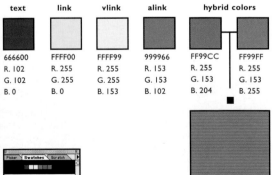

mp02sw　　　　　　　　　　**mp02pat.gif**

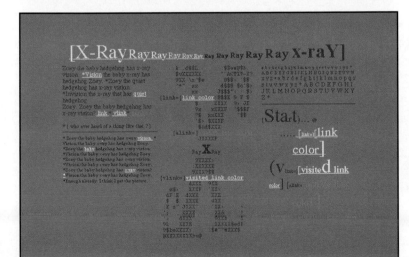

	text	link	vlink	alink	hybrid colors	
	666600	FFFF00	FFFF99	999966	FF99CC	FF99FF
	R. 102	R. 255	R. 255	R. 153	R. 255	R. 255
	G. 102	G. 255	G. 255	G. 153	G. 153	G. 153
	B. 0	B. 0	B. 153	B. 102	B. 204	B. 255

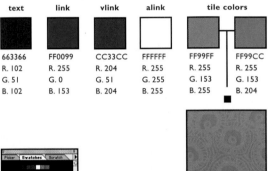

mh02sw　　　　　　　　　　**mh02pat.gif**

web graphics

text	link	vlink	alink	bgcolor
333399	0033FF	666666	0099FF	CC99FF
R. 51	R. 0	R. 102	R. 0	R. 204
G. 51	G. 51	G. 102	G. 153	G. 153
B. 153	B. 255	B. 102	B. 255	B. 255

ms03sw

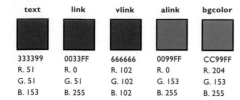

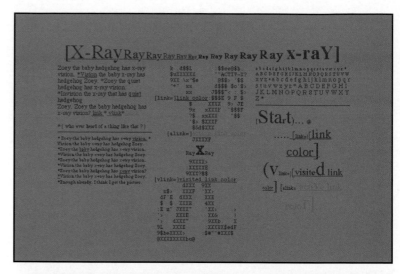

text	link	vlink	alink	tile colors	
993399	FF0000	0000FF	FFCCCC	FF99CC	CC99FF
R. 153	R. 255	R. 0	R. 255	R. 255	R. 204
G. 51	G. 2	G. 0	G. 204	G. 153	G. 153
B. 153	B. 0	B. 255	B. 204	B. 204	B. 255

mp03sw

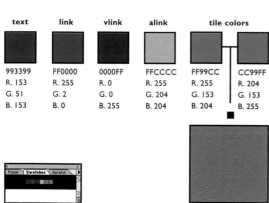

mp03pat.gif

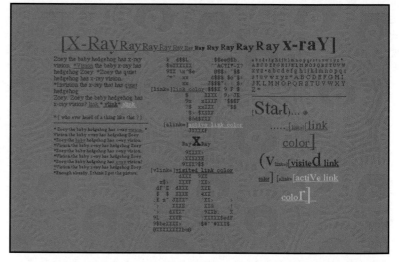

text	link	vlink	alink	hybrid colors	
663399	CC3333	996666	FF0000	FF99CC	CC99FF
R. 102	R. 204	R. 153	R. 255	R. 255	R. 204
G. 51	G. 51	G. 102	G. 0	G. 153	G. 153
B. 153	B. 51	B. 102	B. 0	B. 204	B. 255

mh03sw

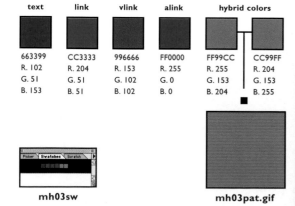

mh03pat.gif

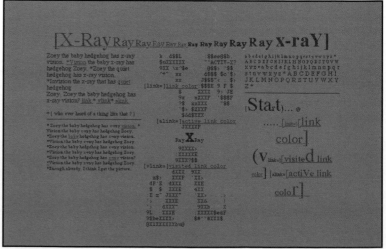

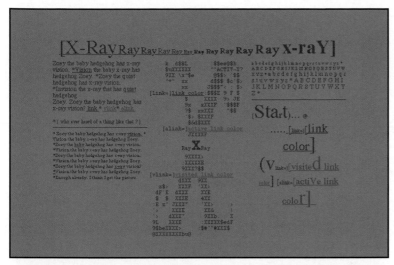

text	link	vlink	alink	bgcolor
663399	0033FF	6666CC	FF00FF	CC99CC
R. 102	R. 0	R. 102	R. 255	R. 204
G. 51	G. 51	G. 102	G. 0	G. 153
B. 153	B. 255	B. 204	B. 255	B. 204

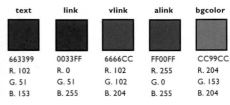

ms04sw

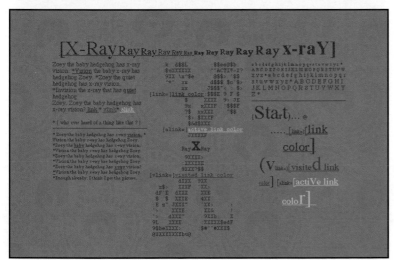

text	link	vlink	alink	tile colors	
990099	0000FF	FF0000	FFCCFF	CC99CC	9999CC
R. 153	R. 0	R. 255	R. 255	R. 204	R. 153
G. 0	G. 0	G. 0	G. 204	G. 153	G. 153
B. 153	B. 255	B. 0	B. 255	B. 204	B. 204

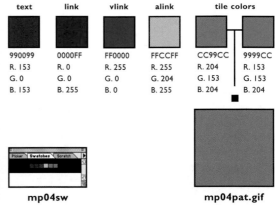

mp04sw

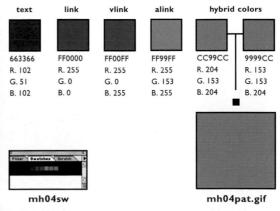

mp04pat.gif

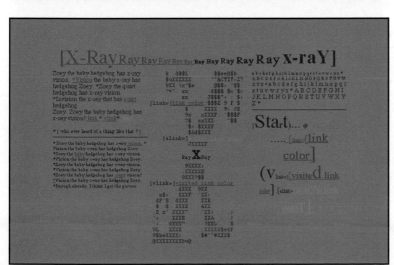

text	link	vlink	alink	hybrid colors	
663366	FF0000	FF00FF	FF99FF	CC99CC	9999CC
R. 102	R. 255	R. 255	R. 255	R. 204	R. 153
G. 51	G. 0	G. 0	G. 153	G. 153	G. 153
B. 102	B. 0	B. 255	B. 255	B. 204	B. 204

mh04sw

mh04pat.gif

text	link	vlink	alink	bgcolor
333300	CC0000	660066	CC6666	FF66FF
R. 51	R. 204	R. 102	R. 204	R. 255
G. 51	G. 0	G. 0	G. 102	G. 102
B. 0	B. 0	B. 102	B. 102	B. 255

ms05sw

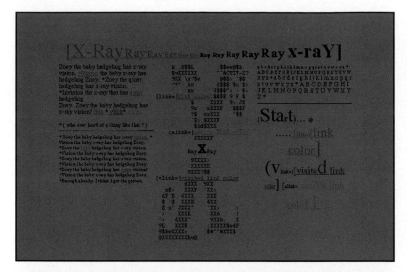

text	link	vlink	alink	tile colors	
990000	FF0000	996633	CCCCCC	FF66FF	CC9999
R. 153	R. 255	R. 153	R. 204	R. 255	R. 204
G. 0	G. 0	G. 102	G. 204	G. 102	G. 153
B. 0	B. 0	B. 51	B. 204	B. 255	B. 153

mp05sw

mp05pat.gif

text	link	vlink	alink	hybrid colors	
FFFFFF	FF0000	CC6633	336666	FF66FF	CC9999
R. 255	R. 255	R. 204	R. 51	R. 255	R. 204
G. 255	G. 0	G. 102	G. 102	G. 102	G. 153
B. 255	B. 0	B. 51	B. 102	B. 255	B. 153

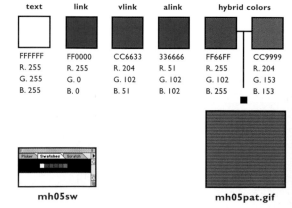

mh05sw

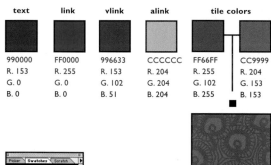

mh05pat.gif

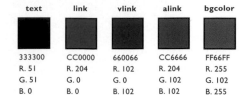

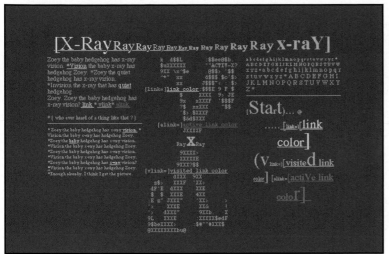

text	link	vlink	alink	bgcolor
FFCCFF	FFFF00	FFCC66	999966	FF33FF
R. 255	R. 255	R. 255	R. 153	R. 255
G. 204	G. 255	G. 204	G. 153	G. 51
B. 255	B. 0	B. 102	B. 102	B. 255

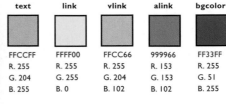

ms06sw

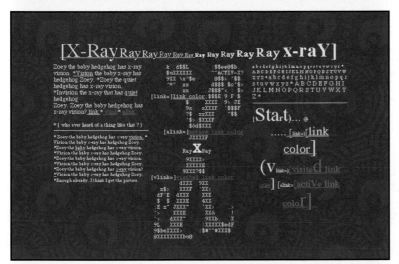

text	link	vlink	alink	tile colors	
FFFFCC	FFFF00	FF9900	FF99FF	CC33FF	FF33FF
R. 255	R. 255	R. 255	R. 255	R. 204	R. 255
G. 255	G. 255	G. 153	G. 153	G. 51	G. 51
B. 204	B. 0	B. 0	B. 255	B. 255	B. 255

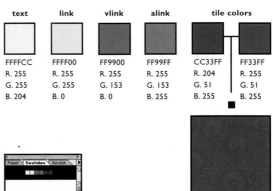

mp06sw

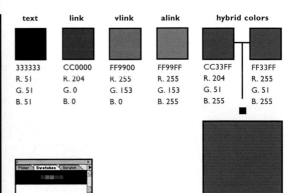

mp06pat.gif

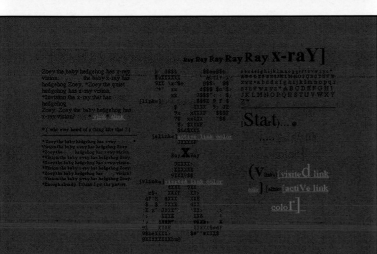

text	link	vlink	alink	hybrid colors	
333333	CC0000	FF9900	FF99FF	CC33FF	FF33FF
R. 51	R. 204	R. 255	R. 255	R. 204	R. 255
G. 51	G. 0	G. 153	G. 153	G. 51	G. 51
B. 51	B. 0	B. 0	B. 255	B. 255	B. 255

mh06sw

mh06pat.gif

text	link	vlink	alink	bgcolor
CCCCCC	FFCC66	99CCFF	CCCCCC	CC66CC
R. 204	R. 255	R. 153	R. 204	R. 204
G. 204	G. 204	G. 204	G. 204	G. 102
B. 204	B. 102	B. 255	B. 204	B. 204

ms07sw

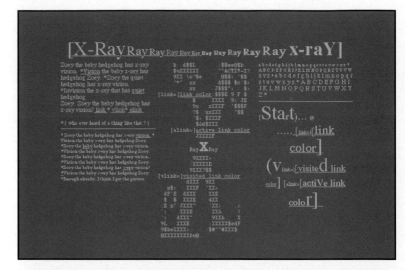

text	link	vlink	alink	tile colors	
FFFFFF	FFFF00	FFCC66	FF00FF	CC66CC	996699
R. 255	R. 255	R. 255	R. 255	R. 204	R. 153
G. 255	G. 255	G. 204	G. 0	G. 102	G. 102
B. 255	B. 0	B. 102	B. 255	B. 204	B. 153

mp07sw

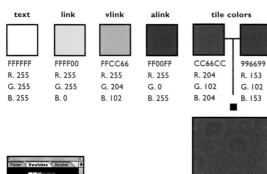

mp07pat.gif

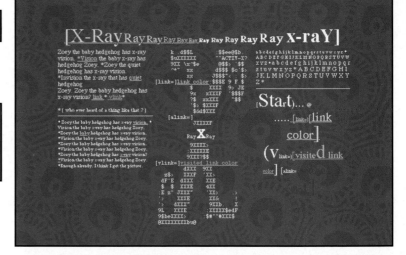

text	link	vlink	alink	hybrid colors	
330066	00FFFF	CCCCFF	CCCCCC	CC66CC	996699
R. 51	R. 0	R. 204	R. 204	R. 204	R. 153
G. 0	G. 255	G. 204	G. 204	G. 102	G. 102
B. 102	B. 255	B. 255	B. 204	B. 204	B. 153

mh07sw

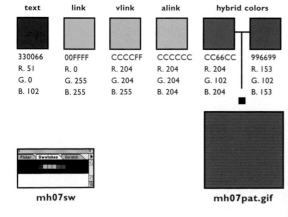

mh07pat.gif

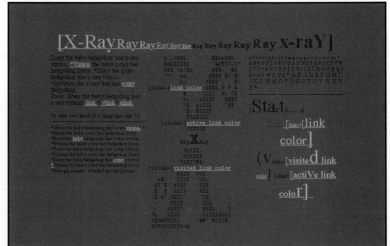

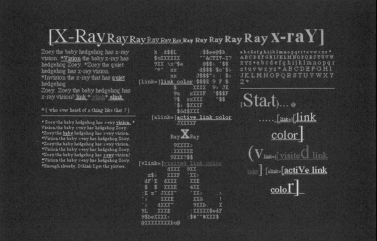

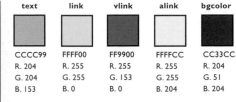

text	link	vlink	alink	bgcolor
CCCC99	FFFF00	FF9900	FFFFCC	CC33CC
R. 204	R. 255	R. 255	R. 255	R. 204
G. 204	G. 255	G. 153	G. 255	G. 51
B. 153	B. 0	B. 0	B. 204	B. 204

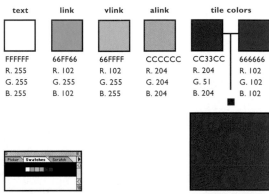

ms08sw

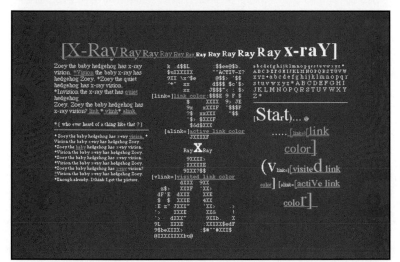

text	link	vlink	alink	tile colors	
FFFFFF	66FF66	66FFFF	CCCCCC	CC33CC	666666
R. 255	R. 102	R. 102	R. 204	R. 204	R. 102
G. 255	G. 255	G. 255	G. 204	G. 51	G. 102
B. 255	B. 102	B. 255	B. 204	B. 204	B. 102

mp08sw

mp08pat.gif

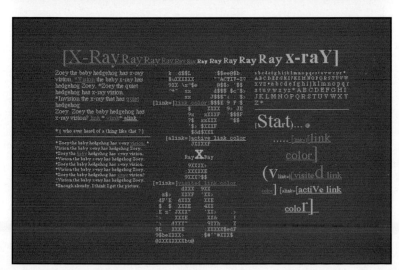

text	link	vlink	alink	hybrid colors	
99CCCC	FF9966	CC99CC	FFCC33	CC33CC	666666
R. 153	R. 255	R. 204	R. 255	R. 204	R. 102
G. 204	G. 153	G. 153	G. 204	G. 51	G. 102
B. 204	B. 102	B. 204	B. 51	B. 204	B. 102

mh08sw

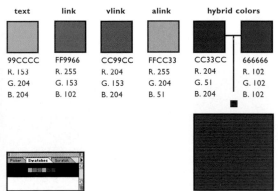

mh08pat.gif

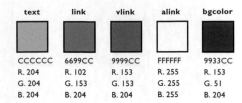

text	link	vlink	alink	bgcolor
CCCCCC	6699CC	9999CC	FFFFFF	9933CC
R. 204	R. 102	R. 153	R. 255	R. 153
G. 204	G. 153	G. 153	G. 255	G. 51
B. 204	B. 204	B. 204	B. 255	B. 204

ms09sw

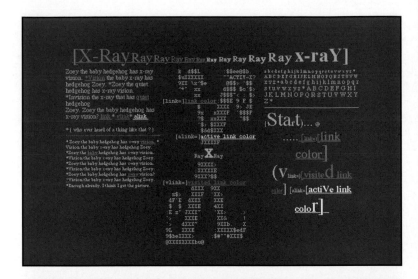

text	link	vlink	alink	tile colors	
CCCCFF	00FFFF	9999FF	CCFFFF	9933CC	CC00FF
R. 204	R. 0	R. 153	R. 204	R. 153	R. 204
G. 204	G. 255	G. 153	G. 255	G. 51	G. 0
B. 255	B. 255	B. 255	B. 255	B. 204	B. 255

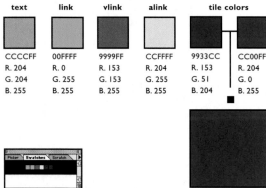

mp09sw

mp09pat.gif

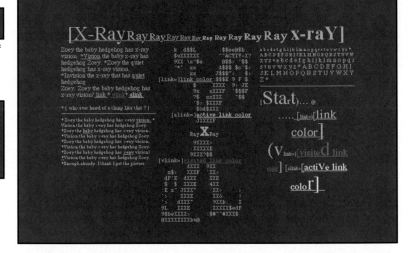

text	link	vlink	alink	hybrid colors	
FFCCCC	FFCC00	CC9900	FF3300	9933CC	CC00FF
R. 255	R. 255	R. 204	R. 255	R. 153	R. 204
G. 204	G. 204	G. 153	G. 51	G. 51	G. 0
B. 204	B. 0	B. 0	B. 0	B. 204	B. 255

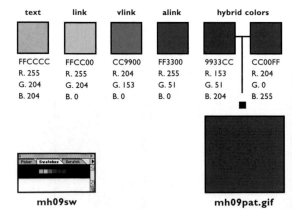

mh09sw

mh09pat.gif

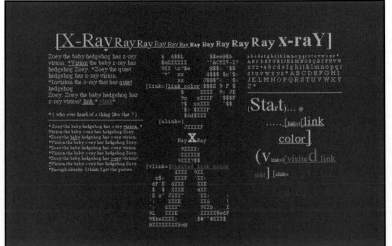

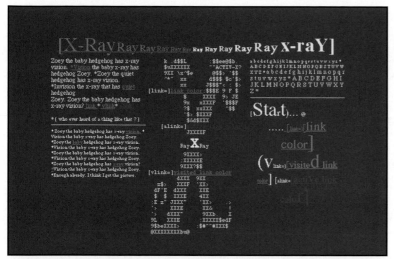

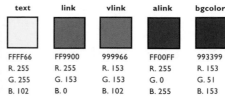

text	link	vlink	alink	bgcolor
FFFF66	FF9900	999966	FF00FF	993399
R. 255	R. 255	R. 153	R. 255	R. 153
G. 255	G. 153	G. 153	G. 0	G. 51
B. 102	B. 0	B. 102	B. 255	B. 153

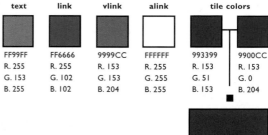

ms10sw

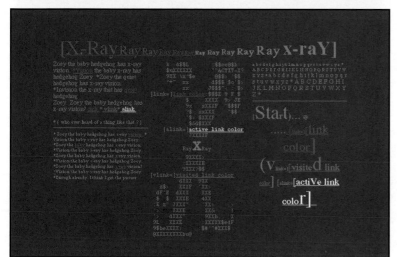

text	link	vlink	alink	tile colors	
FF99FF	FF6666	9999CC	FFFFFF	993399	9900CC
R. 255	R. 255	R. 153	R. 255	R. 153	R. 153
G. 153	G. 102	G. 153	G. 255	G. 51	G. 0
B. 255	B. 102	B. 204	B. 255	B. 153	B. 204

mp10sw

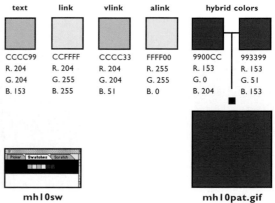

mp10pat.gif

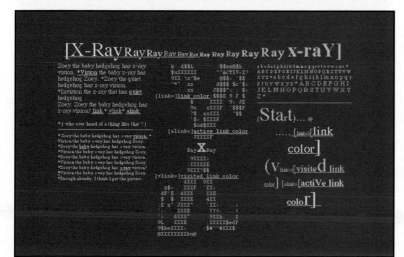

text	link	vlink	alink	hybrid colors	
CCCC99	CCFFFF	CCCC33	FFFF00	9900CC	993399
R. 204	R. 204	R. 204	R. 255	R. 153	R. 153
G. 204	G. 255	G. 204	G. 255	G. 0	G. 51
B. 153	B. 255	B. 51	B. 0	B. 204	B. 153

mh10sw

mh10pat.gif

text	link	vlink	alink	bgcolor
FF99FF	FF9999	993366	FF66CC	996699
R. 255	R. 255	R. 153	R. 255	R. 153
G. 153	G. 153	G. 51	G. 102	G. 102
B. 255	B. 153	B. 102	B. 204	B. 153

ms11sw

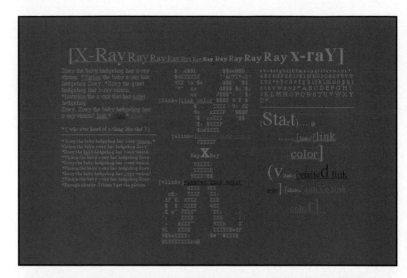

text	link	vlink	alink	tile colors	
FFCCFF	3399FF	00CCFF	00FFFF	666666	996699
R. 255	R. 51	R. 0	R. 0	R. 102	R. 153
G. 204	G. 153	G. 204	G. 255	G. 102	G. 102
B. 255	B. 255	B. 255	B. 255	B. 102	B. 153

mp11sw

mp11pat.gif

text	link	vlink	alink	hybrid colors	
CCCCFF	3333CC	6699CC	000099	996699	666666
R. 204	R. 51	R. 102	R. 0	R. 153	R. 102
G. 204	G. 51	G. 153	G. 0	G. 102	G. 102
B. 255	B. 204	B. 204	B. 153	B. 153	B. 102

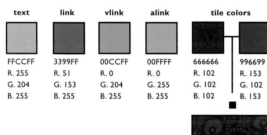

mh11sw

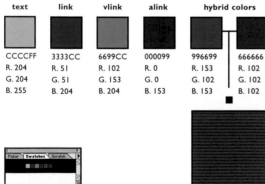

mh11pat.gif

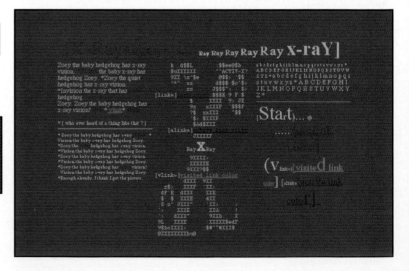

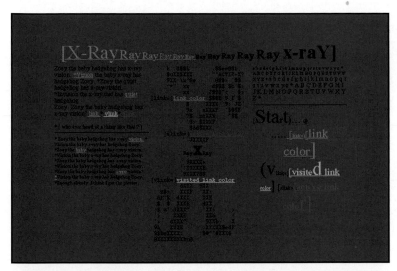

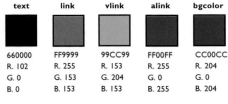

text	link	vlink	alink	bgcolor
660000	FF9999	99CC99	FF00FF	CC00CC
R. 102	R. 255	R. 153	R. 255	R. 204
G. 0	G. 153	G. 204	G. 0	G. 0
B. 0	B. 153	B. 153	B. 255	B. 204

ms12sw

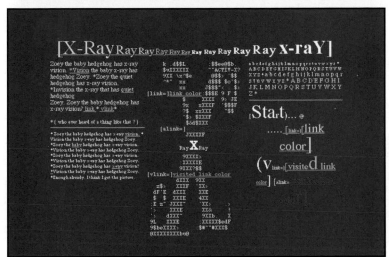

text	link	vlink	alink	tile colors	
FFFFFF	FFFF00	CCCC33	FF0000	CC00CC	9933CC
R. 255	R. 255	R. 204	R. 255	R. 204	R. 153
G. 255	G. 255	G. 204	G. 0	G. 0	G. 51
B. 255	B. 0	B. 51	B. 0	B. 204	B. 204

mp12sw

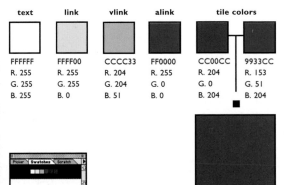

mp12pat.gif

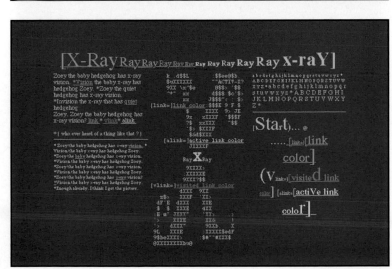

text	link	vlink	alink	hybrid colors	
99FFCC	00FF00	669966	FFFF00	9933CC	CC00CC
R. 153	R. 0	R. 102	R. 255	R. 153	R. 204
G. 255	G. 255	G. 153	G. 255	G. 51	G. 0
B. 204	B. 0	B. 102	B. 0	B. 204	B. 204

mh12sw

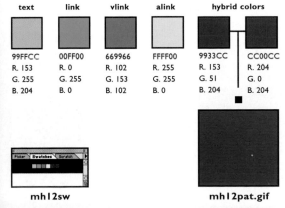

mh12pat.gif

text

FF66FF
R. 255
G. 102
B. 255

link
FF9999
R. 255
G. 153
B. 153

vlink
999900
R. 153
G. 153
B. 0

alink
330033
R. 51
G. 0
B. 51

bgcolor
990099
R. 153
G. 0
B. 153

ms13sw

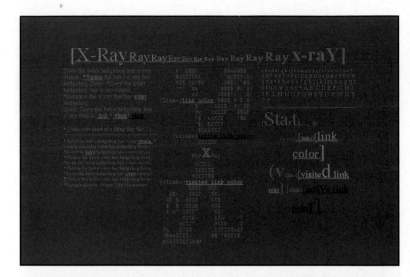

text
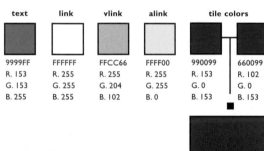
9999FF
R. 153
G. 153
B. 255

link
FFFFFF
R. 255
G. 255
B. 255

vlink
FFCC66
R. 255
G. 204
B. 102

alink
FFFF00
R. 255
G. 255
B. 0

tile colors
990099
R. 153
G. 0
B. 153

660099
R. 102
G. 0
B. 153

mp13sw

mp13pat.gif

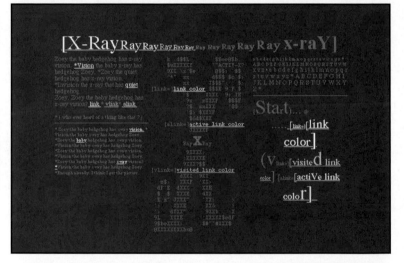

text
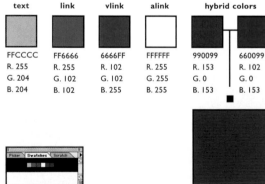
FFCCCC
R. 255
G. 204
B. 204

link
FF6666
R. 255
G. 102
B. 102

vlink
6666FF
R. 102
G. 102
B. 255

alink
FFFFFF
R. 255
G. 255
B. 255

hybrid colors
990099
R. 153
G. 0
B. 153

660099
R. 102
G. 0
B. 153

mh13sw

mh13pat.gif

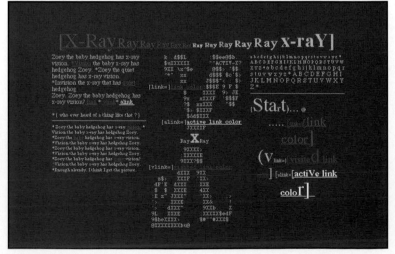

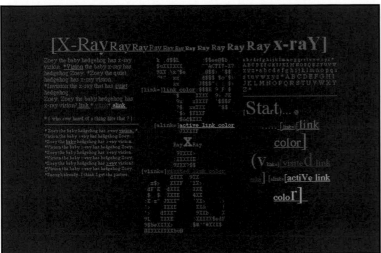

text	link	vlink	alink	bgcolor
999999	999900	CC6666	CCCCCC	660066
R. 153	R. 153	R. 204	R. 204	R. 102
G. 153	G. 153	G. 102	G. 204	G. 0
B. 153	B. 0	B. 102	B. 204	B. 102

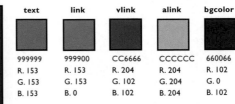

ms14sw

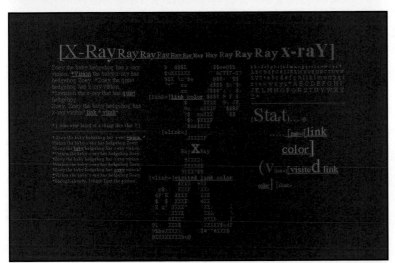

text	link	vlink	alink	tile colors	
FF66FF	FF9999	9999FF	990099	660066	660099
R. 255	R. 255	R. 153	R. 153	R. 102	R. 102
G. 102	G. 153	G. 153	G. 0	G. 0	G. 0
B. 255	B. 153	B. 255	B. 153	B. 102	B. 153

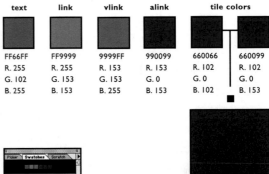

mp14sw

mp14pat.gif

text	link	vlink	alink	hybrid colors	
CC99CC	FF6666	CC6666	999999	660066	660099
R. 204	R. 255	R. 204	R. 153	R. 102	R. 102
G. 153	G. 102	G. 102	G. 153	G. 0	G. 0
B. 204	B. 102	B. 102	B. 153	B. 102	B. 153

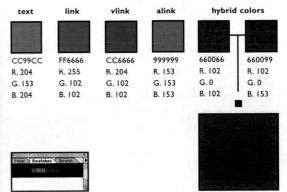

mh14sw

mh14pat.gif

text	link	vlink	alink	bgcolor
9999CC	6666FF	999999	0000FF	663366
R. 153	R. 102	R. 153	R. 0	R. 102
G. 153	G. 102	G. 153	G. 0	G. 51
B. 204	B. 255	B. 153	B. 255	B. 102

ms15sw

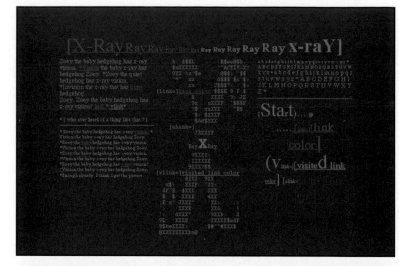

text	link	vlink	alink	tile colors	
CCCCCC	FF66FF	FF6666	FFFFFF	663366	333333
R. 204	R. 255	R. 255	R. 255	R. 102	R. 51
G. 204	G. 102	G. 102	G. 255	G. 51	G. 51
B. 204	B. 255	B. 102	B. 255	B. 102	B. 51

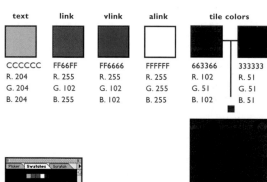

mp15sw

mp15pat.gif

text	link	vlink	alink	hybrid colors	
669999	33CC33	669966	33FF00	663366	333333
R. 102	R. 51	R. 102	R. 51	R. 102	R. 51
G. 153	G. 204	G. 153	G. 255	G. 51	G. 51
B. 153	B. 51	B. 102	B. 0	B. 102	B. 51

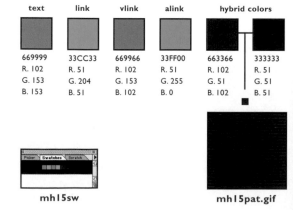

mh15sw

mh15pat.gif

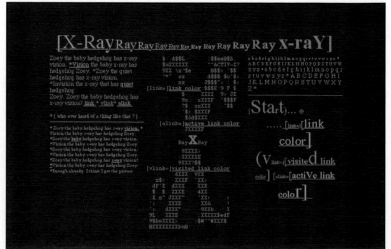

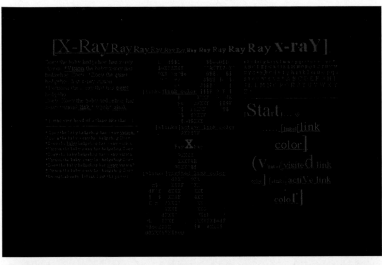

text	link	vlink	alink	bgcolor
666666	CC33CC	993366	666600	330033
R. 102	R. 204	R. 153	R. 102	R. 51
G. 102	G. 51	G. 51	G. 102	G. 0
B. 102	B. 204	0253	B. 0	B. 51

ms16sw

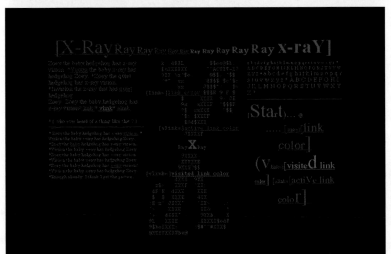

text	link	vlink	alink	tile colors	
CC6666	FF0000	CC9999	996666	330000	330033
R. 204	R. 255	R. 204	R. 153	R. 51	R. 51
G. 102	G. 0	G. 153	G. 102	G. 0	G. 0
B. 102	B. 0	B. 153	B. 102	B. 0	B. 51

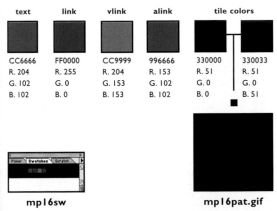

mp16sw **mp16pat.gif**

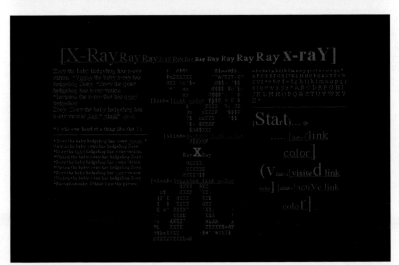

text	link	vlink	alink	hybrid colors	
CC6633	FF00CC	996699	666666	330000	330033
R. 204	R. 255	R. 153	R. 102	R. 51	R. 51
G. 102	G. 0	G. 102	G. 102	G. 0	G. 0
B. 51	B. 204	B. 153	B. 102	B. 0	B. 51

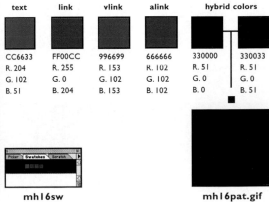

mh16sw **mh16pat.gif**

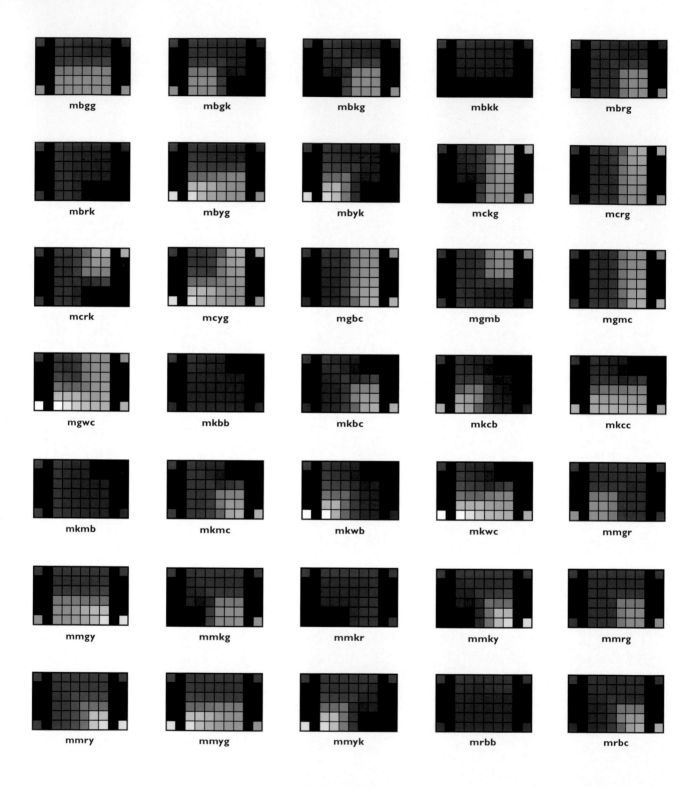

mbgg   mbgk   mbkg   mbkk   mbrg

mbrk   mbyg   mbyk   mckg   mcrg

mcrk   mcyg   mgbc   mgmb   mgmc

mgwc   mkbb   mkbc   mkcb   mkcc

mkmb   mkmc   mkwb   mkwc   mmgr

mmgy   mmkg   mmkr   mmky   mmrg

mmry   mmyg   mmyk   mrbb   mrbc

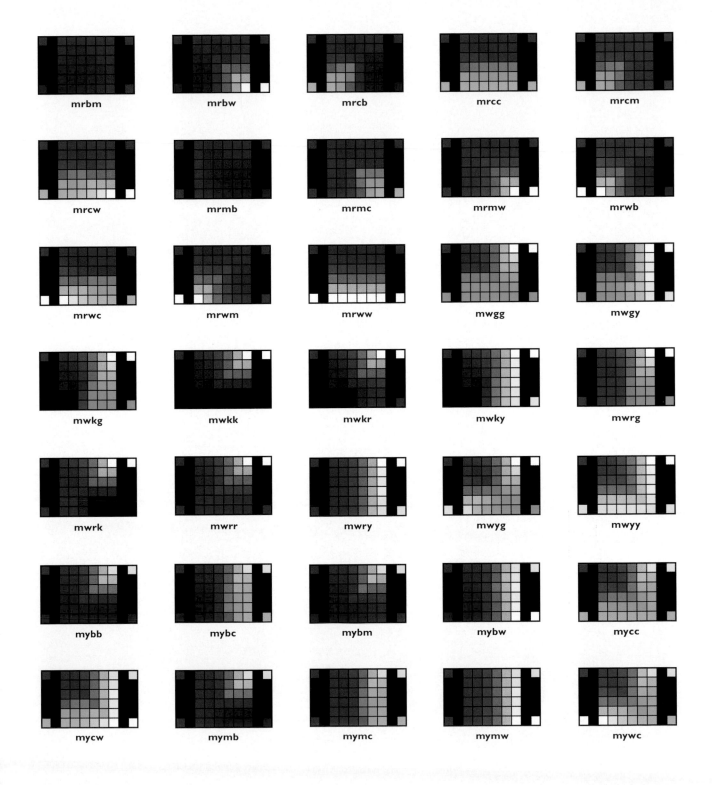

mrbm mrbw mrcb mrcc mrcm

mrcw mrmb mrmc mrmw mrwb

mrwc mrwm mrww mwgg mwgy

mwkg mwkk mwkr mwky mwrg

mwrk mwrr mwry mwyg mwyy

mybb mybc mybm mybw mycc

mycw mymb mymc mymw mywc

YELLOW

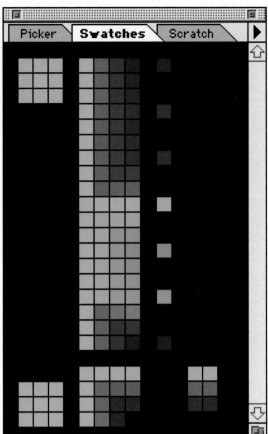

myd

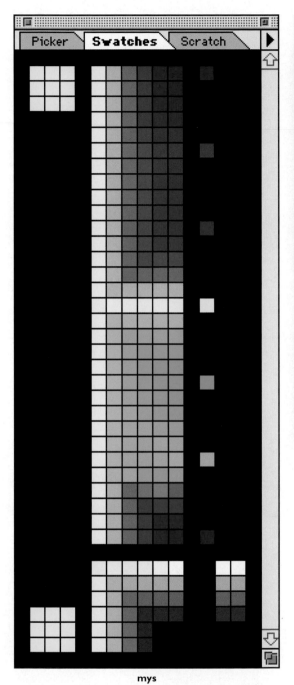

mys

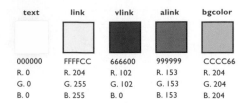

text	link	vlink	alink	bgcolor
000000	FFFFCC	666600	999999	CCCC66
R. 0	R. 204	R. 102	R. 153	R. 204
G. 0	G. 255	G. 102	G. 153	G. 204
B. 0	B. 255	B. 0	B. 153	B. 204

ys01sw

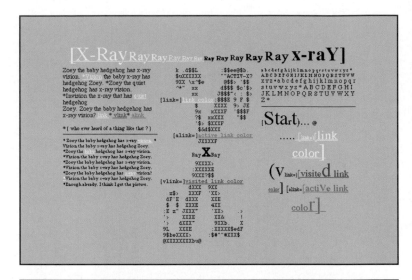

text	link	vlink	alink	tile colors	
000000	FFFF00	999966	666600	CCCCCC	CCCC66
R. 0	R. 255	R. 153	R. 102	R. 204	R. 204
G. 0	G. 255	G. 153	G. 102	G. 204	G. 204
B. 0	B. 0	B. 102	B. 0	B. 204	B. 102

yp01sw

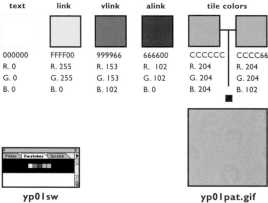

yp01pat.gif

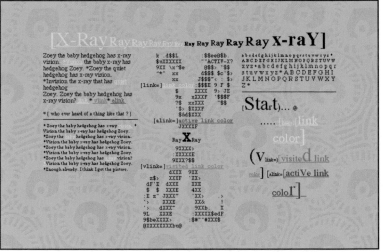

text	link	vlink	alink	hybrid colors	
000000	FFFFCC	999966	666633	CCCC66	CCCCCC
R. 0	R. 255	R. 153	R. 102	R. 204	R. 204
G. 0	G. 255	G. 153	G. 102	G. 204	G. 204
B. 0	B. 204	B. 102	B. 51	B. 102	B. 204

yh01sw

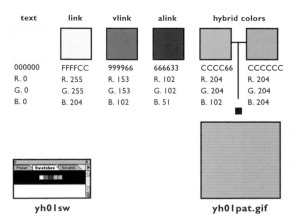

yh01pat.gif

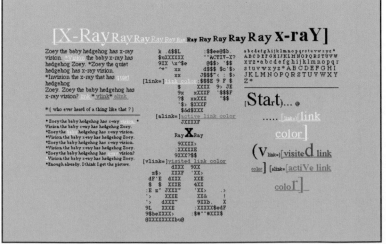

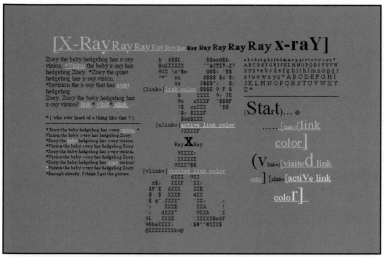

text	link	vlink	alink	bgcolor
333300	CCCC00	CCCC99	FFFF00	999966
R. 51	R. 204	R. 204	R. 255	R. 153
G. 51	G. 204	G. 204	G. 255	G. 153
B. 0	B. 0	B. 153	B. 0	B. 102

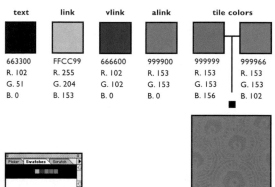

ys02sw

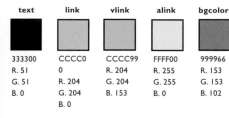

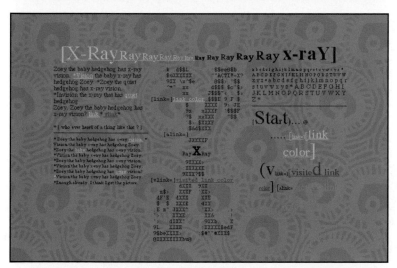

text	link	vlink	alink	tile colors	
663300	FFCC99	666600	999900	999999	999966
R. 102	R. 255	R. 102	R. 153	R. 153	R. 153
G. 51	G. 204	G. 102	G. 153	G. 153	G. 153
B. 0	B. 153	B. 0	B. 0	B. 156	B. 102

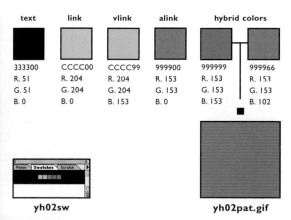

yp02sw

yp02pat.gif

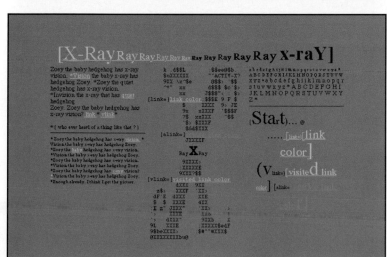

text	link	vlink	alink	hybrid colors	
333300	CCCC00	CCCC99	999900	999999	999966
R. 51	R. 204	R. 204	R. 153	R. 153	R. 153
G. 51	G. 204	G. 204	G. 153	G. 153	G. 153
B. 0	B. 0	B. 153	B. 0	B. 153	B. 102

yh02sw

yh02pat.gif

text	link	vlink	alink	bgcolor
333300	FFFF66	FFFF00	FFFFFF	CCCC33
R. 51	R. 255	R. 255	R. 255	R. 204
G. 51	G. 255	G. 255	G. 255	G. 204
B. 0	B. 102	B. 0	B. 255	B. 51

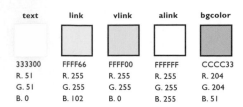

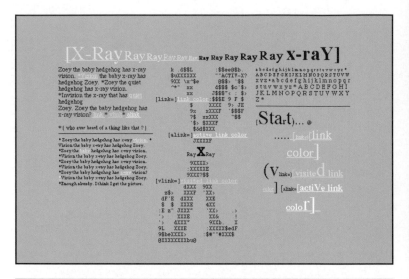

ys03sw

text	link	vlink	alink	tile colors	
333300	FF0000	666633	999966	CCCC33	CCCC66
R. 51	R. 255	R. 102	R. 153	R. 204	R. 204
G. 51	G. 0	G. 102	G. 153	G. 204	G. 204
B. 0	B. 0	B. 51	B. 102	B. 514	B. 102

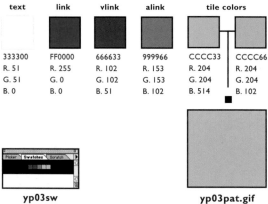

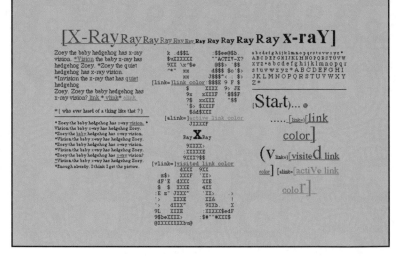

yp03sw

yp03pat.gif

text	link	vlink	alink	hybrid colors	
666633	CC3333	9966CC	996666	CCCC33	CCCC66
R. 102	R. 204	R. 153	R. 153	R. 204	R. 204
G. 102	G. 51	G. 102	G. 102	G. 204	G. 204
B. 0	B. 51	B. 204	B. 102	B. 51	B. 102

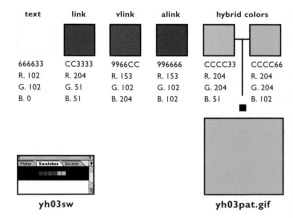

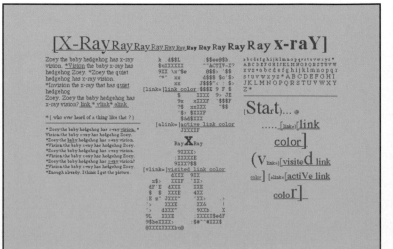

yh03sw

yh03pat.gif

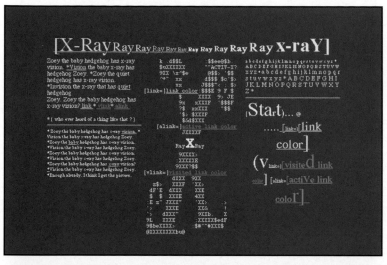

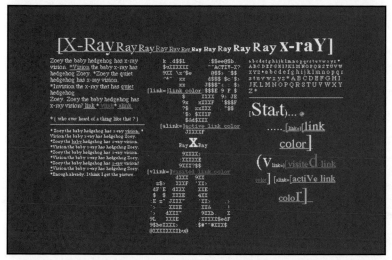

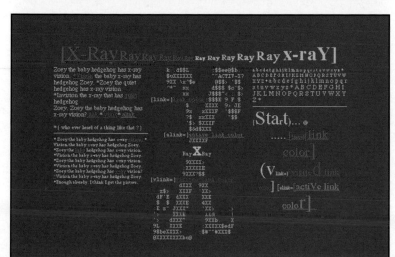

text	link	vlink	alink	bgcolor
FFFFCC	FFFF00	999933	999966	666633
R. 255	R. 255	R. 153	R. 102	R. 102
G. 255	G. 255	G. 153	G. 153	G. 102
B. 204	B. 0	B. 51	B. 102	B. 21

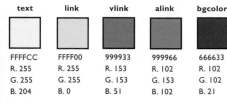

ys04sw

text	link	vlink	alink	tile colors	
FFFFCC	FFFF00	FF9966	FFCC66	666633	666666
R. 255	R. 255	R. 255	R. 255	R. 102	R. 102
G. 255	G. 255	G. 153	G. 204	G. 102	G. 102
B. 204	B. 0	B. 102	B. 102	B. 51	B. 102

yp04sw

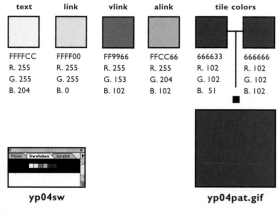

yp04pat.gif

text	link	vlink	alink	hybrid colors	
CCCC99	FF6666	9966CC	FF9999	666666	666633
R. 204	R. 255	R. 153	R. 255	R. 102	R. 102
G. 204	G. 102	G. 102	G. 153	G. 102	G. 102
B. 153	B. 102	B. 204	B. 153	B. 102	B. 51

yh04sw

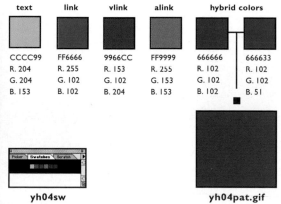

yh04pat.gif

text	link	vlink	alink	bgcolor
CCCC66	FFFF00	CCCCCC	666600	333300
R. 204	R. 255	R. 204	R. 102	R. 204
G. 204	G. 255	G. 204	G. 102	G. 204
B. 102	B. 0	B. 204	B. 0	B. 204

ys05sw

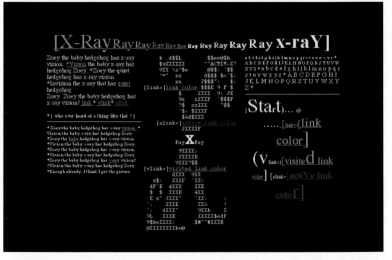

text	link	vlink	alink	tile colors	
FFFFCC	00CCCC	009966	006600	333300	333333
R. 255	R. 0	R. 0	R. 0	R. 51	R. 51
G. 255	G. 204	G. 153	G. 102	G. 51	G. 51
B. 204	B. 204	B. 102	B. 0	B. 51	B. 51

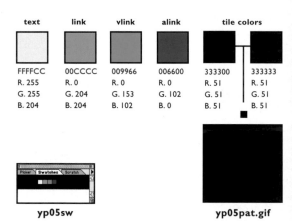

yp05sw

yp05pat.gif

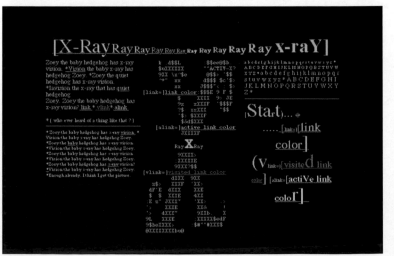

text	link	vlink	alink	hybrid colors	
CCCC99	CCCC00	CC9999	FFFF00	333300	333333
R. 204	R. 204	R. 204	R. 255	R. 51	R. 51
G. 204	G. 204	G. 153	G. 255	G. 51	G. 51
B. 153	B. 0	B. 153	B. 0	B. 0	B. 51

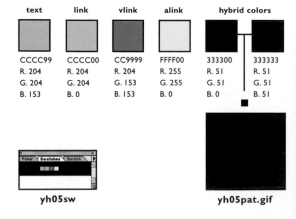

yh05sw

yh05pat.gif

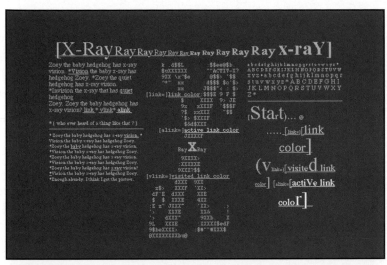

text	link	vlink	alink	bgcolor
CCCC99	CCFF66	CCCC33	FFFFFF	666600
R. 204	R. 204	R. 204	R. 255	R. 102
G. 204	G. 255	G. 204	G. 255	G. 102
B. 153	B. 102	B. 51	B. 255	B. 0

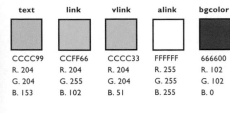

ys06sw

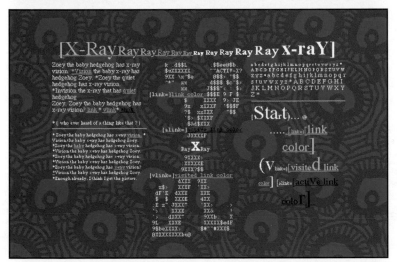

text	link	vlink	alink	tile colors	
FFFFFF	CCFF00	CCCC99	333300	336633	666600
R. 255	R. 204	R. 204	R. 51	R. 51	R. 102
G. 255	G. 255	G. 204	G. 51	G. 102	G. 102
B. 255	B. 0	B. 153	B. 0	B. 51	B. 0

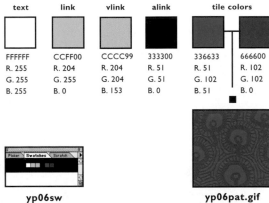

yp06sw

yp06pat.gif

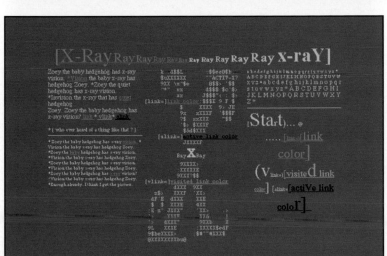

text	link	vlink	alink	hybrid colors	
99FF99	999900	009966	000000	666600	336633
R. 153	R. 153	R. 0	R. 0	R. 102	R. 51
G. 255	G. 153	G. 153	G. 0	G. 102	G. 102
B. 153	B. 0	B. 102	B. 0	B. 0	B. 51

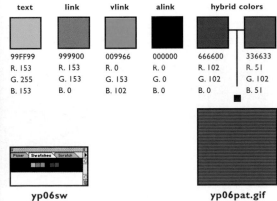

yp06sw

yp06pat.gif

text	link	vlink	alink	bgcolor
000000	CC0000	666666	0000FF	CCCC00
R. 0	R. 204	R. 102	R. 0	R. 204
G. 0	G. 0	G. 102	G. 0	G. 204
B. 0	B. 255	B. 102	B. 255	B. 0

ys07sw

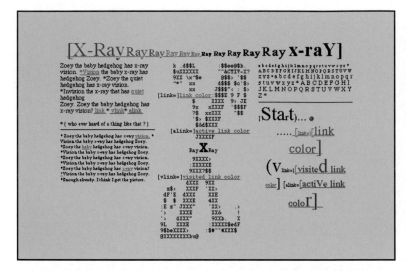

text	link	vlink	alink	tile colors	
333333	FFFFFF	666666	FFFF66	FFCC00	CCCC00
R. 51	R. 255	R. 102	R. 255	R. 2554	R. 204
G. 51	G. 255	G. 102	G. 255	G. 204	G. 204
B. 51	B. 255	B. 102	B. 102	B. 0	B. 0

yp07sw

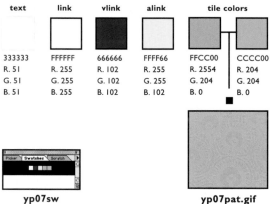

yp07pat.gif

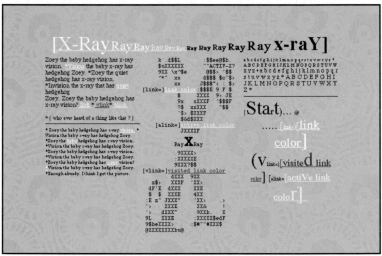

text	link	vlink	alink	hybrid colors	
333333	006633	999900	009999	FFCC00	CCCC00
R. 51	R. 0	R. 153	R. 0	R. 255	R. 204
G. 51	G. 102	G. 153	G. 153	G. 204	G. 204
B. 51	B. 51	B. 0	B. 153	B. 0	B. 0

yh07sw

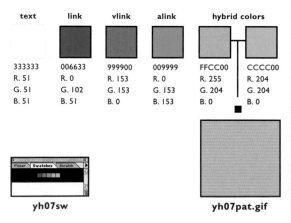

yh07pat.gif

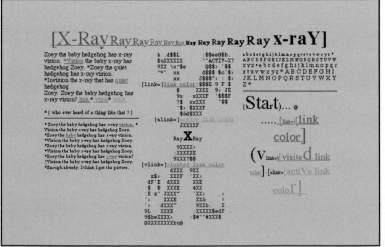

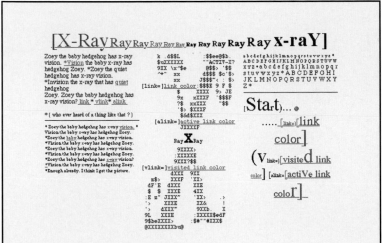

	text	link	vlink	alink	bgcolor
hex	663300	FF0000	CC6600	6666CC	FFFFCC
	R. 102	R. 255	R. 204	R. 102	R. 255
	G. 51	G. 0	G. 102	G. 102	G. 255
	B. 0	B. 0	B. 0	B. 204	B. 204

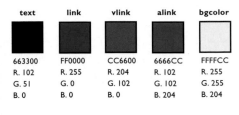

ys08sw

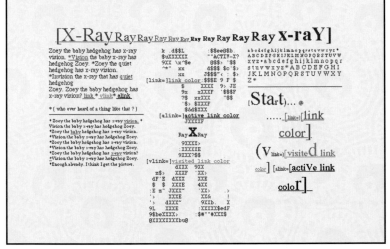

	text	link	vlink	alink	tile colors	
hex	666600	FF3333	FF9900	333300	FFFF99	FFFFCC
	R. 102	R. 255	R. 255	R. 51	R. 255	R. 255
	G. 102	G. 51	G. 153	G. 51	G. 255	G. 255
	B. 0	B. 51	B. 0	B. 0	B. 153	B. 204

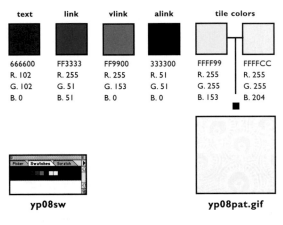

yp08sw

yp08pat.gif

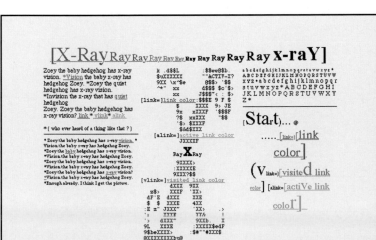

	text	link	vlink	alink	hybrid colors	
hex	333333	006633	999900	009999	FFFF99	FFFFCC
	R. 51	R. 0	R. 153	R. 0	R. 255	R. 255
	G. 51	G. 102	G. 153	G. 153	G. 255	G. 255
	B. 51	B. 51	B. 0	B. 153	B. 153	B. 204

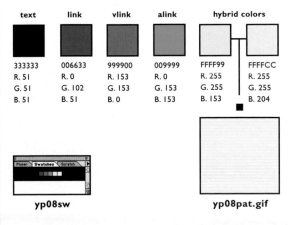

yp08sw

yp08pat.gif

text
996600
R. 153
G. 102
B. 0

link
FF3300
R. 255
G. 51
B. 0

vlink
FF6600
R. 255
G. 102
B. 0

alink
FF0000
R. 255
G. 102
B. 0

bgcolor
FFFF99
R. 255
G. 255
B. 153

ys09sw

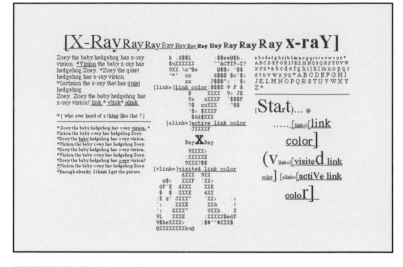

text
660000
R. 102
G. 0
B. 0

link
FF0000
R. 255
G. 0
B. 0

vlink
999900
R. 153
G. 153
B. 0

alink
CC6600
R. 204
G. 102
B. 0

tile colors
FFFF99
R. 255
G. 255
B. 153

FFFF66
R. 255
G. 255
B. 102

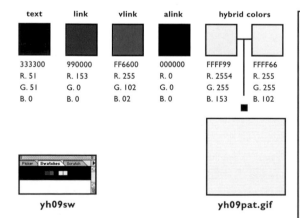

yp09sw

yp09pat.gif

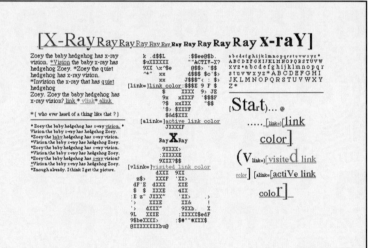

text
333300
R. 51
G. 51
B. 0

link
990000
R. 153
G. 0
B. 0

vlink
FF6600
R. 255
G. 102
B. 02

alink
000000
R. 0
G. 0
B. 0

hybrid colors
FFFF99
R. 2554
G. 255
B. 153

FFFF66
R. 255
G. 255
B. 102

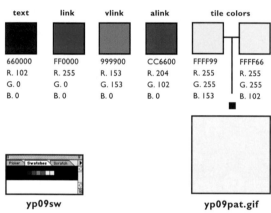

yh09sw

yh09pat.gif

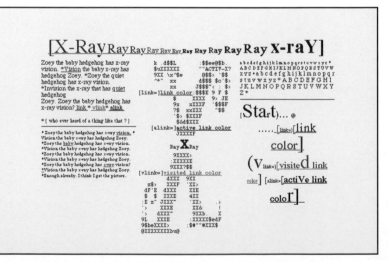

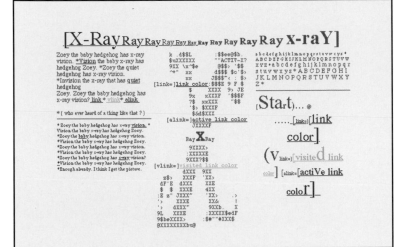

text	link	vlink	alink	bgcolor
336666	0000FF	33CCCC	990099	FFFF66
R. 51	R. 04	R. 51	R. 153	R. 255
G. 102	G. 0	G. 204	G. 0	G. 255
B. 102	B. 255	B. 204	B. 153	B. 102

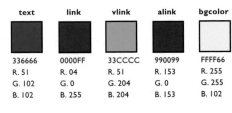

ys10sw

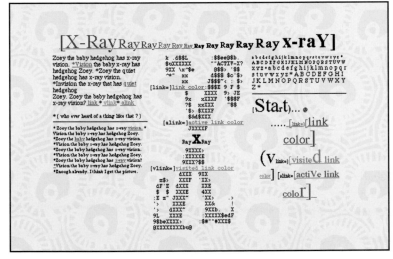

text	link	vlink	alink	tile colors	
000000	FF0000	999900	FF6600	FFFF33	FFFF66
R. 0	R. 255	R. 153	R. 255	R. 255	R. 255
G. 0	G. 0	G. 153	G. 102	G. 255	G. 255
B. 0	B. 0	B. 0	B. 0	B. 51	B. 102

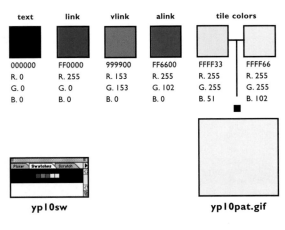

yp10sw   **yp10pat.gif**

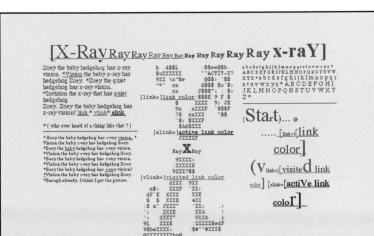

text	link	vlink	alink	hybrid colors	
336600	CC3300	FF6633	660000	FFFF66	FFFF33
R. 51	R. 204	R. 255	R. 102	R. 255	R. 255
G. 102	G. 51	G. 102	G. 0	G. 255	G. 255
B. 0	B. 0	B. 51	B. 0	B. 102	B. 51

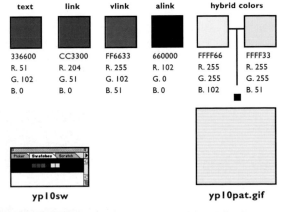

yp10sw   **yp10pat.gif**

text	link	vlink	alink	bgcolor
333333	FFFF00	FFCC66	666600	FF9900
R. 51	R. 255	R. 255	R. 102	R. 255
G. 51	G. 255	G. 204	G. 102	G. 153
B. 51	B. 0	B. 102	B. 0	B. 0

ys11sw

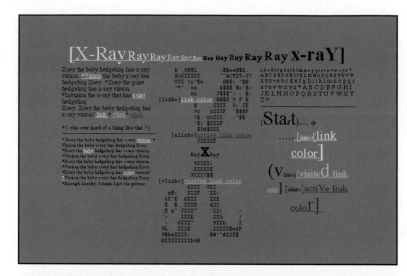

text	link	vlink	alink	tile colors	
003300	006666	336633	FFFF00	FF9900	FF9933
R. 0	R. 0	R. 51	R. 255	R. 255	R. 255
G. 51	G. 102	G. 102	G. 255	G. 153	G. 153
B. 0	B. 102	B. 51	B. 0	B. 0	B. 51

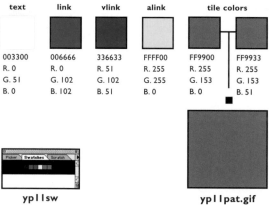

yp11sw

yp11pat.gif

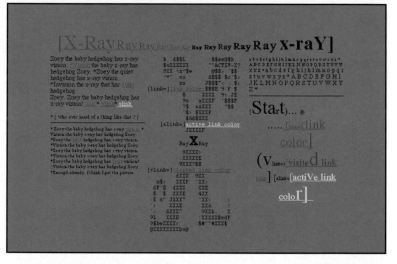

text	link	vlink	alink	hybrid colors	
333333	FFFFCC	CCCCCC	FFFF00	FF9900	FF9933
R. 51	R. 255	R. 204	R. 255	R. 255	R. 255
G. 51	G. 255	G. 204	G. 255	G. 153	G. 153
B. 51	B. 204	B. 204	B. 0	B. 0	B. 51

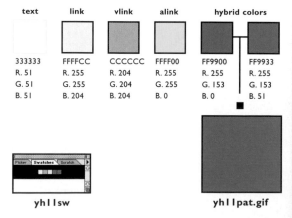

yh11sw

yh11pat.gif

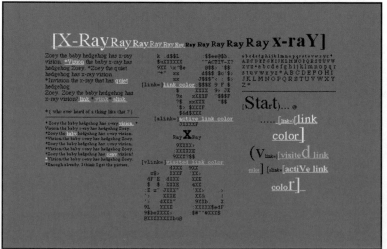

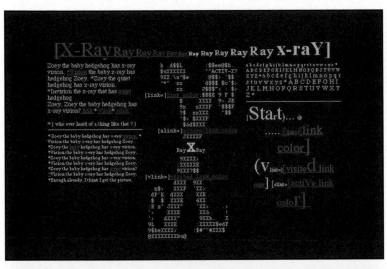

text	link	vlink	alink	bgcolor
FFCC99	FF6600	666699	FF3300	663300
R. 255	R. 255	R. 102	R. 255	R. 102
G. 204	G. 102	G. 102	G. 51	G. 51
B. 153	B. 0	B. 153	B. 0	B. 0

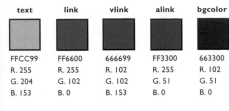

ys12sw

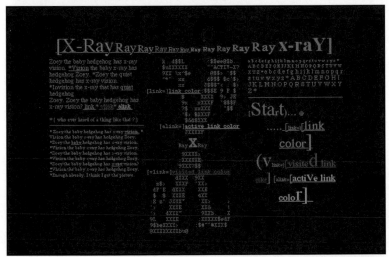

text	link	vlink	alink	tile colors	
9999CC	999900	CC6600	66CC00	333333	663300
R. 153	R. 153	R. 204	R. 102	R. 51	R. 102
G. 153	G. 153	G. 102	G. 204	G. 51	G. 51
B. 214	B. 0	B. 0	B. 0	B. 51	B. 0

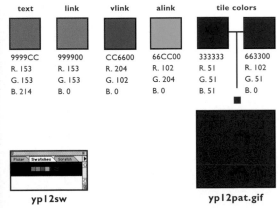

yp12sw

yp12pat.gif

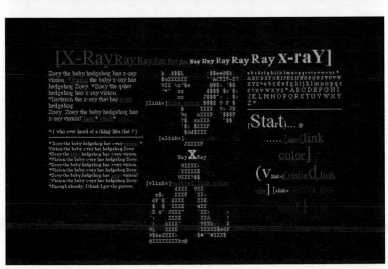

text	link	vlink	alink	hybrid colors	
CCCCFF	6666FF	666666	0000FF	333333	663300
R. 204	R. 102	R. 102	R. 0	R. 51	R. 102
G. 204	G. 102	G. 102	G. 0	G. 51	G. 51
B. 255	B. 255	B. 102	B. 255	B. 51	B. 0

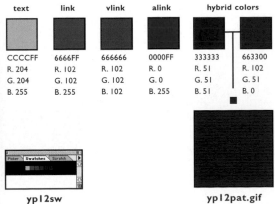

yp12sw

yp12pat.gif

text	link	vlink	alink	bgcolor
333333	006633	999900	009999	FFCC99
R. 51	R. 0	R. 153	R. 0	R. 255
G. 51	G. 102	G. 153	G. 153	G. 204
B. 51	B. 51	B. 0	B. 153	B. 153

ys13sw

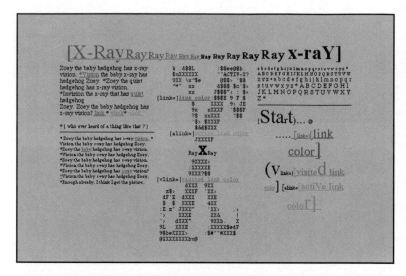

text	link	vlink	alink	tile colors	
663300	CC6600	666666	FF3300	FFCC66	FFCC99
R. 102	R. 204	R. 102	R. 255	R. 255	R. 255
G. 51	G. 102	G. 102	G. 51	G. 204	G. 204
B. 0	B. 0	B. 102	B. 0	B. 102	B. 153

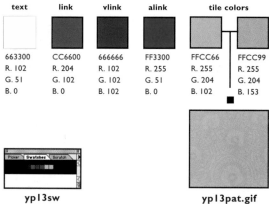

yp13sw

yp13pat.gif

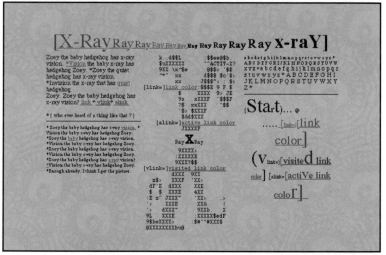

text	link	vlink	alink	hybrid colors	
663300	FF6600	999900	FF3300	FFCC66	FFCC99
R. 102	R. 255	R. 153	R. 255	R. 255	R. 255
G. 51	G. 102	G. 153	G. 51	G. 204	G. 204
B. 0	B. 0	B. 0	B. 0	B. 102	B. 153

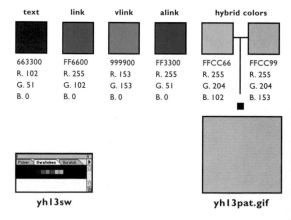

yh13sw

yh13pat.gif

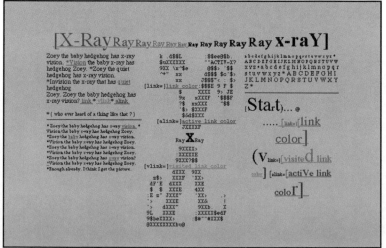

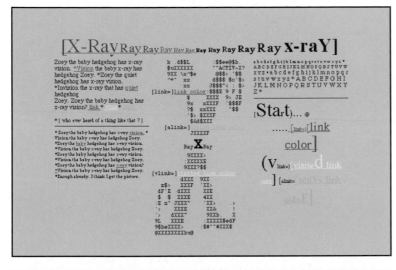

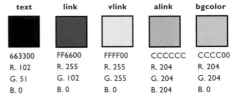

text	link	vlink	alink	bgcolor
663300	FF6600	FFFF00	CCCCCC	CCCC00
R. 102	R. 255	R. 255	R. 204	R. 204
G. 51	G. 102	G. 255	G. 204	G. 204
B. 0	B. 0	B. 0	B. 204	B. 0

ys14sw

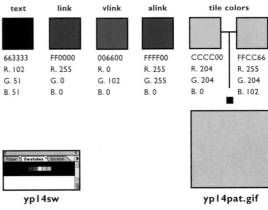

text	link	vlink	alink	tile colors	
663333	FF0000	006600	FFFF00	CCCC00	FFCC66
R. 102	R. 255	R. 0	R. 255	R. 204	R. 255
G. 51	G. 0	G. 102	G. 255	G. 204	G. 204
B. 51	B. 0	B. 0	B. 0	B. 0	B. 102

yp14sw   yp14pat.gif

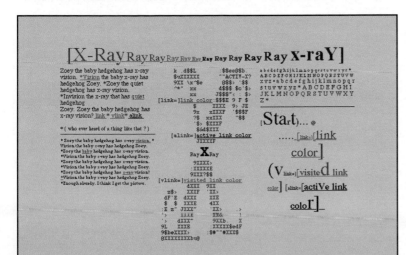
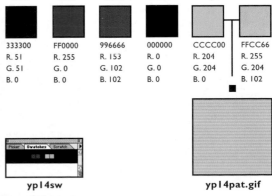

text	link	vlink	alink	hybrid colors	
333300	FF0000	996666	000000	CCCC00	FFCC66
R. 51	R. 255	R. 153	R. 0	R. 204	R. 255
G. 51	G. 0	G. 102	G. 0	G. 204	G. 204
B. 0	B. 0	B. 102	B. 0	B. 0	B. 102

yp14sw   yp14pat.gif

text	link	vlink	alink	bgcolor
660099	FF3399	669966	CC3333	FFFFCC
R. 102	R. 255	R. 102	R. 204	R. 255
G. 0	G. 51	G. 153	G. 51	G. 255
B. 153	B. 153	B. 102	B. 51	B. 204

ys15sw

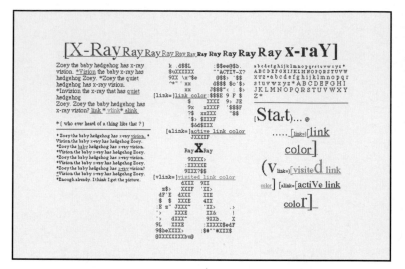

text	link	vlink	alink	tile colors	
660033	FF0000	999900	FF00FF	CCCCCC	FFFFCC
R. 102	R. 255	R. 153	R. 255	R. 204	R. 255
G. 0	G. 0	G. 153	G. 0	G. 204	G. 255
B. 51	B. 0	B. 0	B. 255		B. 204

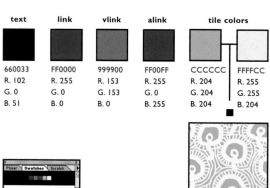

yp15sw

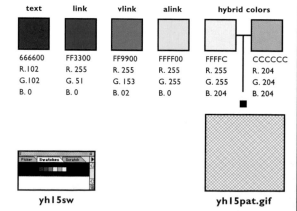

yp15pat.gif

text	link	vlink	alink	hybrid colors	
666600	FF3300	FF9900	FFFF00	FFFFC	CCCCCC
R.102	R. 255	R. 255	R. 255	R. 255	R. 204
G.102	G. 51	G. 153	G. 255	G. 255	G. 204
B. 0	B. 0	B. 02	B. 0	B. 204	B. 204

yh15sw

yh15pat.gif

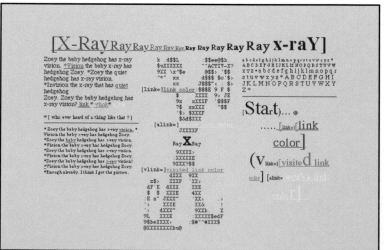

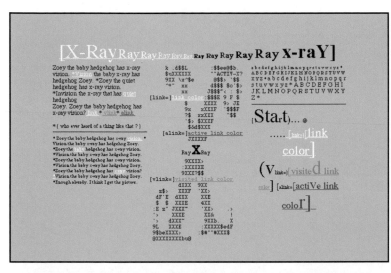

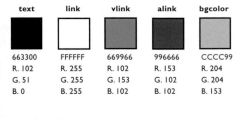

	text	link	vlink	alink	bgcolor
	663300	FFFFFF	669966	996666	CCCC99
	R. 102	R. 255	R. 102	R. 153	R. 204
	G. 51	G. 255	G. 153	G. 102	G. 204
	B. 0	B. 255	B. 102	B. 102	B. 153

ys16sw

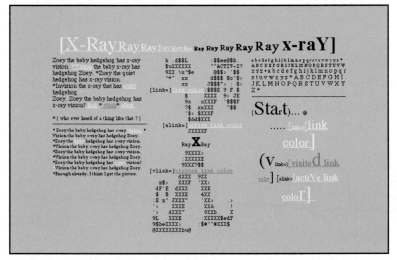

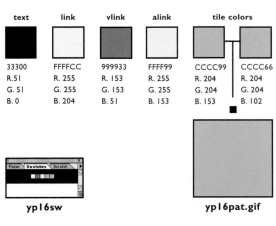

	text	link	vlink	alink	tile colors	
	33300	FFFFCC	999933	FFFF99	CCCC99	CCCC66
	R.51	R. 255	R. 153	R. 255	R. 204	R. 204
	G. 51	G. 255	G. 153	G. 255	G. 204	G. 204
	B. 0	B. 204	B. 51	B. 153	B. 153	B. 102

yp16sw   **yp16pat.gif**

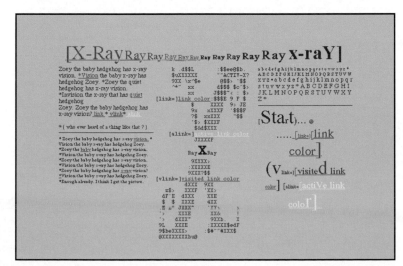

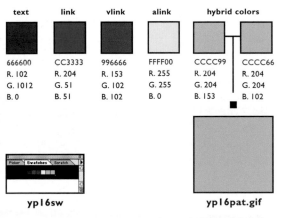

	text	link	vlink	alink	hybrid colors	
	666600	CC3333	996666	FFFF00	CCCC99	CCCC66
	R. 102	R. 204	R. 153	R. 255	R. 204	R. 204
	G. 1012	G. 51	G. 102	G. 255	G. 204	G. 204
	B. 0	B. 51	B. 102	B. 0	B. 153	B. 102

yp16sw   **yp16pat.gif**

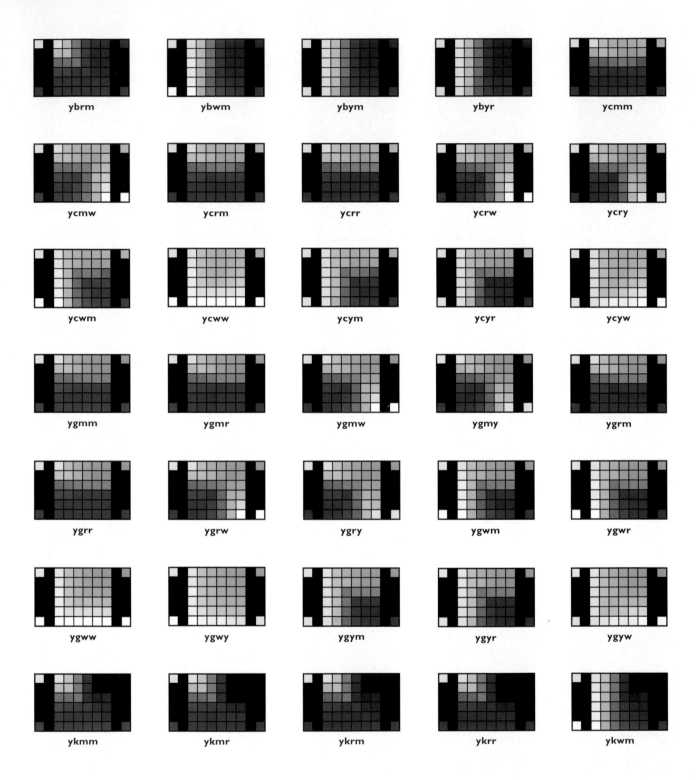

ybrm	ybwm	ybym	ybyr	ycmm
ycmw	ycrm	ycrr	ycrw	ycry
ycwm	ycww	ycym	ycyr	ycyw
ygmm	ygmr	ygmw	ygmy	ygrm
ygrr	ygrw	ygry	ygwm	ygwr
ygww	ygwy	ygym	ygyr	ygyw
ykmm	ykmr	ykrm	ykrr	ykwm

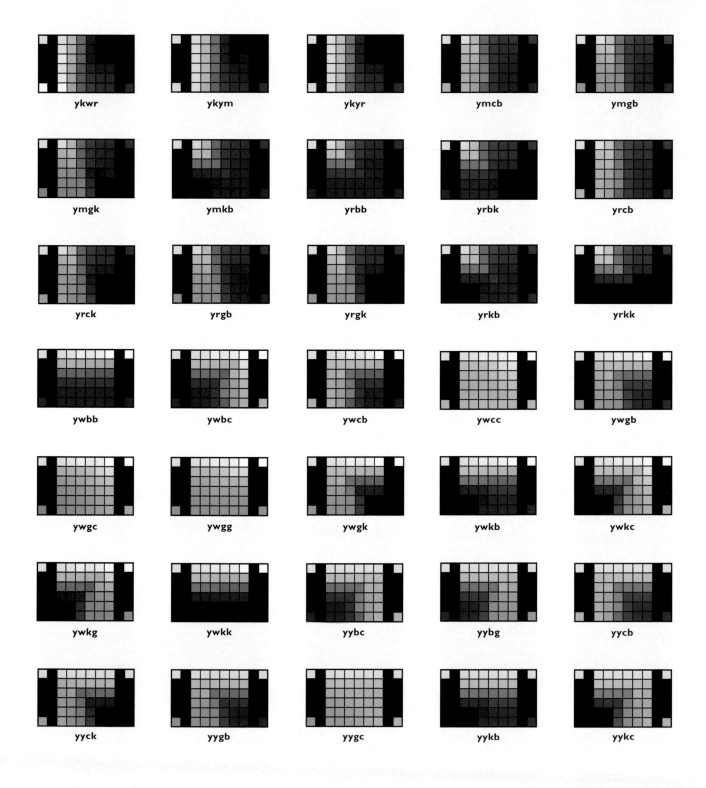

ykwr	ykym	ykyr
ymcb	ymgb	
ymgk	ymkb	yrbb
yrbk	yrcb	
yrck	yrgb	yrgk
yrkb	yrkk	
ywbb	ywbc	ywcb
ywcc	ywgb	
ywgc	ywgg	ywgk
ywkb	ywkc	
ywkg	ywkk	yybc
yybg	yycb	
yyck	yygb	yygc
yykb	yykc	

MONOCHROMATIC

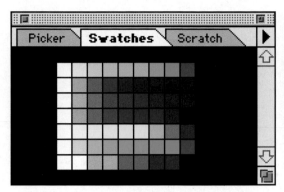

odd06

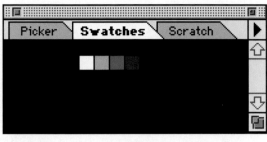

odd04

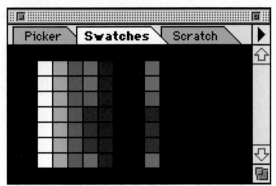

med

text	link	vlink	alink	bgcolor
339933	33FF00	666666	666600	000000
R. 51	R. 51	R. 102	R. 102	R. 0
G. 153	G. 255	G. 102	G. 102	G. 0
B. 51	B. 0	B. 102	B. 0	B. 0

ks01sw

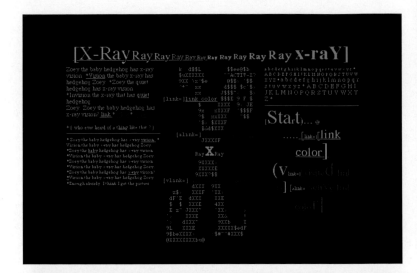

text	link	vlink	alink	bgcolor
CC6666	FF0000	CC3333	990000	000000
R. 204	R. 255	R. 204	R. 153	R. 0
G. 102	G. 0	G. 51	G. 0	G. 0
B. 102	B. 0	B. 51	B. 0	B. 0

ks02sw

text	link	vlink	alink	bgcolor
999966	FFFF00	999933	FFFF99	000000
R. 153	R. 255	R. 153	R. 255	R. 0
G. 153	G. 255	G. 153	G. 255	G. 0
B. 102	B. 0	B. 51	B. 153	B. 0

ks03sw

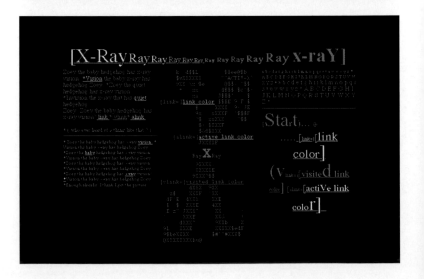

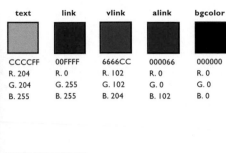

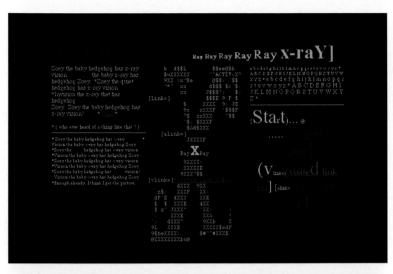

text	link	vlink	alink	bgcolor
CCCCFF	00FFFF	6666CC	000066	000000
R. 204	R. 0	R. 102	R. 0	R. 0
G. 204	G. 255	G. 102	G. 0	G. 0
B. 255	B. 255	B. 204	B. 102	B. 0

ks04sw

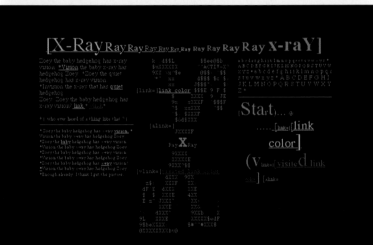

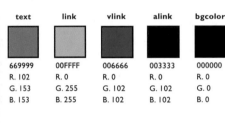

text	link	vlink	alink	bgcolor
669999	00FFFF	006666	003333	000000
R. 102	R. 0	R. 0	R. 0	R. 0
G. 153	G. 255	G. 102	G. 102	G. 0
B. 153	B. 255	B. 102	B. 102	B. 0

ks05w

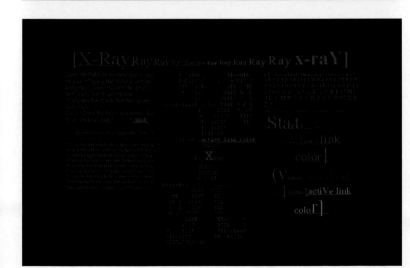

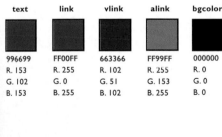

text	link	vlink	alink	bgcolor
996699	FF00FF	663366	FF99FF	000000
R. 153	R. 255	R. 102	R. 255	R. 0
G. 102	G. 0	G. 51	G. 153	G. 0
B. 153	B. 255	B. 102	B. 255	B. 0

ks06sw

text	link	vlink	alink	bgcolor
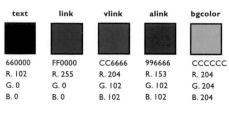				
660000	FF0000	CC6666	996666	CCCCCC
R. 102	R. 255	R. 204	R. 153	R. 204
G. 0	G. 0	G. 102	G. 102	G. 204
B. 0	B. 0	B. 102	B. 102	B. 204

gls01sw

text	link	vlink	alink	bgcolor
663366	FF00FF	990099	FFFFFF	CCCCCC
R. 153	R. 255	R. 153	R. 255	R. 204
G. 51	G. 0	G. 0	G. 255	G. 204
B. 153	B. 255	B. 153	B. 255	B. 204

gls02sw

text	link	vlink	alink	bgcolor
333366	0000FF	6666FF	9999FF	CCCCCC
R. 51	R. 0	R. 153	R. 153	R. 204
G. 51	G. 0	G. 153	G. 153	G. 204
B. 102	B. 255	B. 255	B. 255	B. 204

gls03sw

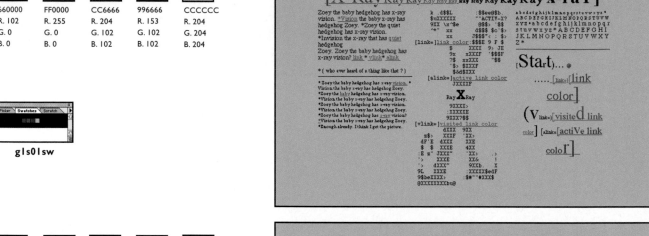

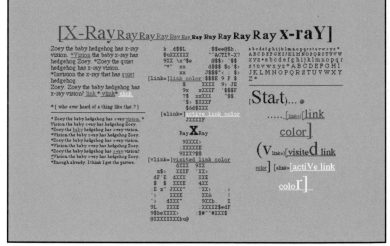

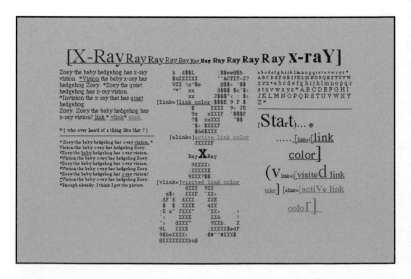

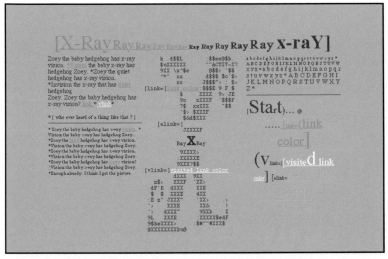

text	link	vlink	alink	bgcolor
336666	009999	FFFFFF	00FFFF	CCCCCC
R. 51	R. 0	R. 255	R. 0	R. 204
G. 102	G. 153	G. 255	G. 255	G. 204
B. 102	B. 153	B. 255	B. 255	B. 204

gls04sw

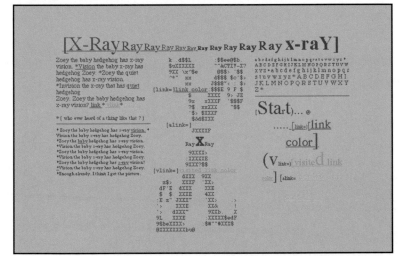

text	link	vlink	alink	bgcolor
336633	006600	00CC00	99CC99	CCCCCC
R. 51	R. 0	R. 0	R. 153	R. 204
G. 102	G. 102	G. 204	G. 204	G. 204
B. 51	B. 0	B. 0	B. 153	B. 204

gls05sw

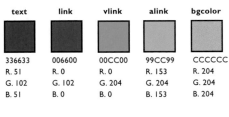

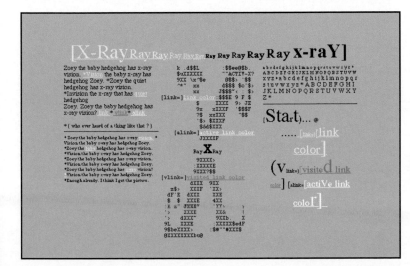

text	link	vlink	alink	bgcolor
333300	FFFFCC	999933	FFFFFF	CCCCCC
R. 51	R. 255	R. 153	R. 255	R. 204
G. 51	G. 255	G. 153	G. 255	G. 204
B. 0	B. 204	B. 51	B. 255	B. 204

gls06sw

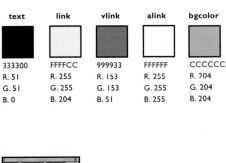

text	link	vlink	alink	bgcolor
333300	FFFF00	CCCC33	FFFF99	999999
R. 51	R. 255	R. 204	R. 255	R. 153
G. 51	G. 255	G. 204	G. 255	G. 153
B. 0	B. 0	B. 51	B. 153	B. 153

g2s01sw

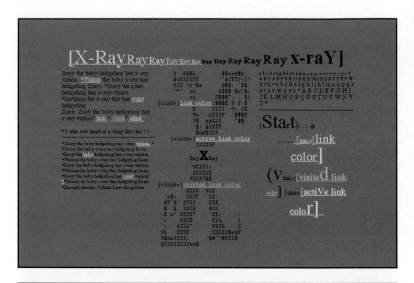

text	link	vlink	alink	bgcolor
FFFFFF	FF00FF	993399	FF66FF	999999
R. 255	R. 255	R. 153	R. 255	R. 153
G. 255	G. 0	G. 51	G. 102	G. 153
B. 255	B. 255	B. 153	B. 255	B. 153

g2s02sw

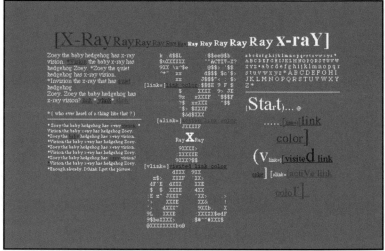

text	link	vlink	alink	bgcolor
663333	FF0000	CC3333	660000	999999
R. 102	R. 255	R. 204	R. 102	R. 153
G. 51	G. 0	G. 51	G. 0	G. 153
B. 51	B. 0	B. 51	B. 0	B. 153

g2s03sw

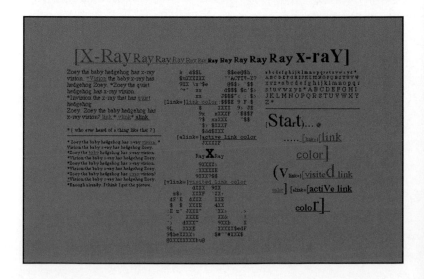

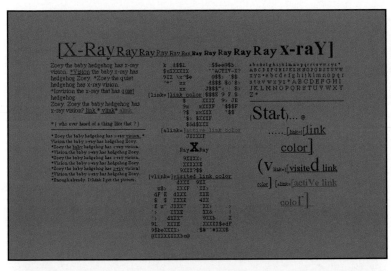

text	link	vlink	alink	bgcolor
333366	0000FF	000066	6666FF	999999
R. 51	R. 0	R. 0	R. 102	R. 153
G. 51	G. 0	G. 0	G. 102	G. 153
B. 102	B. 255	B. 102	B. 255	B. 153

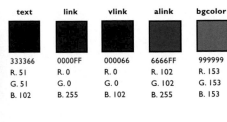

g2s04sw

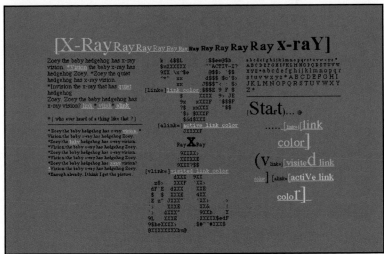

text	link	vlink	alink	bgcolor
003333	00FFFF	66CCCC	99FFFF	999999
R. 0	R. 0	R. 102	R. 153	R. 153
G. 51	G. 255	G. 204	G. 255	G. 153
B. 51	B. 255	B. 204	B. 255	B. 255

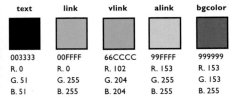

g2s05sw

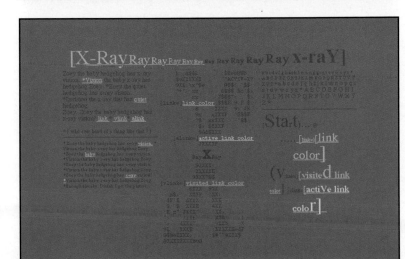

text	link	vlink	alink	bgcolor
006600	99FF99	99CC99	CCFFCC	999999
R. 0	R. 153	R. 153	R. 204	R. 153
G. 102	G. 255	G. 204	G. 255	G. 153
B. 0	B. 153	B. 153	B. 204	B. 153

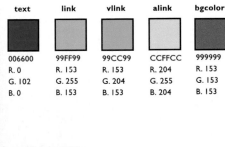

g2s06sw

text	link	vlink	alink	bgcolor
99CCCC	00FFFF	66CCCC	CCFFFF	666666
R. 153	R. 0	R. 102	R. 204	R. 102
G. 204	G. 255	G. 204	G. 255	G. 102
B. 204	B. 255	B. 204	B. 255	B. 102

g3s01sw

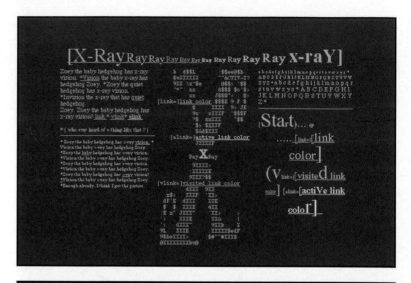

text	link	vlink	alink	bgcolor
99CC99	00FF00	CCFFCC	003300	666666
R. 153	R. 0	R. 204	R. 0	R. 102
G. 204	G. 255	G. 255	G. 51	G. 102
B. 153	B. 0	B. 204	B. 0	B. 102

g3s02sw

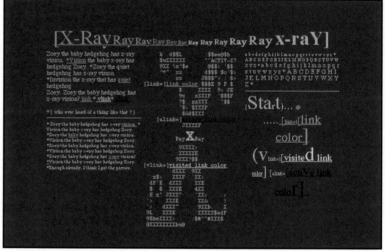

text	link	vlink	alink	bgcolor
CCCC99	FFFF00	FFFF99	999900	666666
R. 204	R. 255	R. 255	R. 153	R. 102
G. 204	G. 255	G. 255	G. 153	G. 102
B. 153	B. 0	B. 153	B. 0	B. 102

g3s03sw

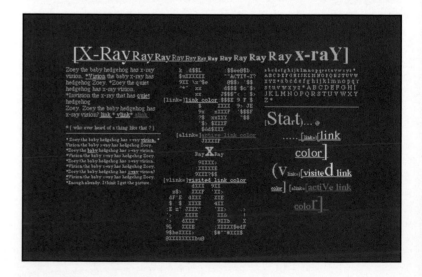

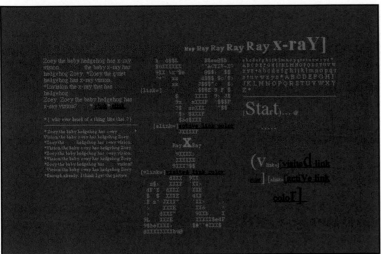

text	link	vlink	alink	bgcolor
FF9999	CC0000	663333	330000	666666
R. 255	R. 204	R. 102	R. 51	R. 102
G. 153	G. 0	G. 51	G. 0	G. 102
B. 153	B. 0	B. 51	B. 0	B. 102

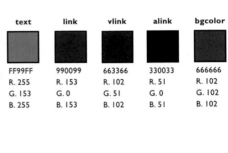

g3s04sw

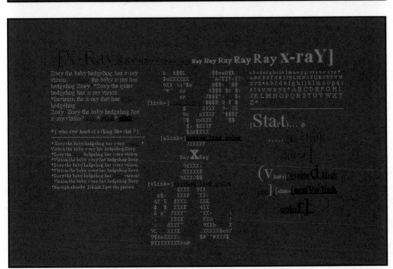

text	link	vlink	alink	bgcolor
FF99FF	990099	663366	330033	666666
R. 255	R. 153	R. 102	R. 51	R. 102
G. 153	G. 0	G. 51	G. 0	G. 102
B. 255	B. 153	B. 102	B. 51	B. 102

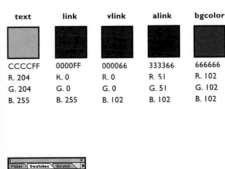

g3s05sw

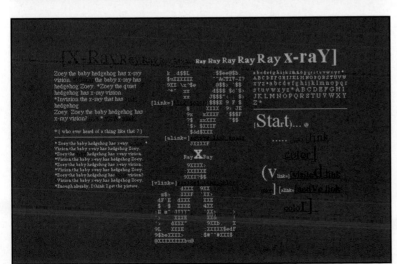

text	link	vlink	alink	bgcolor
CCCCFF	0000FF	000066	333366	666666
R. 204	R. 0	R. 0	R. 51	R. 102
G. 204	G. 0	G. 0	G. 51	G. 102
B. 255	B. 255	B. 102	B. 102	B. 102

g3s06sw

text	link	vlink	alink	bgcolor
669999	00FFFF	66CCCC	CCFFFF	333333
R. 102	R. 0	R. 51	R. 204	R. 51
G. 153	G. 255	G. 204	G. 255	G. 51
B. 153	B. 255	B. 204	B. 255	B. 51

g4s01sw

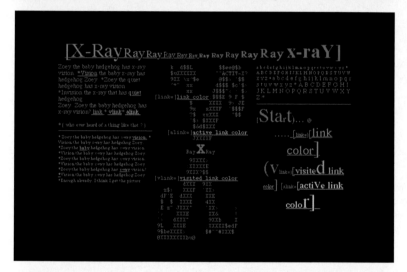

text	link	vlink	alink	bgcolor
669966	33CC33	99CC99	CCFFCC	333333
R. 102	R. 51	R. 153	R. 204	R. 51
G. 153	G. 204	G. 204	G. 255	G. 51
B. 102	B. 51	B. 153	B. 204	B. 51

g4s02sw

text	link	vlink	alink	bgcolor
999966	CCCC33	CCCC99	FFFFCC	333333
R. 153	R. 204	R. 204	R. 255	R. 51
G. 153	G. 204	G. 204	G. 255	G. 51
B. 102	B. 51	B. 153	B. 204	B. 51

g4s03sw

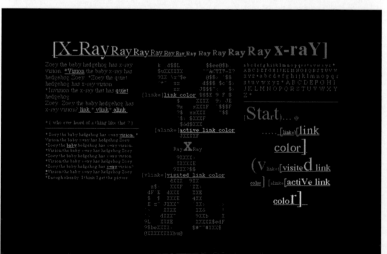

g4s04sw

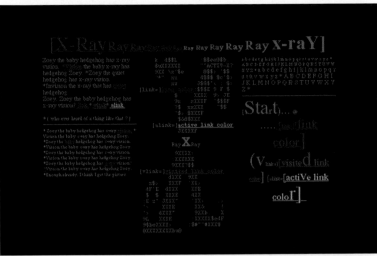

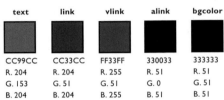

text	link	vlink	alink	bgcolor
CC9999	CC3333	FF6666	FFCCCC	333333
R. 204	R. 204	R. 255	R. 255	R. 51
G. 153	G. 51	G. 102	G. 204	G. 51
B. 153	B. 51	B. 102	B. 204	B. 51

Picker | Swatches | Scratch

g4s04sw

g4s05sw

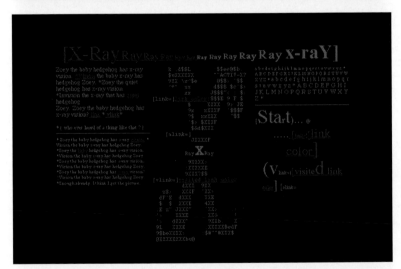

text	link	vlink	alink	bgcolor
CC99CC	CC33CC	FF33FF	330033	333333
R. 204	R. 204	R. 255	R. 51	R. 51
G. 153	G. 51	G. 51	G. 0	G. 51
B. 204	B. 204	B. 255	B. 51	B. 51

Picker | Swatches | Scratch

g4s05sw

g4s06sw

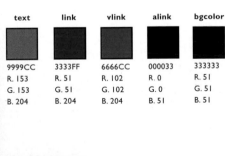

text	link	vlink	alink	bgcolor
9999CC	3333FF	6666CC	000033	333333
R. 153	R. 51	R. 102	R. 0	R. 51
G. 153	G. 51	G. 102	G. 0	G. 51
B. 204	B. 204	B. 204	B. 51	B. 51

Picker | Swatches | Scratch

g4s06sw

text	link	vlink	alink	bgcolor
333333	000000	999999	FFFFFF	CCCCCC
R. 51	R. 0	R. 153	R. 255	R. 204
G. 51	G. 0	G. 153	G. 255	G. 204
B. 51	B. 0	B. 153	B. 255	B. 204

g1s07sw

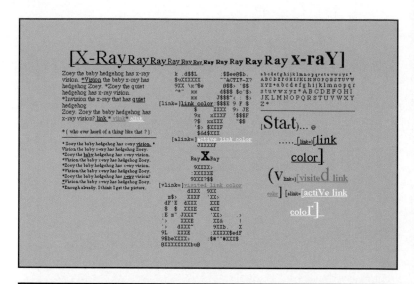

text	link	vlink	alink	bgcolor
333333	000000	666666	FFFFFF	999999
R. 51	R. 0	R. 102	R. 255	R. 153
G. 51	G. 0	G. 102	G. 255	G. 153
B. 51	B. 0	B. 102	B. 255	B. 153

g2s07sw

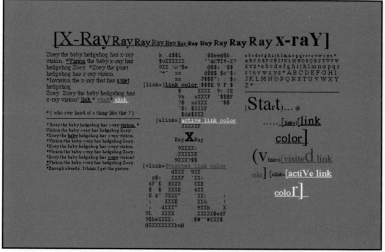

text	link	vlink	alink	bgcolor
FFFFFF	000000	999999	CCCCCC	666666
R. 255	R. 0	R. 153	R. 204	R. 102
G. 255	G. 0	G. 153	G. 204	G. 102
B. 255	B. 0	B. 153	B. 204	B. 102

g3s07sw

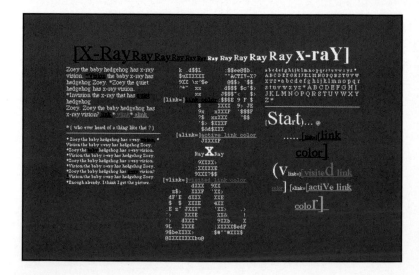

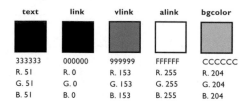

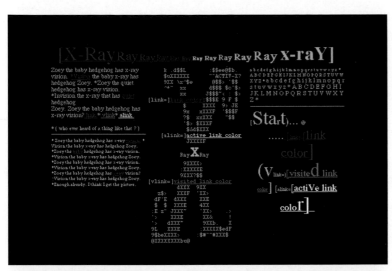

text	link	vlink	alink	bgcolor
CCCCCC	666666	999999	FFFFFF	333333
R. 204	R. 102	R. 153	R. 255	R. 51
G. 204	G. 102	G. 153	G. 255	G. 51
B. 204	B. 102	B. 153	B. 255	B. 51

g4s07sw

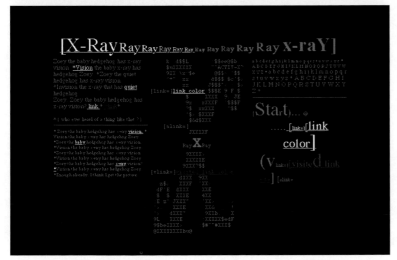

text	link	vlink	alink	bgcolor
999999	FFFFFF	666666	333333	000000
R. 153	R. 255	R. 102	R. 51	R. 0
G. 153	G. 255	G. 102	G. 51	G. 0
B. 153	B. 255	B. 102	B. 51	B. 0

ks07sw

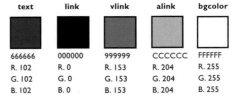

text	link	vlink	alink	bgcolor
666666	000000	999999	CCCCCC	FFFFFF
R. 102	R. 0	R. 153	R. 204	R. 255
G. 102	G. 0	G. 153	G. 204	G. 255
B. 102	B. 0	B. 153	B. 204	B. 255

ws07sw

text	link	vlink	alink	bgcolor
996666	FF0000	663333	FF9999	FFFFFF
R. 153	R. 255	R. 102	R. 255	R. 255
G. 102	G. 0	G. 51	G. 153	G. 255
B. 102	B. 0	B. 51	B. 153	B. 255

ws01sw

text	link	vlink	alink	bgcolor
996699	990099	663366	FF00FF	FFFFFF
R. 153	R. 153	R. 102	R. 255	R. 255
G. 102	G. 0	G. 51	G. 0	G. 255
B. 153	B. 153	B. 102	B. 255	B. 255

ws02sw

text	link	vlink	alink	bgcolor
666699	3333FF	333366	0000CC	FFFFFF
R. 102	R. 51	R. 51	R. 0	R. 255
G. 102	G. 51	G. 51	G. 0	G. 255
B. 153	B. 255	B. 102	B. 204	B. 255

ws03sw

text	link	vlink	alink	bgcolor
336666	009999	66CCCC	00FFFF	FFFFFF
R. 51	R. 0	R. 102	R. 0	R. 255
G. 102	G. 153	G. 204	G. 255	G. 255
B. 102	B. 153	B. 204	B. 255	B. 255

ws04sw

text	link	vlink	alink	bgcolor
669966	009900	336633	00FF00	FFFFFF
R. 102	R. 0	R. 51	R. 0	R. 255
G. 153	G. 153	G. 102	G. 255	G. 255
B. 102	B. 0	B. 51	B. 0	B. 255

ws05sw

text	link	vlink	alink	bgcolor
999966	CCCC00	666633	FFFF66	FFFFFF
R. 153	R. 204	R. 102	R. 255	R. 255
G. 153	G. 204	G. 102	G. 255	G. 255
B. 102	B. 0	B. 51	B. 102	B. 255

ws06sw

ODDBALL

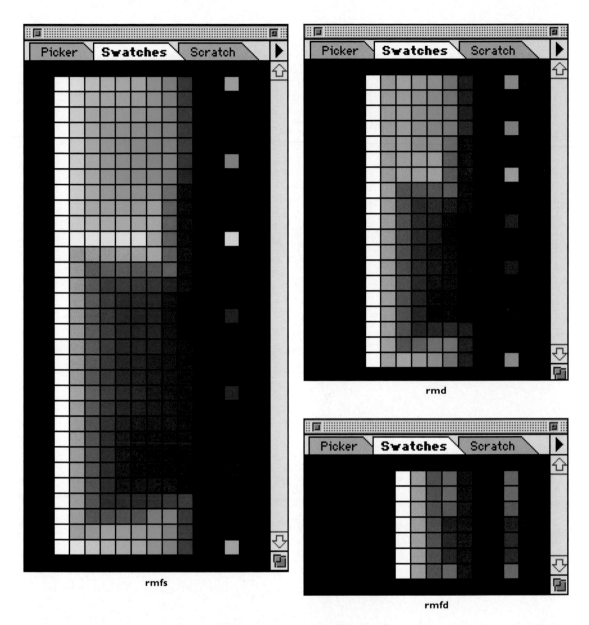

rmfs

rmd

rmfd

The oddball swatches compose all the colors of the cube, organized in different ways. Load these palettes when you don't have an exact color scheme in mind—you'll find they help organize the colors into workable relationships.

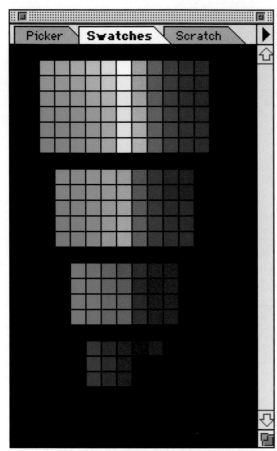

odd22

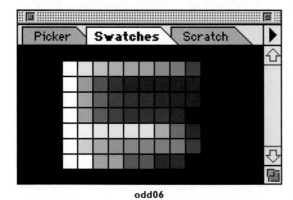

odd06

odd05

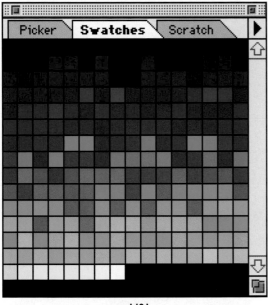

odd01

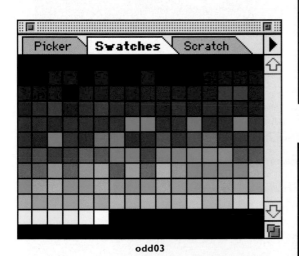

odd03

odd02

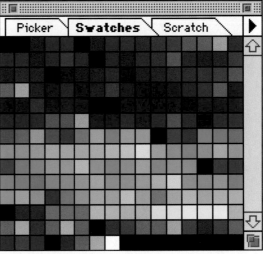

odd04

huesw

lumsw

The **huesw** and **lumsw** files match the browser-safe color charts at the end of Chapter 3, "Browser-Safe Color."

Analagous

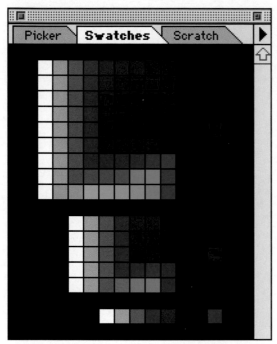

ba

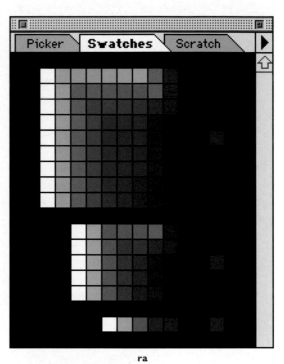

ra

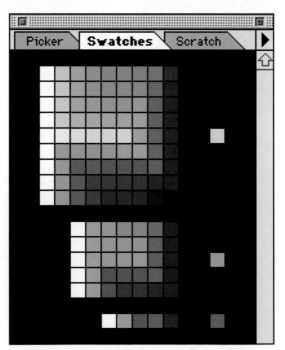

ya

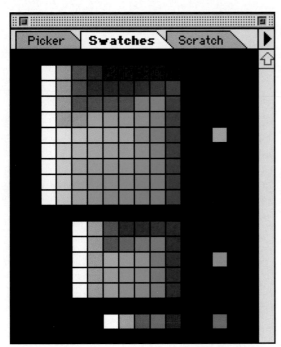

ca

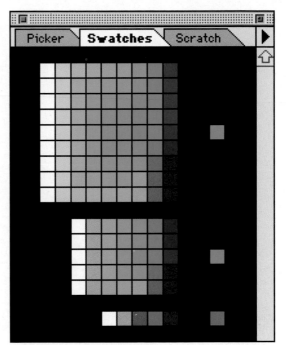

ga

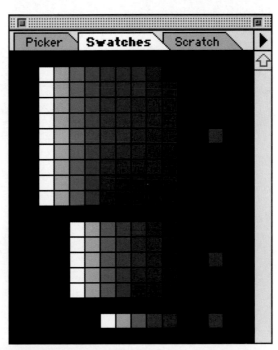

ma

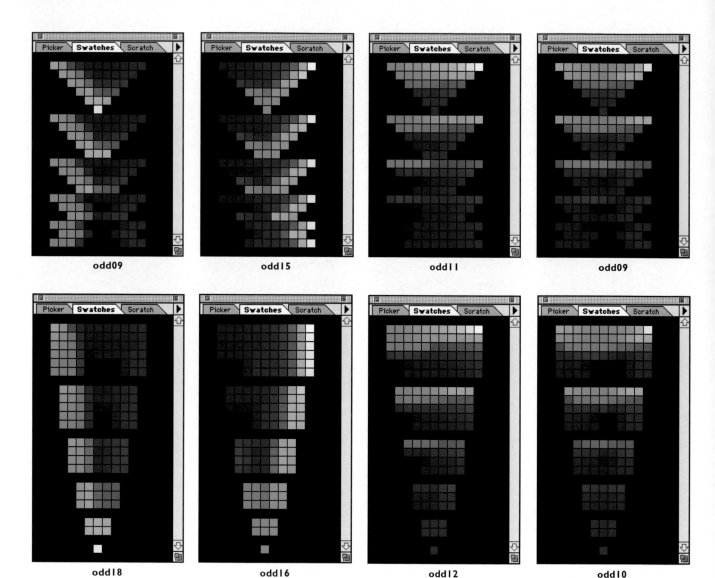

odd09

odd15

odd11

odd09

odd18

odd16

odd12

odd10

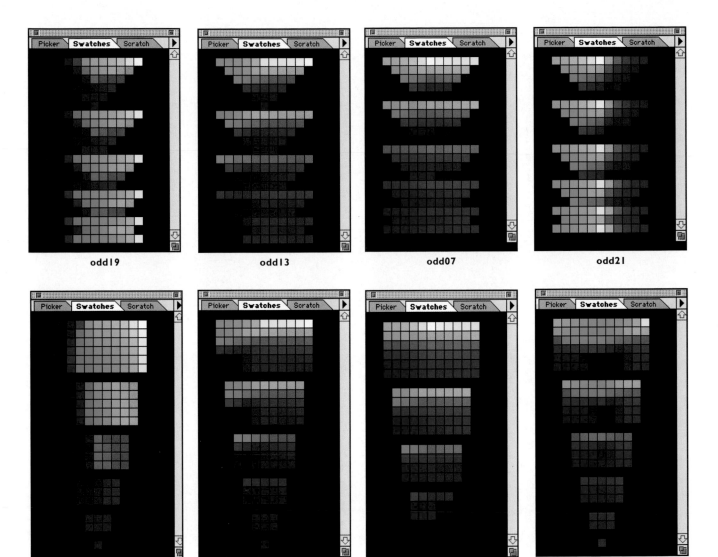

odd19 odd13 odd07 odd21

odd20 odd14 odd08 odd10

Clipart

The browser-safe tiles, buttons, and rules included in this chapter are located on the *Coloring Web Graphics* CD-rom inside the CLIPART folder.

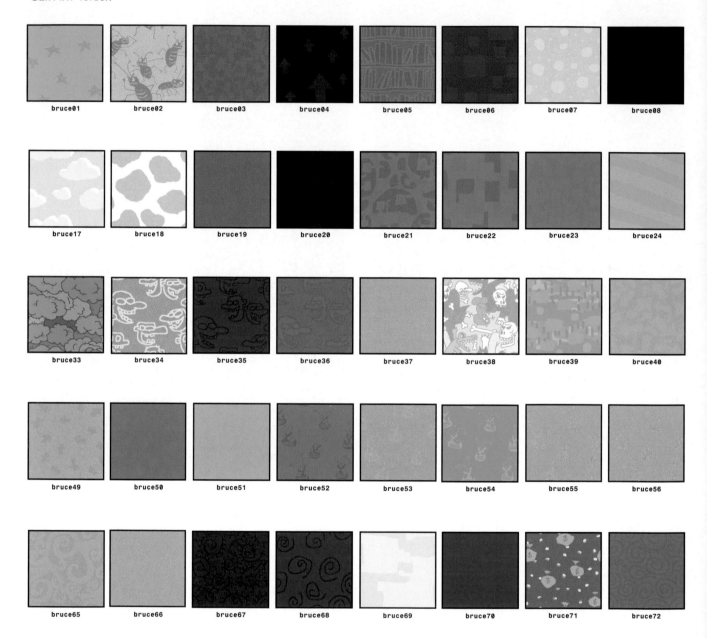

bruce01   bruce02   bruce03   bruce04   bruce05   bruce06   bruce07   bruce08

bruce17   bruce18   bruce19   bruce20   bruce21   bruce22   bruce23   bruce24

bruce33   bruce34   bruce35   bruce36   bruce37   bruce38   bruce39   bruce40

bruce49   bruce50   bruce51   bruce52   bruce53   bruce54   bruce55   bruce56

bruce65   bruce66   bruce67   bruce68   bruce69   bruce70   bruce71   bruce72

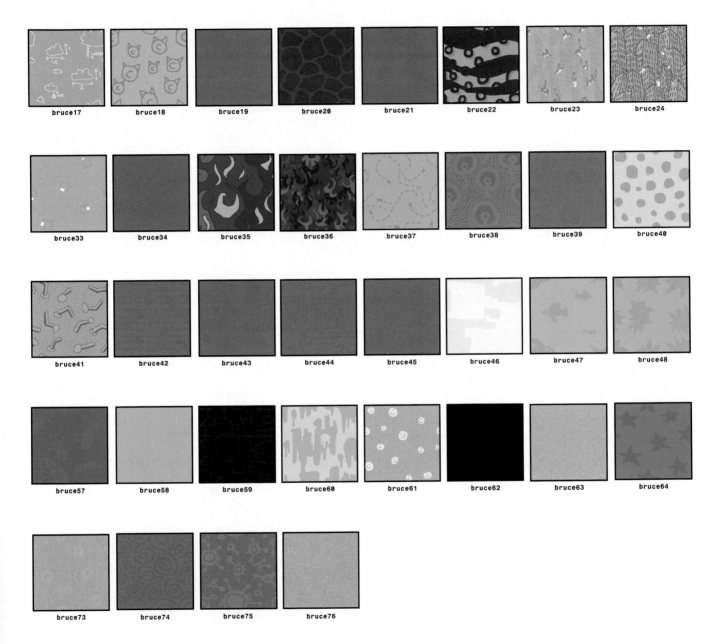

bruce17   bruce18   bruce19   bruce20   bruce21   bruce22   bruce23   bruce24

bruce33   bruce34   bruce35   bruce36   bruce37   bruce38   bruce39   bruce40

bruce41   bruce42   bruce43   bruce44   bruce45   bruce46   bruce47   bruce48

bruce57   bruce58   bruce59   bruce60   bruce61   bruce62   bruce63   bruce64

bruce73   bruce74   bruce75   bruce76

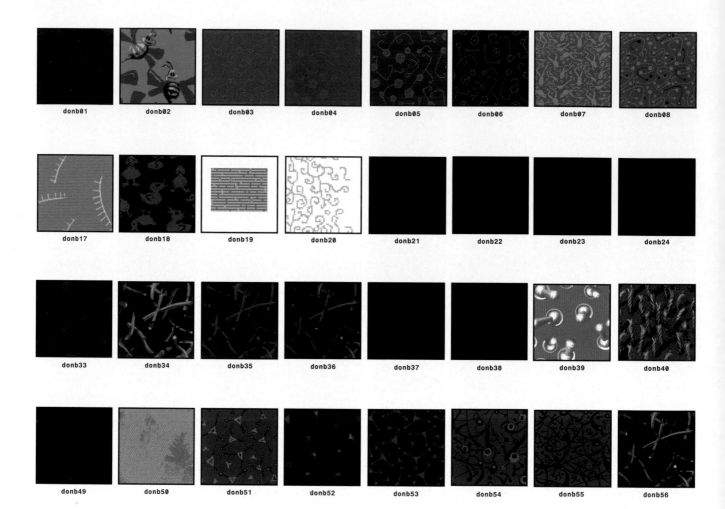

donb01   donb02   donb03   donb04   donb05   donb06   donb07   donb08

donb17   donb18   donb19   donb20   donb21   donb22   donb23   donb24

donb33   donb34   donb35   donb36   donb37   donb38   donb39   donb40

donb49   donb50   donb51   donb52   donb53   donb54   donb55   donb56

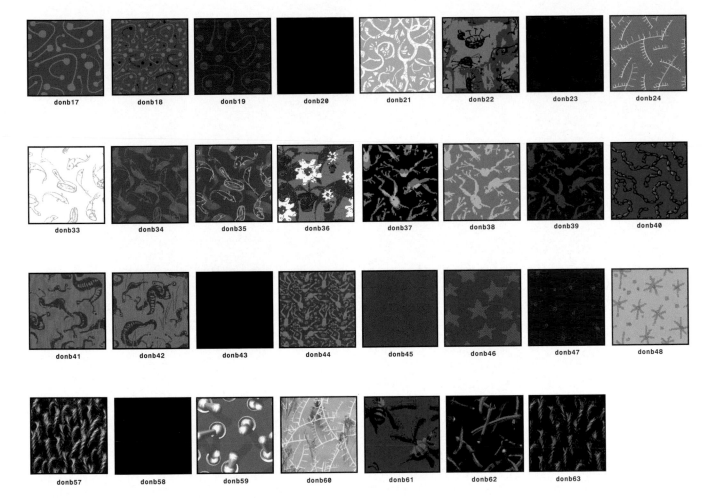

donb17　donb18　donb19　donb20　donb21　donb22　donb23　donb24

donb33　donb34　donb35　donb36　donb37　donb38　donb39　donb40

donb41　donb42　donb43　donb44　donb45　donb46　donb47　donb48

donb57　donb58　donb59　donb60　donb61　donb62　donb63

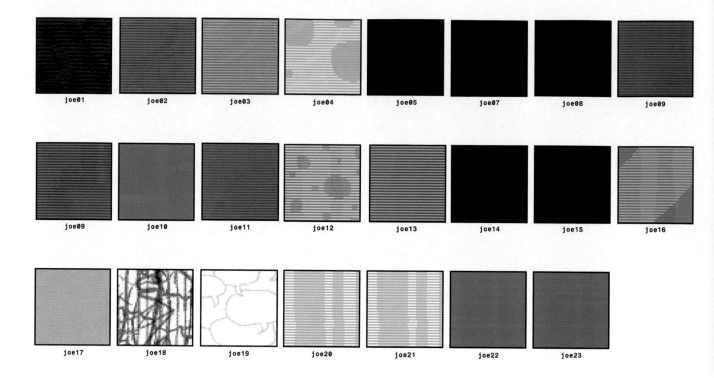

joe01 joe02 joe03 joe04 joe05 joe07 joe08 joe09

joe09 joe10 joe11 joe12 joe13 joe14 joe15 joe16

joe17 joe18 joe19 joe20 joe21 joe22 joe23

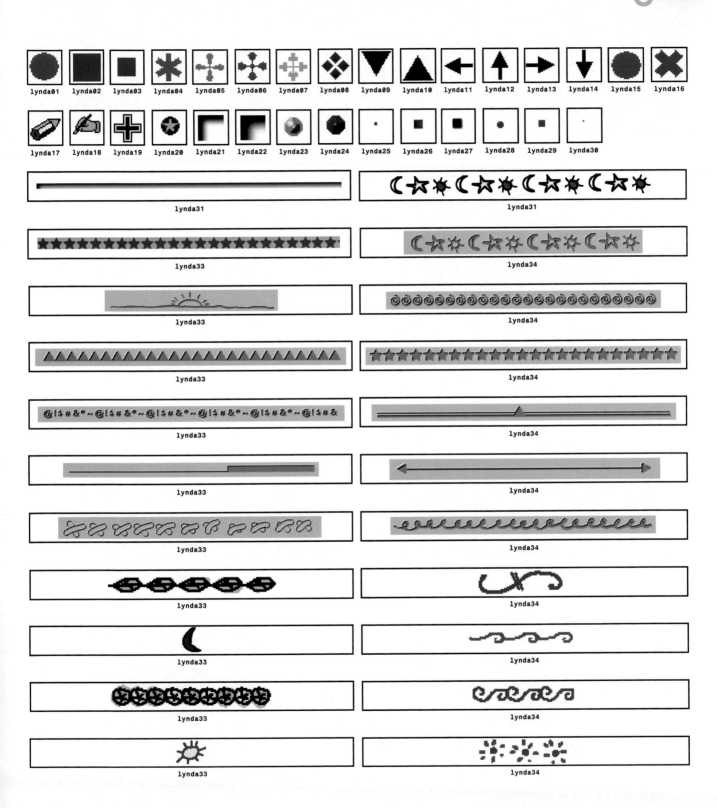

lynda01 lynda02 lynda03 lynda04 lynda05 lynda06 lynda07 lynda08 lynda09 lynda10 lynda11 lynda12 lynda13 lynda14 lynda15 lynda16

lynda17 lynda18 lynda19 lynda20 lynda21 lynda22 lynda23 lynda24 lynda25 lynda26 lynda27 lynda28 lynda29 lynda30

lynda31

lynda31

lynda33

lynda34

lynda33

lynda34

lynda33

lynda34

lynda33

lynda34

lynda33

lynda34

lynda33

lynda34

lynda33

lynda34

lynda33

lynda34

lynda33

lynda34

lynda33

lynda34

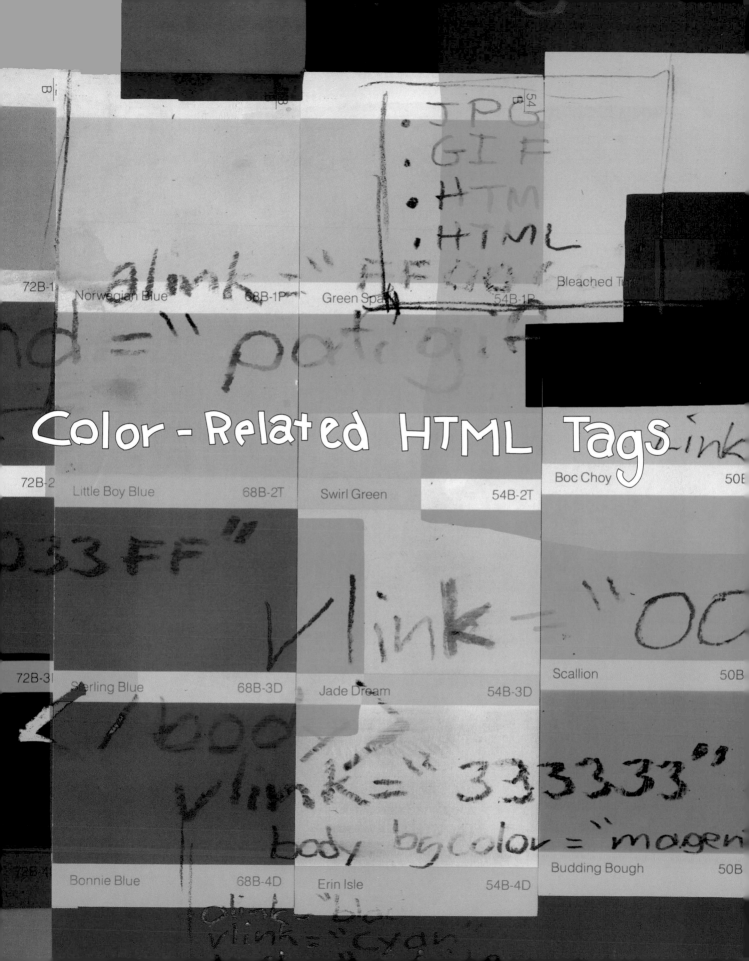

Color - Related HTML Tags

Color-Related HTML Tags

Now for the fun (?) part. How does this all this come together on a Web page? Web pages are written in a low-level programming language called HTML (**H**yper**T**ext **M**arkup **L**anguage). You can write HTML code in a standard text editor, dedicated HTML editor, or WYSIWYG (**W**hat**Y**ou**S**ee**I**s**W**hat**Y**ou**G**et) HTML editor. Some WYSIWYG editors allow you to edit HTML source code directly, and some do not. Because some of the color tags discussed in this chapter may not be supported by WYSIWYG editors, you may have to edit your files later to add the foreign HTML tags. You can always begin a page in a WYSIWYG editor and then later edit the source code in a text editor in order to add additional tags.

The Basic Structure of HTML

HTML code has a basic structure, which dictates where certain markup tags belong. Here is the most basic HTML structure:

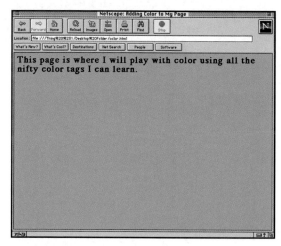

This is a basic Web page with no color added.

1 `<HTML>`
2 `<HEAD>`
3 `<TITLE>Adding Color to My Page</TITLE>`
`</HEAD>`
4 `<BODY>`
5 `<H1>This page is where I will play with color using all the nifty color tags I can learn. </H1>`
`</BODY>`
`</HTML>`

1 `<HMTL>, </HTML>` An HTML document must open and close with this identifying tag.

2 `<HEAD>,</HEAD>` Header information, such as the title of the document, must open and close with this tag.

3 `<TITLE>, </TITLE>` is where you name the title of your HTML document. If you leave this undone, the document will appear as Untitled in Web browsers.

4 `<BODY>,</BODY>` The body of the document, such as text, images, links, and multimedia content, goes in between these opening and closing tags.

5 `<H1>, </H1>` A header tag for first-level headers. In some browsers, this causes the text contained within it to be sized larger than normal text and to be bold.

Adding Color to a Web Page

To add variety within HTML, you include special tags called attributes. Attributes modify the existing material; applying italic to text is an example of using an attribute. When used in HTML, attributes are nested within their parent tags. So, to add color to the body text, you would place the attribute within the <BODY> tag. To add color to the page in our example, you would add the following HTML code:

Color was added to this page using hexadecimal RGB values and attributes of BGCOLOR and TEXT placed within the <BODY> tag.

```
    <HTML>
    <HEAD>
    <TITLE>Adding Color to my Page</TITLE>
1   </HEAD>
    <BODY BGCOLOR="330033"
    LINK="ccccff"
    VLINK="ccffcc"
    ALINK="66ffcc"
    TEXT="cc66cc">
    <H1>
    This<A
    HREF="http://www.lynda.com/">page</A>
    is where I will play
    <A HREF="http://color.com/">color</A>
    using all the
    <A HREF="www.bearheart.net">nifty </A>
    color tags I can learn.
    </H1>
    </BODY>
    </HTML>
```

1 BGCOLOR, LINK, VLINK, ALINK, and TEXT are attributes that are nested inside the <BODY> tag. Here's a list of possible attributes that relate to color within the <BODY> tag:

BGCOLOR	Color of the background of the Web page
TEXT	Color of the text
LINK	Color of the link
VLINK	Color of the link after it has been visited
ALINK	Color of the active link while the mouse is depressed on a link

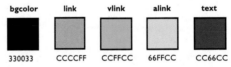

bgcolor	link	vlink	alink	text
330033	CCCCFF	CCFFCC	66FFCC	CC66CC

Each of these color chips represents the hexadecimal color used in the example on this page.

Using Color Names Instead of Hex

You don't have to use hexadecimal numbers inside the color attribute tags; you can use words, too. Here's a list of color names that will work in Netscape.

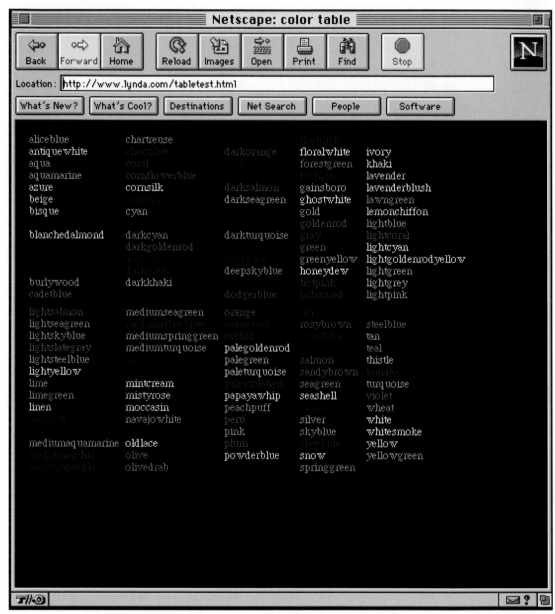

Using any of the names inside the color attribute tags will generate colored text in Netscape.

Here's an example of using color names instead of hexadecimal values to define color.

```
<HTML>
<HEAD>
<TITLE>Adding Color to My Page</TITLE>
</HEAD>
```
1 `<BODY BGCOLOR="lightgreen"`
```
TEXT="darkgreen">
<H1>This page is where I will play
with color using all the nifty color
tags I can learn.
</H1>
</BODY>
</HTML>
```

1 You don't have to use hexadecimal numbers to define color—certain color names work as well. Here's an example of using "lightgreen" and "darkgreen" as color names within the <BODY> tag.

Warning: Color Names Are Rarely Browser Safe

Here are charts showing how the color names translate to hex values. Notice how very few of them are browser safe. Since browsers, when viewed in 256 colors, will convert the color names to their own palettes on the fly, we also show a column of numbers that refers to how the browser-safe colors round up or down in a 256-color environment. In some cases the colors round off differently on Macs and PCs. The few existing browser-safe colors are highlighted as well. Note: for the purpose of this demonstration, we have chosen the abbreviation "B-S" to represent the term browser-safe.

B-S	Color Name	HEX 24-bit Mac/PC	256 MAC	256 PC
	aliceblue	F0F8FF	99CC00	99CC00
	antiquewhite	FAEBD7	FFFFCC	FFFFCC
■	**aqua**	**00FFFF**	**00FFFF**	**00FFFF**
	aquamarine	7FFFD4	66FFCC	66FFCC
	azure	F0FFFF	FFFFFF	FFFFFF
	beige	F5F5DC	FFFFCC	FFFFCC
	bisque	FFE4C4	FFFFCC	FFCCCC
■	**black**	**000000**	**000000**	**000000**
	blanchedalmond	FFEBCD	FFFFCC	FFFFCC
■	**blue**	**0000FF**	**0000FF**	**0000FF**
	blueviolet	8A2BE2	9933FF	9933CC
	brown	A52A2A	993333	993333
	burlywood	DEB887	CCCC99	CCCC99
	cadetblue	5F9EA0	669999	669999
	chartreuse	7FFF00	66FF00	66FF00
	chocolate	D2691E	CC6600	CC6633
	coral	FF7F50	FF6666	FF6666
	cornflowerblue	6495ED	6699FF	6699FF
	cornsilk	FFF8DC	FFFFCC	FFFFCC
	crimson	DC143C	CC0033	CC0033
■	**cyan**	**00FFFF**	**00FFFF**	**00FFFF**
	darkblue	00008B	000099	000099
	darkcyan	008B8B	009999	009999
	darkgoldenrod	B8860B	CC9900	CC9900
	darkgray	A9A9A9	CC00FF	CC00CC
	darkgreen	006400	006600	006600
	darkkhaki	BDB76B	CCCC66	CCCC66
	darkmagenta	8B008B	990099	990099
	darkolivegreen	556B2F	666633	666633
	darkorange	FF8C00	FF9900	FF9900
	darkorchid	9932CC	9933CC	9933CC
	darkred	8B0000	990000	990000
	darksalmon	E9967A	FF9966	FF9966
	darkseagreen	8FBC8F	99CC99	99CC99
	darkslateblue	483D8B	333399	333399
	darkslategray	2F4F4F	333333	336666
	darkturquoise	00CED1	00CCCC	00CCCC

B-S	Color Name	HEX 24-bit Mac/PC	256 MAC	256 PC
	darkviolet	9400D3	9900CC	9900CC
	deeppink	FF1493	FF0099	FF0099
	deepskyblue	00BFFF	00CCFF	00CCFF
	dimgray	696969	666666	666666
	dodgerblue	1E90FF	0099FF	3399FF
	firebrick	B22222	CC3333	993333
	floralwhite	FFFAF0	FFFFFF	FFFFFF
	forestgreen	228B22	339933	339933
■	**fuchsia**	**FF00FF**	**FF00FF**	**FF00FF**
	gainsboro	DCDCDC	CCCCCC	CCCCCC
	ghostwhite	F8F8FF	FFFFFF	FFFFFF
	gold	FFD700	FFCC00	FFCC00
	goldenrod	DAA520	CC9933	CC9933
	gray	808080	999999	999999
	green	008000	009900	009900
	greenyellow	ADFF2F	99FF33	99FF33
	honeydew	F0FFF0	FFFFFF	FFFFFF
	hotpink	FF69B4	FF66CC	FF66CC
	indianred	CD5C5C	CC6666	CC6666
	indigo	4B0082	330099	330099
	ivory	FFFFF0	FFFFFF	FFFFFF
	khaki	F0E68C	FFFF99	FFFF99
	lavender	E6E6FA	FFFFFF	FFFFFF
	lavenderblush	FFF0F5	FFFFFF	FFFFFF
	lawngreen	7CFC00	66FF00	66FF00
	lemonchiffon	FFFACD	FFFFCC	FFFFCC
	lightblue	ADD8E6	99CCFF	99CCFF
	lightcoral	F08080	FF9999	FF9999
	lightcyan	E0FFFF	FFFFFF	CCFFFF
	lightgoldenrodyellow	FAFAD2	FFFFCC	FFFFCC
	lightgreen	90EE90	99FF99	99FF99
	lightgrey	D3D3D3	CCCCCC	CCCCCC
	lightpink	FFB6C1	FFCCCC	FFCCCC
	lightsalmon	FFA07A	FF9966	FF9966
	lightseagreen	20B2AA	33CC99	339999
	lightskyblue	87CEFA	99CCFF	99CCFF
	lightslategray	778899	669999	669999

B-S	Color Name	HEX 24-bit Mac/PC	256 MAC	256 PC
	lightsteelblue	B0C4DE	CCCCCC	99CCCC
	lightyellow	FFFFE0	FFFFFF	FFFFFF
■	**lime**	**00FF00**	**00FF00**	**00FF00**
	limegreen	32CD32	33CC33	33CC33
	linen	FAF0E6	FFFFFF	FFFFFF
■	**magenta**	**FF00FF**	**FF00FF**	**FF00FF**
	maroon	800000	990000	990000
	mediumaquamarine	66CDAA	66CC99	66CC99
	mediumblue	0000CD	0000CC	0000CC
	mediumorchid	BA55D3	CC66CC	CC66CC
	mediumpurple	9370DB	9966CC	9966CC
	mediumseagreen	3CB371	33CC66	33CC66
	mediumslateblue	7B68EE	6666FF	6666FF
	mediumspringgreen	00FA9A	00FF99	00FF99
	mediumturquoise	48D1CC	33CCCC	33CCCC
	mediumvioletred	C71585	CC0099	CC0099
	midnightblue	191970	000066	000066
	mintcream	F5FFFA	FFFFFF	FFFFFF
	mistyrose	FFE4E1	FFFFFF	FFFFFF
	moccasin	FFE4B5	FFFFCC	FFFFCC
	navajowhite	FFDEAD	FFCC99	FFCC99
	navy	000080	000099	000099
	oldlace	FDF5E6	FFFFFF	FFFFFF
	olive	808000	999900	999900
	olivedrab	6B8E23	669933	669933
	orange	FFA500	FF9900	FF9900
	orangered	FF4500	FF3300	FF3300
	orchid	DA70D6	CC66CC	CC66CC
	palegoldenrod	EEE8AA	FFFF99	FFFF99
	palegreen	98FB98	99FF99	99FF99
	paleturquoise	AFEEEE	99FFFF	99FFFF
	palevioletred	DB7093	CC6699	CC6699
	papayawhip	FFEFD5	FFFFCC	FFFFCC
	peachpuff	FFDAB9	FFCCCC	FFCCCC
	peru	CD853F	CC9933	CC9933
	pink	FFC0CB	FFCCCC	FFCCCC
	plum	DDA0DD	CC99CC	CC99CC

B-S	Color Name	HEX 24-bit Mac/PC	256 MAC	256 PC
	powderblue	B0E0E6	CCFFFF	99CCFF
	purple	800080	990099	990099
■	**red**	**FF0000**	**FF0000**	**FF0000**
	rosybrown	BC8F8F	CC9999	CC9999
	royalblue	4169E1	3366FF	3366CC
	saddlebrown	8B4513	993300	993300
	salmon	FA8072	FF9966	FF9966
	sandybrown	F4A460	FF9966	FF9966
	seagreen	2E8B57	339966	339966
	seashell	FFF5EE	FFFFFF	FFFFFF
	sienna	A0522D	996633	996633
	silver	C0C0C0	CCCCCC	CCCCCC
	skyblue	87CEEB	99CCFF	99CCFF
	slateblue	6A5ACD	6666CC	6666CC
	slategray	708090	669999	669999
	snow	FFFAFA	FFFFFF	FFFFFF
	springgreen	00FF7F	00FF66	00FF66
	steelblue	4682B4	3399CC	3399CC
	tan	D2B48C	CCCC99	CCCC99
	teal	008080	009999	009999
	thistle	D8BFD8	CCCCCC	CCCCCC
	tomato	FF6347	FF6633	FF6633
	turquoise	40E0D0	33FFCC	33CCCC
	violet	EE82EE	FF99FF	FF99FF
	wheat	F5DEB3	FFCCCC	FFCCCC
■	**white**	**FFFFFF**	**FFFFFF**	**FFFFFF**
	whitesmoke	F5F5F5	FFFFFF	FFFFFF
■	**yellow**	**FFFF00**	**FFFF00**	**FFFF00**
	yellowgreen	9ACD32	99CC33	99CC33

Coloring Individual Lines of Text

You can also assign specific colors to individual lines of text by using the <FONT> tag. Here's some sample code:

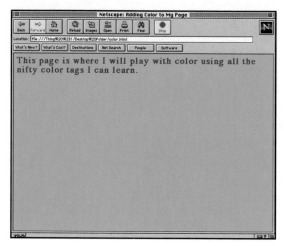

Here's an example of using the <FONT> tag to insert color attributes so that individual words or letters can be colored.

```
<HTML>
<HEAD>
<TITLE>Adding Color to My Page</TITLE>
</HEAD>
<BODY BGCOLOR="660099"
TEXT="CCCCFF">
<H1>This page is where I
<FONT COLOR="99FFFF">will </FONT>
<FONT COLOR="CCFF99">play </FONT>
<FONT COLOR="CC99CC">with</FONT>
<FONT COLOR="CC0000">color </FONT>
using all the nifty color tags I can
learn.
</H1>
</BODY>
</HTML>
```

1 The <FONT> tag can contain a color attribute, which can be specified using color names or hex numbers. It must be closed with a </FONT> tag each time you want the specific colored text attribute to end.

Coloring Links

Link color can affect the border color around linked images or the color of linked text. Here's an example of how to set this up in an HTML document.

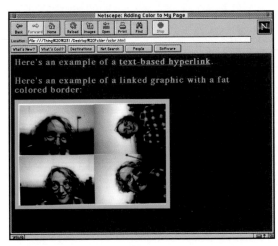

Here's an example of creating colored links. The border around the graphic was made wider with the BORDER attribute.

1 The LINK attribute within the <BODY> tag establishes the color for the linked text or graphic. The <A HREF></A> tag is producing linked text.

2 The IMG SRC tag inserts an image, and the BORDER attribute enables you to set a width for the border, measured in pixels. Note: If you don't want a border, you can set this to BORDER=0.

```
<HTML>
<HEAD>
<TITLE>Adding Color to My Page</TITLE>
</HEAD>
<BODY
BGCOLOR="660099"
TEXT="CCCCFF"
LINK="CCFF00">
<H1>Here's an example of a <a
href="http://www.stinkabod.com">text-based
hyperlink</a>
<p>
Here's an example of a linked graphic with
a fat, colored border: </H1>
<p>
<a href="http://www.stinkabod.com"><img
src="fourlynda.gif" border=10></a>
</BODY>
</HTML>
```
(markers **1** appears at the TEXT="CCCCFF" line and **2** appears at the `<a href="http://www.stinkabod.com"><img` line)

Inserting a Background Image

Chapter 2, "Browser-Safe Color," shows how to insert a hybrid-safe tile into a page. That same technique will work for a solid color background tile or a pattern tile. Here's how to set up this technique:

Here's an example of inserting a background image. You can insert a solid color image, a hybrid color image, a repeating tile image, or a seamless tile image. It's the same code, just a different graphic file!

```
<HTML>
<HEAD>
<TITLE>Adding Color to My Page</TITLE>
</HEAD>
<BODY
```
1 `BACKGROUND="tile.gif"`
```
TEXT="CCCCFF"
LINK="CCFF00">
<center>
<a href="http://www.stinkabod.com"><img
src="fourlynda.gif" border=10></a>
<center>
</BODY>
</HTML>
```

1 The BACKGROUND attribute within the <BODY> tag enables you to insert an image into the background of the Web page. This image can be any kind of image (.jpeg or .gif), and could be a solid color, a hybrid color, a seamless tile image, or a repeating tile image.

< coloring

Adding Color to Tables

The BGCOLOR attribute works in table cells as well as the body of the HTML document. Here's some sample code that demonstrates this technique:

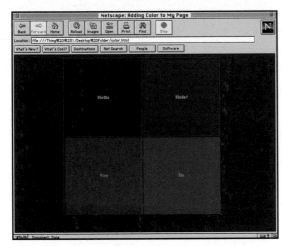

Here's an example of coloring cells within a table, using the BGCOLOR attribute within the <TABLE> tag.

1 The <CENTER> tag instructs the table to be centered in the page.

2 The <TABLE> tag establishes the beginning of the table command. The BORDER attribute assigns an embossed border to the table.

3 <TR> initiates a table row. TH stands for table header. Everything within the <TH> tag will automatically be bold and centered. The BGCOLOR attribute allows a color to be established within the table cell, and can be specified using hexadecimal color or color names. The HEIGHT and WIDTH tags assign dimensions to the table cells, using pixel-based measurements. The ALIGN=middle attribute centers the text within the table cells.

```
<HTML>
<HEAD>
<TITLE>Adding Color to My Page</TITLE>
</HEAD>
<BODY BGCOLOR="660099"
TEXT="CCCCFF">
```
1 `<center>`
2 `<table border >`
3
```
<tr><th bgcolor="003366" height=200
width=200>Hello</th>
<th bgcolor="990033" height=200
width=200>Hola!</th>
<tr ><td bgcolor="666600" height=200
width=200 align=middle>You</td><td
bgcolor="996666" height=200width=200
align=middle>Me</td>
</table>
</center>
</BODY>
</HTML>
```

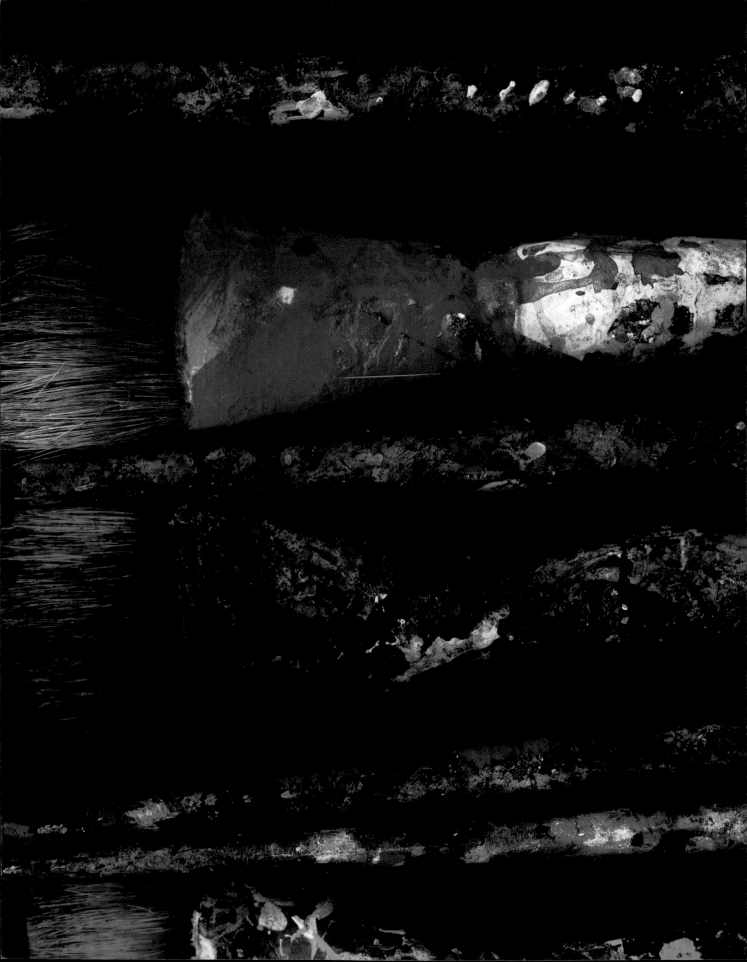

Glossary

Glossary

8-bit graphics: A color or grayscale graphic or movie that has 256 colors or less.

16-bit graphics: A color image or movie that has 65,500 colors.

24-bit graphics: A color image or movie that has 16.7 million colors.

32-bit graphics: A color image or movie that has 16.7 million colors, plus an 8-bit masking channel.

adaptive dithering: A form of dithering in which the program looks to the image to determine the best set of colors when creating an 8-bit or smaller palette. See dithering.

additive color: The term for RGB color space that uses projected light to mix color.

aliasing: In bitmapped graphics, the jagged boundary along the edges of different-colored shapes within an image. See anti-aliasing.

analagous colors: Brackets a color hue on either side of the color wheel.

anti-aliasing: A technique for reducing the jagged appearance of aliased bitmapped images, usually by inserting pixels that blend at the boundaries between adjacent colors.

artifacts: Image imperfections caused by compression.

bit-depth: The number of bits used to represent the color of each pixel in a given movie or still image. Specifically: Bit-depth of 2=black-and-white pixels. Bit-depth of 4=16 colors or grays. Bit-depth of 8=256 colors or grays. Bit-depth of 16=65,536 colors. Bit-depth of 24=(approximately) 16 million colors.

bitmapped graphics: Graphics that are pixel-based, as opposed to object-oriented. Bitmapped graphics are what the computer can display, because it's a pixel-based medium, whereas object-oriented graphics can be viewed in high resolution once they are sent to a printer. Graphics on the Web are bitmapped because they are viewed from a computer screen-based delivery system.

brightness: Adds white or tints an image, whereas lack of brightness adds black or tones an image.

browser: An application that enables you to access World Wide Web pages. Most browsers provide the capability to view Web pages, copy and print material from Web pages, download files over the Web, and navigate throughout the Web.

browser-safe colors: The 216 colors that do not shift between platforms, operating systems, or most Web browsers.

CLUT: Color LookUp Table. An 8-bit or lower image file uses a CLUT to define its palette.

color mapping: A color map refers to the color palette of an image. Color mapping means assigning colors to an image.

complementary colors: Created from opposing color hues on the color wheel.

compression: Reduction of the amount of data required to re-create an original file, graphic, or movie. Compression is used to reduce the transmission time of media and application files across the Web.

contrast: The degree of separation between values.

dithering: The positioning of different-colored pixels within an image that uses a 256-color palette to simulate a color that does not exist in the palette. A dithered image often looks noisy, or composed of scattered pixels. See adaptive dithering.

dpi: Dots Per Inch is a term used mostly by print graphics-based programs and professionals, and is a common measurement related to the resoluton of an image. See screen resolution.

extension: Abbreviated code at the end of a file that tells the browser what kind of file it's looking at. Example: a JPEG file would have the extension .jpg.

fixed palette: An established palette that is fixed. When a fixed palette Web browser views images, it will convert images to its colors and not use the colors from the original.

gamma: Gamma measures the contrast that affects the midtones of an image. Adjusting the gamma lets you change the brightness values of the middle range of gray tones without dramatically altering the shadows and highlights.

gamut: A viewable or printable color range.

GIF: A bitmapped color graphics file format. GIF is commonly used on the Web because it employs an efficient compression method. See JPEG.

GIF89a: A type of GIF file that supports transparency and multi-blocks. Multi-blocks create the illusion of animation. GIF89a files are sometimes referred to as "transparent GIFs" or "animated GIFs."

hexadecimal: A base 16 mathematics calculation, often used in scripts and code. Hexadecimal code is required by HTML to describe RGB values of color for the Web.

HTML: HyperText Markup Language. The common language for interchange of hypertext between the World Wide Web client and server. Web pages must be written using HTML. See hypertext.

hue: Defines a linear spectrum of the color wheel.

hypertext: Text formatted with links that enable the reader to jump among related topics. See HTML.

interlaced GIFs: The GIF file format allows for "interlacing," which causes the GIF to load quickly at low or chunky resolution and then come into full or crisp resolution.

JPEG: Acronym for Joint Photographic Experts Group, but commonly used to refer to a lossy compression technique that can reduce the size of a graphics file by as much as 96 percent. See GIF.

links: Emphasized words in a hypertext document that act as pointers to more information on that specific subject. Links are generally underlined and may appear in a different color. When you click on a link, you can be transported to a different Web site that contains information about the word or phrase used as the link. See hypertext.

lossless compression: A data compression technique that reduces the size of a file without sacrificing any of the original data. In lossless compression, the expanded or restored file is an exact replica of the original file before it was compressed. See compression.

lossy compression: A data compression technique in which some data is deliberately discarded in order to achieve massive reductions in the size of the compressed file.

mask: The process of blocking out areas in a computer graphic.

moiré: A pattern that results when dots overlap.

Postscript: A sophisticated page description language used for printing high-quality text and graphics on laser printers and other high-resolution printing devices.

primary colors: The theory behind primary colors is that these colors are the starting point from which any other colors can be mixed. On the computer, the primary colors are red, green, and blue because color mixing is additive (created with light). With pigment the primary colors are red, blue, and yellow because color mixing is subtractive.

progressive JPEG: A type of JPEG that produces an interlaced effect as it loads, and that can be 30 percent smaller than standard JPEGs. It is not currently supported by many Web browsers.

saturation: Defines the intensity of color.

screen resolution: Screen resolution generally refers to the resolution of common computer monitors. 72 dpi is an agreed upon average, though you will also hear of 96 dpi being the resolution of larger displays.

secondary colors: The colors in between primary colors.

tables: Tables create rows and columns, like in a spreadsheet, and can be used to align data and images.

tag: ASCII text indicators with which you surround text and images to designate certain formats or styles.

transparent GIFs: A subset of the original GIF file format that adds header information to the GIF file, which signifies that a defined color will be masked out.

true color: The quality of color provided by 24-bit color depth. 24-bit color depth results in 16.7 million colors, which is usually more than adequate for the human eye.

value: The range from light to dark in an image.

WYSIWYG: Pronounced wizzy-wig. A design philosophy in which formatting commands directly affects the text displayed on-screen, so that the screen shows the appearance of the printed text.

■ colophon

The preliminary art direction for *Coloring Web Graphics* was sketched on paper. This book was then designed and pro-duced using QuarkXPress, Adobe Photoshop, and Microsoft Word on a Power Macintosh 7100/80. All of the text was set in the Adobe Gill Sans family except for the HTML/CODE, which was set in Macmillan's MCPDigital, and the red square Zapf Dingbats. *Coloring Web Graphics* was printed on 80lb. Influence Soft Gloss paper and was produced digitally using Adobe software. Prepress consisted of Postscript computer-to-plate technology (filmless process) printed by Shepard Poorman, Indianapolis, Indiana. The cover illustration was painted with acrylics and crayons and then drum scanned. *Coloring Web Graphics* was first printed in an edition of twenty thousand copies.

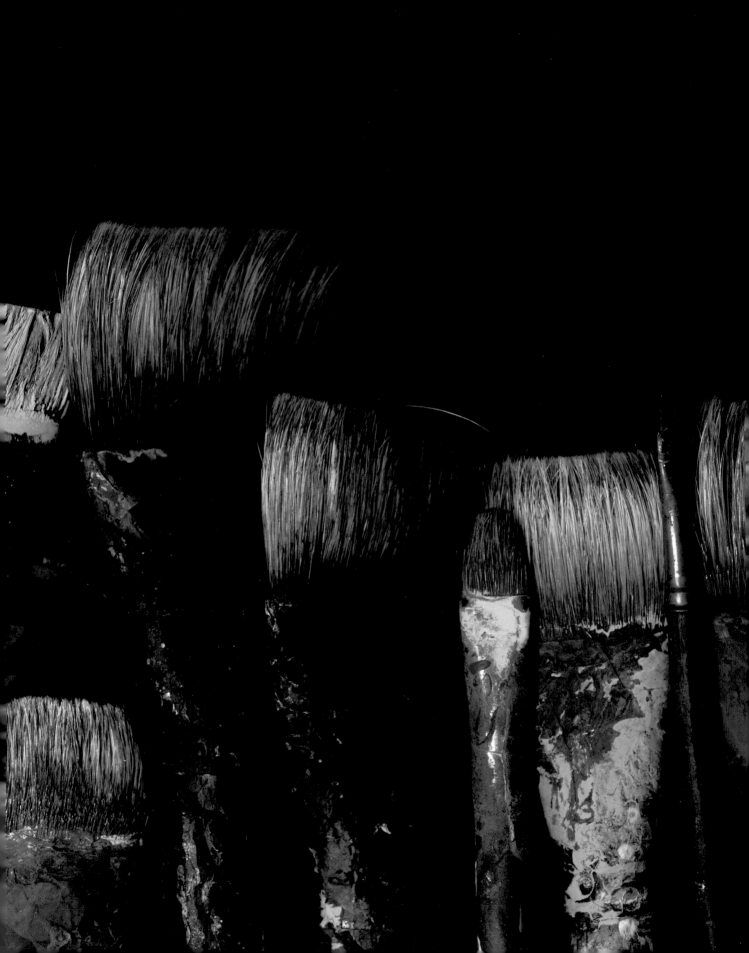

Index

Numbers and Symbols

1-bit transparency, 51
6x6x6 cube, 25
6x6x6 palette, 25
8-bit graphics, 280
8-bit transparency, 51
16-bit graphics, 280
24-bit graphics, 280
32-bit graphics, 280
216clut.cpl file, 81, 98

A

<A HREF>...<\A> tag, 59, 275
.aco file extension, 30, 78, 114-115
adaptive dithering, 280
adaptive palette, 12-13, 44-45, 86
additive color, 280
Adobe Illustrator, 98-99
Adobe PageMill, 101
aliased graphics, 42, 92
aliasing, 280
alpha channel-based transparency, 51
analogous color swatches, 70
analogous colors, 64, 280
animated GIFs, 39, 52-53
    common palette, 94-95, 97
    file sizes, 52
    palette flashing, 94
    references, 52
animation, 39
    streaming, 52
anti-aliased graphics, 42, 92
anti-aliasing, 280
    GIF (Graphics Interchange Format) file format,
    41
Apple Color Picker, 101
artifacts, 280
attributes, 269

B

background images, 276
background tiles with high noise contrast, 67
banding, 12-13
Barnett, Don, 28, 29, 42, 105, 109
batch processing, 97
BBEdit, 101
bclut2.aco file, 90-91
bit-depth, 10-11, 280
    calculation of, 10
    monitors, 14-15
bitmapped graphics, 98, 280
black-and-white monitor contrast, 67
blended color sets, 114
<body background> tag and hybrid color files, 29
<BODY>...<\BODY> tag, 268
    ALINK attribute, 269
    BACKGROUND attribute, 29, 276
    BGCOLOR attribute, 269
    color names, 271
    LINK attribute, 269, 275
    TEXT attribute, 269
    VLINK attribute, 269
Boutell, Thomas, 93
brightness, 65, 67, 280
browser-safe color palette, 25, 44
    full saturation palette, 27
    hexadecimal values, 25
    hybrid-safe colors, 28-29
    low saturation palette, 27
    middle saturation palette, 27
    Paint Shop Pro, 80
    Painter, 82
    PhotoPaint, 81
    Photoshop, 77
    reorganizing, 26-27
    RGB values, 25

browser-safe colors, 20, 24, 280
  applying to existing artwork, 83
  file format conversion and images, 89-90
  GIF (Graphics Interchange Format) file format, 42
  illustration-based artwork color conversion, 22
  limited palette, 21
  organized by hue, 32-33
  organized by luminance, 34-35
  photograph-based artwork, 23
  removing unwanted, 91
  working with, 29
browser-safe swatch set, 78
browsers, 280
  adaptive or nearest color palettes, 45
  converting non-browser-safe colors, 21
  function of, 20
  GIF (Graphics Interchange Format) file format, 39
interlacing, 48

C

calibration, 7
<CENTER> tag, 277
ckrbd.gif file, 103
Claris Homepage, 101
CLUT (Color LookUp Table), 83, 280
clut.bcs file, 100
CMYK (cyan, magenta, yellow, black) color, 6
color
  adding to Web pages, 269
  adding/replacing in swatch set, 78
  analogous, 64
  assigning to images, 83
  brightness, 65
  browser-safe, 20-35
  CMYK (cyan, magenta, yellow, black), 6
  combining hue, value, and saturation, 65
  common within system palettes, 20
  complementary, 64
  computers, 4
  contrast, 65
  converting RGB values to hexadecimal numbers, 16-17
  desaturation, 68
  file formats, 38
  hexadecimal-based values, 21
  hue, 65
  hybrid-safe, 28-29
  intensity measurement, 68
  limited palette, 21
  links, 275
  meaning of, 62
  noise, 69
  patterns, 69
  primary, 64
  pushed in two directions, 65
  relativity of, 71
  RGB (red, blue, green), 6
  saturation, 65, 68
  screen-based, 4-17
  secondary, 64
  shifting, 21
  simulating printing inks, 6
  subtracting in swatch set, 78
  symbolism, 62
  tables, 277
  terminology, 64
  text, 274
  texture, 69
  unifying, 70
  tValue, 65
  Web, 5
color mapping, 280
  GIF (Graphics Interchange Format) file format, 44

color names
  hexadecimal equivalents of, 272-273
  HTML (HyperText Markup Language) and,
    270-271
color picker-based applications, 101
color principles
  children's view of, 63
  meaning of color, 62
color swatches, analogous, 70
Color Wheel, 64
color-related HTML tags, 268-277
color-safe palettes in Macromedia Director, 102
Coloring Web Graphics CD-ROM
  216clut.cpl file, 98
  .aco swatch files, 83
  bclut2.aco file, 90-91
  blended color sets, 114
  browser-safe color files, 29
  browser-safe color palettes, 27
  ckrbd.gif file, 103
  CLIPART folder, 112-113, 115
  CLIPART\BRUCE\TILES folder, 103
  CLIPART\DON\TILES folder, 105
  CLIPART\LICENSOR\BRUCE folder, 115
  CLUT folder, 80, 112-113
  clut.bcs file, 100
  CLUT\PAINTER folder, 82
  CLUT\WIN16 folder, 88
  file organization, 114-115
  ga.aco and ga.gif files, 70
  GIF folder, 30
  hybrid-safe color files, 29
  lines.gif file, 103
  master color palettes, 115
  mini color sets, 114
  PSP folder, 31
  shmancy.gif file, 105
  SWATCH/GIF folder, 79
  Swatches folder, 30, 112-113
  SWATCHES\ACO folder, 77

SWATCHES\BLEND folder, 114
SWATCHES\MASTER folder, 115
SWATCHES\MINI folder, 114
SWATCH\ODDBALL folder, 109
Xray.psd file, 109
ColorWeb, 101
common palette, 94-95
complementary colors, 64, 280
compression, 281
  loseless, 39
  lossy, 55, 89
  LZW (Lempel-Ziv & Welch) compression
    scheme, 39-40
  run-length, 40
computers
  color, 4
  primary colors, 64
contrast, 65, 67, 281
Corel Draw, 98
custom palettes, 86
  Shockwave, 102

D

DeBabelizer, 97
desaturation, 68
dithering, 12-13, 22, 281
  photographs, 46
  screen, 12-13
dpi (dots per inch), 8, 281
DreamWorks Interactive SKG site, 28

E

embedding images and HTML (HyperText Markup
  Language), 59
Exact palette, 86
Excellent GIF transparency tutorial site, 93
extension, 281

F

fast-loading graphics, 38
file extensions for file formats, 59
file formats
   color, 38
   file extensions for, 59
   GIF (Graphics Interchange Format), 38-53
   JPEG (Joint Photographic Experts Group), 38, 54-58
   Web, 38
files and high vs. low resolution, 8-9
fixed palette, 281
<FONT>...<\FONT> tag color attributes, 274
Freehand, 98, 100
full saturation palette, 27

G

ga.aco file, 70
ga.gif file, 70
gamma, 7, 281
   sites for more information on, 7
gamut, 281
GIF (Graphics Interchange Format) file format, 30, 38-53, 281
   animated GIF references, 52
   animated GIFs, 52-53
   animation, 94-95, 97
   anti-aliasing, 41
   bit-depth, 43
   bitmapped artwork, 98
   browser-safe colors, 42
   color mapping, 44
   fewer colors, 41
   GIF87a, 39
   GIF89a, 39
   graphics, 41
   illustration-style imagery, 41-42
   indexed color, 39
   interlaced GIFs, 48-49
   loseless compression, 39

LZW (Lempel-Ziv & Welch) compression
   scheme, 39-40
   masked regions, 50
   photographic imagery, 43-47
   photographs, 41
   popular authoring tools, 52
   precise color control, 90
   reducing colors in Photoshop, 84
   small files, 40, 47
   swatch sets, 79
   transparent GIFs, 50-51, 92-93
Gif Construction Set, 52, 96
gif file extension, 79, 114-115
GIF87a format, 39
GIF89a format, 39, 281
   animated GIFs, 52
   animation, 94
   custom palette handling, 94
GIFBuilder/freeware
   FAQ site, 52
   custom palette, 96
graphics. See also images
   aliased, 42
   animation, 39
   anti-aliased, 42
   banding, 12-13
   bit depth, 10-11
   compression of, 38-53
   deleting border of linked, 59
   dithering, 12-13
   fast-loading, 38
   GIF (Graphics Interchange Format) file format, 41-42
   high vs. low resolution, 8-9
   inserting into HTML page, 59
   interlacing, 39
   linking to another graphic or HTML page, 59
   moire, 13
   number of colors in, 10
   screen resolution, 9
   transparency, 39
   tValue, 65

H

<H1>...<\H1> tag, 268
Heavin, Bruce, 28, 42, 106- 107
hexadecimal numbers, 281
    converting RGB values to, 16-17
hexadecimal-based color values, 21
high vs. low resolution files, 8-9
Homegurrl site, 53
Hot Hot Hot site, 42
HTML (HyperText Markup Language), 281
adding color to Web pages, 269
    attributes, 269
    background images, 276
    color names, 270-271
    color-related tags, 268-277
    coloring individual lines of text, 274
    coloring links, 275
    deleting border of linked image, 59
    embedding images, 59
    hexadecimal equivalents of color names, 272-
    273
    inserting graphics into HTML page, 59
    linking graphics to another graphic or HTML
    page, 59
    structure, 268
    table color, 277
    text editors, 268
HTML (HyperText Markup Language) documents
    active link color, 269
    background color, 269
    body, 268
    first-level headers, 268
    header information, 268
    inserting graphics, 59
    link color, 269
    linking graphics to, 59
    opening and closing tags, 268

    text color, 269
    title, 268
    visted link color, 269
<HTML>...<\HTML> tag, 268
hue, 65, 281
    browser-safe colors organized by, 32-33
hybrid-safe colors, 28
    background tile creation, 103
    coloring tiles, 104
    working with, 29
hypertext, 281

I

illustration-based artwork color conversion, 22
images. See also graphics
    aliased, 92
    anti-aliased, 92
    assigning color to, 83
    background, 276
    brightness, 67
    contrast, 67
    glow, 92
    HTML for embedding, 59
    reading, 66
    relativity of, 73
    remaining browser-safe during file format con-
    version, 89-90
    shadow, 92
    too much color and saturation, 68
    value, 66
    vector-based, 98-100
imaging techniques, 76
    adding/replacing color in swatch set, 78
    CLUT (Color LookUp Table), 83
    Paint Shop Pro, 80
    Painter, 82
    Photo-Paint, 81

reducing colors in GIF files with Photoshop, 84
saving new swatch set, 78
subtracting color in swatch set, 78
swatch sets for other programs, 79
<IMG SCR> tag, 59, 275
interlaced GIFs, 48-49, 281
essential graphics and, 49
transparency, 49
interlacing graphics, 39
Internet Explorer
animated GIFs, 52
GIF (Graphics Interchange Format) file format, 39
palette-management process, 20
progressive JPEGs, 58

J

JPEG, 281
JPEG (Joint Photographic Experts Group) file format, 38, 54-58
bitmapped artwork, 98
decompression and compression, 55
imprecise color information, 89
lossy compression, 55
photographs, 54-55
progressive vs. standard, 58
solid color compression, 55
subtle gradations, 54
time required to decompress, 55
variety of compression levels, 56-57
limited palette, 21
lines.gif file, 103
links, 281
color, 275
logo for tiled background, 108
lossless compression, 39, 282
lossy compression, 55, 89, 282
low saturation palette, 27

luminance, browser-safe colors organized by, 34-35
LZW (Lempel-Ziv & Welch) compression scheme, 39-40

M

Macintosh
changing monitor bit depth, 15
color shifting, 21
monitor factory settings, 7
Monitors control panel, 15
progressive JPEG tools, 58
Sights and Sound control panel, 15
system palette, 20, 44
Macromedia Director, 102
Maller, Joe, 29
mask, 282
master color palettes, 115
middle saturation palette, 27
mini color sets, 114
moire, 13, 282
monitors
average user's, 14
bit-depth, 14-15
calibration, 7
changing bit depth, 15
contrast, 67
dpi (dots per inch), 8
factory settings, 7
gamma, 7
pixels, 6
ppi (pixels per inch), 8
Mosaic
animated GIFs, 52
GIF (Graphics Interchange Format) file format, 39
palette-management process, 20
progressive JPEGs, 58
multiblock GIFs, 52

N

nearest color, 44-45
Netscape Navigator
    animated GIFs, 52
    GIF (Graphics Interchange Format) file format, 39
    HTML color names, 270-271
    palette-management process, 20
    progressive JPEGs, 58
netscape.pal file, 31, 80
noise, 69
    photographs, 46

O

Offset Filter, 106-108
Online Transparent GIF creation site, 93

P

Paint Shop Pro
    custom palettes, 31
    Decrease Color Depth - X Colors dialog box, 88
    default image setting, 9
    dithering, 47
    loading browser-safe palette, 80
    nearest color palette, 44
    netscape.pal file, 80
    netscape.pal palette, 31
    organizing .pal files by palette, 31
    reducing colors in, 88
    RGB color space, 6
Painter, loading browser-safe palette, 82
palette flashing, 94
palettes
    adaptive, 44-45, 86
    browser-safe, 44
    custom, 86
    exact, 86
    nearest color, 44-45
    previous, 86
    system, 86
Park, Yuryeong, 42
patterns, 69
    coloring tiles, 104
PCs
    changing monitor bit depth, 15
    color shifting, 21
    monitor factory settings, 7
    progressive JPEG tools, 58
Photo-Paint, 81, 87, 98
    216clut.cpl file, 81, 98
    converting Corel Draw artwork, 98
    dither types, 87
    loading browser-safe palette, 81
    palette types, 87
    reducing colors in, 87
photograph-based artwork browser-safe colors, 23
photographs
    compression of, 38
    dithering, 46
    GIF (Graphics Interchange Format) file format, 41, 43-47
    JPEG (Joint Photographic Experts Group) file format, 54, 55
    noise, 46
Photoshop
    72 dpi, 9
    aco file extension, 30, 778
    adaptive palette, 44, 86
    adding/replacing color in swatch set, 78
    appending swatch set, 77
    applying browser-safe colors to existing artwork, 83

bclut2.aco file, 90-91
bit-depth of image, 85
CLUT (Color LookUp Table), 83
Color Table dialog box, 83, 94-95
coloring hybrid tiles, 104
coloring pattern tiles, 104
colors used in image, 85
common palettes, 94-95
Custom palette, 30, 86, 90
dither settings, 86
dithering, 47
dithering colors not in palette, 86
Exact palette, 86, 90-91
flat colors to represent colors, 86
hybrid color background tile creation, 103
Indexed Color dialog box, 83-85
JPEG compression settings, 56
loading browser-safe palette into, 77
logo for tiled background, 108
Offset Filter, 106-108
palette settings, 86
PICT file format, 51
Previous palette, 86
previsualizing tiles, 105
previsualizing Web pages, 109
ProJPEG plug-in, 58
reducing colors in GIF files, 84
removing unwanted browser-safe colors, 91
resolution settings, 85
RGB color space, 6, 9
saving new swatch set, 78
screen reduction mode, 85
scripting feature, 97
seamless tile creation, 106-107
shortcuts for filling, 104
subtracting color in swatch set, 78
Swatch palettes, 30
swatch set usage, 77
System palette, 86
TGA file format, 51
uniform pattern dither, 86

pixels, 6
PNG file format site, 51
Postscript, 282
ppi (pixels per inch), 8
previous palette, 86
previsualizing
    tiles, 105
    Web pages, 109
primary colors, 64, 282
programs
Adobe Illustrator, 98-99
Adobe PageMill, 101
BBEdit, 101
Claris Homepage, 101
color picker-based, 101
ColorWeb, 101
Corel Draw, 98
DeBabelizer, 97
Freehand, 100
GIFBuilder, 52, 96
Mosaic, 20, 39, 52, 58
Netscape Navigator, 20, 39, 52, 270-271
Paint Shop Pro, 6, 9, 31, 44, 47, 80, 88
Painter, 82
Photo-Paint, 81, 87, 98
Photoshop, 9, 30, 44, 47, 77-78, 83, 85-86, 90-91,
    94-95, 103-104
Shockwave plug-in, 102
progressive JPEGs, 58, 282
ProJPEG plug-in, 58

R

reading, 66
RGB (red, blue, green) color, 6
    converting values to hexadecimal numbers, 16-17
Rosenthal, Amy, 82, 100
Royal Frazier's site, 52
run-length compression, 40

S

saturation, 65, 68, 282
    relativity of, 71
    varying, 68
screen
    dithering, 12-13
    resolution, 282
screen-based color, 4-6
    banding, 12-13
    bit depth, 10-11
    calibration, 7
    dithering, 12-13
    gamma, 7
    hexadecimal number conversion, 16-17
    high vs. low resolution files, 8-9
    monitor bit depth, 14-15
    pixels, 6
seamless tiles, 106-107
secondary colors, 64, 282
SGI monitor factory settings, 7
shmancy.gif file, 105
Shockwave plug-in, 102
standard JPEGs, 58
streaming animation, 52
super palette, 94-95, 97
swatch sets
    adding/replacing color in, 78
    appending, 77
    GIF files, 79
    other programs, 79
    saving new, 78
    subtracting color in, 78
symbolism and color, 62
system palettes, 20, 86

T

<TABLE>...<\TABLE> tag, 277
    BORDER attribute, 277
tables, 282
    color, 277
tags, 282
text, color, 274
text editors, 268
texture, 69
<TH> tag
    ALIGN=middle attribute, 277
    BGCOLOR attribute, 277
    HEIGHT attribute, 277
    WIDTH attribute, 277
<TITLE>...<\TITLE> tag, 268
<TR> tag, 277
transparent GIFs, 39, 50-51, 282
    1-bit transparency, 51
    8-bit transparency, 51
    common problems with, 92-93
    halos, fringes, or matte lines, 92
    masks, 92
    URLs for, 93
transparent graphics, 39
true color value, 282
tValue, 65

U

unifying colors, 70
user's average monitor, 14

V

value, 66
    relativity of, 71-72
    Web graphics, 66
vector-based artwork
    Adobe Illustrator, 99
    Corel Draw, 98
    Freehand, 100

W

Walter, Chip, 93
Web
 color, 5
 file formats, 38
 speedy graphics, 38
Web pages
 adding color, 269
 previsualizing, 109
Weinman, Jamie, 63
Weinman, Lynda, 29
win16.clut file, 88
Windows 3.1
 changing monitor bit depth, 15
 native palette, 88
 system palette, 20
 win16.clut file, 88
Windows 95
 changing monitor bit depth, 15
 native palette, 88
 system palette, 20
 win16.clut file, 88
WWW FAQ on Transparency site, 93
WYSIWYG, 282

X

Xray.psd file, 109

Here's What People Are Saying About Designing Web Graphics, also by Lynda Weinman:

"No Digital Fluff! Do you need to know it all and know it fast? Then *Designing Web Graphics* is the answer."
-**Russell Brown**, Sr. Creative Director, Adobe Systems, Inc.

"Your book has been incredibly useful for answering questions and providing inspiration. One of my team members made this comment: 'There are a lot of books out there that supposedly will answer all your questions about how to do things for the Web, but Lynda's book actually does!' I just love the logical and concise organization, and thorough discussion of each topic. And the 'Browser CLUT Palette' —that's worth 50 bucks all by itself!"
-**Dave Roh**, Simon & Schuster Elementary Group

"I just picked up your book *Designing Web Graphics*. Although I was already aware of about 75 percent of what your book covers, I still found it VERY, VERY helpful. It is well written and seems to keep in mind the fact that designers will be reading it. So in short, I'd like to thank you for providing me with a tool I can both learn from and hand off to others to help teach them the ins and outs of online design."
-**Dom Moreci**, Monnens-Addis Design

"I just want to let you know that I am sooo glad someone has finally assembled such a complete and useful reference on the subject. As a graphic designer who is increasingly finding himself asked to design graphics for Web sites, I have been feeling my way around in the dark on matters such as color palettes and cross-platform issues. Your book pulls everything together in one place and I will not hesitate to recommend it to colleagues in the same situation as myself."
-**Mark Fitzgerald**

"Your book is excellent!! It rocks!! It was a total lifesaver on my redesign project. Thank you, thank you, thank you!! It was so refreshing to read a book that isn't written by a 'tech-head' who is only interested in technology—you did a wonderful job of giving me not only the details, but also how they fit into the bigger picture and why they matter. I really appreciate writing that puts things in perspective. Your book does an excellent job. Your sense of humor definitely made it a fun read—I can't think of any better title for cross-platform issues than 'Platform Hell!'"
-**Dana Giles**

"I am a designer in the Philadelphia area—new to designing Web stuff—I just bought your book and WOW it is very good! Wish I had had a teacher like you in art school. Anyway, just wanted to say I am enjoying your book and home page—you have a refreshing style (open and fun)."
-**Victoria Land**

"You opened doors to so many problems I was encountering and had nowhere to go for the answers. Your book CLEARLY defines and illustrates every detail. I just can't thank you enough for taking the time for this project."
-**Joan Smith**

"Love the book! You made it easy and gave excellent samples that are easy to learn and expand on."
-**Julie A. Kreiner**, JAK Graphic Solutions, Chicago, IL

Fold Here

BUSINESS REPLY MAIL
FIRST-CLASS MAIL PERMIT NO. 9918 INDIANAPOLIS IN

POSTAGE WILL BE PAID BY THE ADDRESSEE

NEW RIDERS PUBLISHING
201 W 103RD ST
INDIANAPOLIS IN 46290-9058

REGISTRATION CARD

Coloring Web Graphics

Name _____ Title _____

Company _____ Type of business _____

Address _____

City/State/ZIP _____

E-mail/Internet _____ Phone _____

Would you like to be placed on our preferred mailing list?   ❑ yes   ❑ no

Have you used/purchased New Riders books before?   ❑ yes   ❑ no

Where did you purchase this book? Check one.
- ❑ Bookstore chain
- ❑ Wholesale club
- ❑ Independent bookstore
- ❑ College bookstore
- ❑ Computer store
- ❑ Other _____

What influenced your decision to purchase this title? _____

_____

Which of the following operating systems do you use? Check all that apply.
- ❑ Windows 3.x
- ❑ Macintosh
- ❑ Windows 95
- ❑ SGI
- ❑ Windows NT
- ❑ Other _____

What are the names of the software programs you use currently? _____

_____

_____

Which of the following best describes your work environment? Check one.
- ❑ Self-employed
- ❑ Small business
- ❑ Large business

Which of the following do you create/develop for? Check all that apply.
- ❑ Games
- ❑ Print
- ❑ Motion pictures
- ❑ Other
- ❑ Web sites

What online services and Web sites do you visit on a regular basis? _____

_____

What trade shows do you attend? _____

What computer book titles do you consider your most valuable sources of information?

_____

What applications/technologies would you like to see us publish in the future?

_____

LICENSE AGREEMENT

THIS SOFTWARE LICENSE AGREEMENT CONSTITUTES AN AGREEMENT BETWEEN YOU AND NEW RIDERS PUBLISHING, LYNDA WEINMAN, AND BRUCE HEAVIN ("LICENSOR" HEREINAFTER, BOTH JOINTLY AND INDIVIDUALLY). YOU SHOULD CAREFULLY READ THE FOLLOWING TERMS AND CONDITIONS BEFORE OPENING THIS ENVELOPE. COPYING THIS SOFTWARE TO YOUR MACHINE, BREAKING THE SEAL, OR OTHERWISE REMOVING OR USING THE SOFTWARE INDICATES YOUR ACCEPTANCE OF THESE TERMS AND CONDITIONS. IF YOU DO NOT AGREE TO BE BOUND BY THE PROVISIONS OF THIS LICENSE AGREEMENT, YOU SHOULD PROMPTLY DELETE THE SOFTWARE FROM YOUR MACHINE.

TERMS AND CONDITIONS:

1. GRANT OF LICENSE. In consideration of payment of the License Fee, which was a part of the price you paid for this product, LICENSOR grants to you (the "Licensee") a non-exclusive right to use and display this copy of a Software program, along with any updates or upgrade releases of the Software for which you have paid (all parts and elements of the Software as well as the Software as a whole are hereinafter referred to as the "Software") on a single computer only (i.e., with a single CPU) at a single location, all as more particularly set forth and limited below. LICENSOR reserves all rights not expressly granted to you as Licensee in this License Agreement.

2. OWNERSHIP OF SOFTWARE. The license granted herein is not a sale of the original Software or of any copy of the Software. As Licensee, you own only the rights to use the Software as described herein and the magnetic or other physical media on which the Software is originally or subsequently recorded or fixed. LICENSOR retains title and ownership of the Software recorded on the original disk(s), as well as title and ownership of any subsequent copies of the Software irrespective of the form of media on or in which the Software is recorded or fixed. This license does not grant you any intellectual or other proprietary or other rights of any nature whatsoever in the Software.

3. USE RESTRICTIONS. As Licensee, you may use the Software only as expressly authorized in this License Agreement under the terms of paragraph 4. You may physically transfer the Software from one computer to another provided that the Software is used on only a single computer at any one time. You may not: (i) electronically transfer the Software from one computer to another over a network; (ii) make the Software available through a time-sharing service, network of computers, or other multiple user arrangement; (iii) distribute copies of the Software or related written materials to any third party, whether for sale or otherwise; (iv) modify, adapt, translate, reverse engineer, decompile, disassemble, or prepare any derivative work based on the Software or any element thereof; (v) make or distribute, whether for sale or otherwise, any hard copy or printed version of any of the Software nor any portion thereof nor any work of yours containing the Software or any component thereof; (vi) use any of the Software nor any of its components in any other work.

4. THIS IS WHAT YOU CAN AND CANNOT DO WITH THE SOFTWARE. Even though in the preceding paragraph and elsewhere LICENSOR has restricted your use of the Software, the following are the only things you can do with the Software and the various elements of the Software. There are several different kinds of folders in the Software, each containing different materials and different restrictions.

a) THE FOLDER MARKED CLUTS: THE MATERIAL CONTAINED IN THIS FOLDER MAY NOT BE USED IN ANY MANNER WHATSOEVER OTHER THAN TO VIEW THE SAME ON YOUR COMPUTER AND MAY BE USED IN YOUR DESIGN OR OTHER WORK ON YOUR COMPUTER ONLY BUT NOT OTHERWISE. THIS MATERIAL IS SUBJECT TO ALL OF THE RESTRICTION PROVISIONS OF THIS SOFTWARE LICENSE. SPECIFICALLY BUT NOT IN LIMITATION OF THESE RESTRICTIONS, YOU MAY NOT DISTRIBUTE OR TRANSFER THIS PART OF THE SOFTWARE DESIGNATED AS "CLUTS" NOR ANY OF YOUR DESIGN OR OTHER WORK CONTAINING ANY OF THE SOFTWARE DESIGNATED AS "CLUTS" NOR ANY OF YOUR DESIGN OR OTHER WORK CONTAINING ANY SUCH "CLUTS," ALL AS MORE PARTICULARLY RESTRICTED IN THE WITHIN SOFTWARE LICENSE.

b) THE FOLDER MARKED CLIPART\LICENSOR: THE MATERIAL CONTAINED IN THIS FOLDER MAY BE USED ONLY ON YOUR PERSONAL, NON-COMMERCIAL WEB SITE BUT NOT OTHERWISE. YOU MAY NOT OTHERWISE DISTRIBUTE OR TRANSFER IT.

c) THE FOLDER MARKED SWATCHES: THE MATERIAL CONTAINED IN THIS FOLDER MAY NOT BE USED IN ANY MANNER WHATSOEVER OTHER THAN TO VIEW THE SAME ON YOUR COMPUTER AND MAY BE USED IN YOUR DESIGN OR OTHER WORK ON YOUR COMPUTER ONLY BUT NOT OTHERWISE. THIS MATERIAL IS SUBJECT TO ALL OF THE RESTRICTION PROVISIONS OF THIS SOFTWARE LICENSE. SPECIFICALLY BUT NOT IN LIMITATION OF THESE RESTRICTIONS, YOU MAY NOT DISTRIBUTE OR TRANSFER THIS PART OF THE SOFTWARE DESIGNATED AS "SWATCHES" NOR ANY OF YOUR DESIGN OR OTHER WORK CONTAINING ANY OF THE SOFTWARE DESIGNATED AS "SWATCHES" NOR ANY OF YOUR DESIGN OR OTHER WORK CONTAINING ANY SUCH "SWATCHES," ALL AS MORE PARTICULARLY RESTRICTED IN THE WITHIN SOFTWARE LICENSE.

d) THE FOLDER MARKED CLIPART\3rd PARTY: THE MATERIAL CONTAINED IN THIS FOLDER MAY BE USED ONLY IN ACCORDANCE WITH ALL OF THE PROVISIONS OF ANY THIRD PARTY LICENSES CONTAINED IN THE SOFTWARE AND FOLDER. READ ALL FILES PROVIDED, INCLUDING BUT NOT LIMITED TO "READ ME" FILES FOR SUCH RESTRICTIONS. NOTHING CONTAINED IN THIS LICENSE AGREEMENT SHALL BE DEEMED TO GRANT TO YOU ANY PERMISSION OR RIGHTS OF ANY NATURE WHATSOEVER WITH REGARD TO SUCH MATERIALS CONTROLLED BY THIRD PARTIES.

e) OTHER THAN THESE EXCEPTIONS IN 4a) THROUGH d), ALL OF THE RESTRICTIONS CONTAINED IN THIS LICENSE APPLY IN FULL.

5. COPY RESTRICTIONS. The Software and accompanying written materials are protected under United States copyright laws. Unauthorized copying and/or distribution of the Software and/or the related written materials is expressly forbidden. You may be held legally responsible for any copyright infringement that is caused, directly or indirectly, by your failure to abide by the terms of this License Agreement. Subject to the terms of this License Agreement and if the software is not otherwise copy protected, you may make one copy of the Software for backup purposes only. The copyright notice and any other proprietary notices which were included in the original Software must be reproduced and included on any such backup copy.

6. TRANSFER RESTRICTIONS. The licensee herein granted is personal to you, the Licensee. You may not transfer the Software nor any of its components or elements to anyone else, nor may you sell, lease, loan, sublicense, assign, or otherwise dispose of the Software nor any of its components or elements without the express written consent of LICENSOR, which consent may be granted or withheld at LICENSOR's sole discretion.

7. TERMINATION. The license herein granted hereby will remain in effect until terminated. This license will terminate automatically without further notice from LICENSOR in the event of the violation of any of the provisions hereof. As Licensee, you agree that upon such termination you will promptly destroy any and all copies of the Software which remain in your possession and, upon request, will certify to such destruction in writing to LICENSOR.